Guide to Madagascar

Hilary Bradt

2nd Edition

BRADT PUBLICATIONS, UK
HUNTER PUBLISHING, USA

First edition published in 1988 by Bradt Publications, 41 Nortoft Road, Chalfont St Peter, Bucks, SL9 0LA, England. Distributed in the U.S.A. by Hunter Publishing Inc., 300 Rariton Center Parkway, CN94, Edison, NJ 08818.

Second updated printing 1988.

Second edition published May 1990.

British Library Cataloguing in Publication Data
Bradt, Hilary, 1941-
  Guide to Madagascar.
  2nd ed.
  1.Madagascar. Visitors' guides
  916.91045

ISBN 0-946983-48-8

Made and printed in Great Britain by
The Guernsey Press Co. Ltd., Guernsey, Channel Islands.

Galidia elegans   HB

Maps by Hans van Well.
Photos and line drawings by the author, unless otherwise stated.
Cover photos. Front: Ring-tailed lemur and infant. Photo by Hilary Bradt.
Back: Woman returning from market, Mahafaly country. Photo by John R. Jones.

THE AUTHOR

I haven't written the rest of the book in the third person so don't see why I should now, despite convention. I have visited Madagascar eight or so times since 1976, both as an independent traveller and as leader for Wilderness Travel (California). Between times I run Bradt Publications. Recently a reader of the first edition commented to a friend: 'Hilary Bradt? I used his book and thought he was a jolly good chap!' So I should, perhaps, point out that I am a woman.

THE CONTRIBUTORS

Dick Byrne (*Nocturnal lemurs*, etc).
A lecturer at St Andrews University, Dick researches and teaches primate behaviour.

Sally Crook (*Village life in the South, the Sarimanok Expedition, Sambatra*).
The only woman on the 8-crew *Sarimanok* Expedition, Sally Crook is a nutritionist who has worked for the VSO in West Africa and travelled widely, and solo, in Madagascar. She took part in the Ankarana Expedition led by Jane Wilson.

Ed Fletcher (*baobabs*).
Ed is a specialist in bonsai trees and is the only person growing baobabs in Great Britain.

John R.Jones (Photographs)
John is a professional travel photographer who has visited Madagascar twice. His photographs appeared in *Madagascar* (Aston Publications) and he was awarded 'commended' for his portrait of a lepilemur in the 1989 Wildlife Photographer of the Year competition at the Natural History Museum.

Gordon and Merlin Munday (*Flora, Man and Nature*).
A retired physicist/medical practioner team, the Mundays have a strong interest in conservation and botany, specialising in succulents and tropical vegetation.

Alison Richard (*Conservation*).A professor of Anthropology at Yale University, Alison Richard is one of Madagascar's leading conservationists. Her work in the field includes the new reserve of Beza Mahafaly in the south, and overseeing student studies in the east.

Jane Wilson (Health)
A medical doctor with a degree in biology, Jane Wilson has organised expeditions to many parts of the world. Her two expeditions to Madagascar (1981 and 1986) were to Ankarana. In addition to studies on the natural history of the reserve, Jane investigated Bilharzia.

ACKNOWLEDGEMENTS

No one person can thoroughly know a country as large and rich in interest as Madagascar, and for the first edition I made much use of information supplied by residents, naturalists and other specialists in their fields. For background information my grateful thanks go to Sir Mervyn Brown, former British Ambassador to Madagascar, whose book *Madagascar Rediscovered* was the source of the history sections, and who generously gave his time correcting the sections on history. Alison Jolly's *A World Like our Own* gave inspiration and information on natural history, and John Mack, of the Museum of Mankind, provided valuable help and corrections on the pages dealing with traditional practices. The author of *A Glance at Madagascar* (who wishes to remain anonymous) shared his wealth of miscellaneous knowledge acquired during 30-odd years of residence in Madagascar.

My continuing gratitude to travellers and researchers who provided vital information for the first edition: S. and E. Garnett, Bob Gillam, Oenone Hammersley, Olivier Langrand, Jytte Arnfred Larson, Patrick Marks, Sheila O'Connor and Mark Pidgeon, and Harry Sutherland-Hawes. They were joined in the second printing by Jean-Marie de La Beaujardière, the Rev. J. Hardiman, Simon Hale, Ted Jackson, Julian Tennant, and Raniero Leto.

In this new edition there were several readers whose detailed letters provided just the right blend of enthusiasm and hard information: I am particularly grateful to Liz Roberts, Helena Drysdale, Benjamin Freed, David Bonderman and Laurie Michaels, Ceinwen Sinclair, Tim Cross, Evelyn Horn Wootton, Sheila Tunstall and Martin Kitzen, and Robert Stewart and Robert Howie for sharing so many of their hard-earned experiences and carefully recorded recommendations. Also included here is the French woman, whose letter with the unreadable signature and no address, was most helpful.

Every reader's letter is valuable, and further thanks are due to Edith Beveridge, David Carr, Eleanor Clarke, Sally and Ian Durant, Petra Jenkins, Peter Elliott, Keith Hern, Hugh Hadley, Erik Kon, J.M.Layman, Angela Newport, Beverly Menheim, David Orchard, and M.J. Sherman.

My thanks to the WWF in Switzerland for permission to reproduce some of their maps from *Madagascar: Revue de la conservation et des aires protégées*.

Last, but certainly not least, my undying gratitude to Alan Hickling and Monique Rodriguez whose constant flow of faxes has enabled me to keep bang up to date with developments in a fast-changing country.

PERSPECTIVES ON MADAGASCAR

"[Madagascar is] the chiefest paradise this day upon earth."
Richard Boothby, 1630.

"I could not but endeavour to dissuade others from undergoing the miseries that will follow the persons of such as adventure themselves for Madagascar ... from which place, God divert the residence and adventures of all good men."
Powle Waldegrave, 1649.

Madagascar is my favourite country. My love affair has lasted fourteen years and like any lover I am fulsome in my praise and intolerant of any criticism of my beloved. That my feelings are not shared by everyone is brought home to me from time to time as I lead parties of tourists around the island, and also by the occasional letter from travellers unseduced by the charms of Madagascar. This is not a holiday island, it is not even a tourist island in that it lacks tangible tourist sights and events. As one traveller pointed out: 'I need to be hit in the face with garish temples, outrageous costumes, bizarre practices. I agree toying with Grandad's bones is pretty bizarre but what chance has a tourist like me of seeing a *famadihana*?...'

Last year in Diego Suarez a tourist asked me with dismayed curiosity 'But what is it you *like* about Madagascar?' Eloquent from punch au coco, I told her (as I tell you later in this section). But I didn't describe that day's serendipity. Wandering around the back streets I came across a 'church bazaar'. Stalls had been set up, music was blaring, and the locals were enjoying all the fun of the fair. Neat stacks of cans tested your aim with a ball: knock them all down and win a prize; a tub of sawdust hid goodies: take a lucky dip; you could buy an icecream, or – if you had no money – stand around talking and laughing. That's what most people were doing. I thought about the fun fairs at home, the tired parents and children whimpering for yet more money for a ride on the space rocket, and I was stirred by nostalgia for what our culture has lost, grateful for a chance to experience this time warp.

These are a few of my favourite things:

The natural history. I have seen spectacular wildlife in many parts of the world, but nothing to equal the surprises of Madagascar's small-scale marvels, such as the Uroplatus, the spiny tenrec, the spiders with their golden webs, weird and wonderful beetles. Nor have I seen any mammals more endearing than lemurs. For the anthropomorphic, gooey brigade they are winners!

The snorkelling. I have been told disdainfully that the snorkelling around Madagascar could not compare with Tahiti. I wouldn't know. All I can say is that the underwater world around Nosy Tanikely (off Nosy Be) is so wonderful I have difficulty not gasping with delight and drowning.

The beauty of the Malagasy people. I remember sitting in a bus and gazing at the faces around me as though I were in an art gallery. I never get tired of their infinite variety. That it is combined with friendliness and courtesy is an added delight.

The tragic drama of Madagascar seen from the air. Erosion has caused great red fissures in the overgrazed hillsides. From a plane these terracotta fingers clawing the soft green landscape are beautiful, as are the emerald green rectangles of rice paddies in the valleys and stacked like tiles up the mountainsides.

Antananarivo. Surely the most attractive capital of any Third World country – a multicoloured tumble of buildings behind the white umbrellas of the *Zoma* (market). And is there any better market anywhere? The colour, the variety of goods and the relative lack of sales-pressure make it very special.

The food. The abundance of sea food – oysters, lobster and shrimp – and the good French and Chinese cooking in the larger towns more than compensate for the mounds of sticky rice and tough meat that is sometimes all that is available. Nor does a wonderful meal have to be expensive: several people have written to tell me about 'the best meal I've ever had', often in an out of the way place.

Now for the negative aspects, which irritate or depress all visitors, and are the last straw for some:

The towns. Apart from Antananarivo, there are very few attractive Malagasy towns. All are shabby, and some are in an advanced state of decay. There are exceptions, of course, but even places like Antsirabe and Ambositra, which come as a pleasant surprise for those still coming to terms with the likes of Tuléar, are only relatively pretty.

The poverty. About 1,500 people in Antananarivo live exclusively off rubbish tips. Despite the ever-present laughter, seeing such deprivation is profoundly saddening to many visitors.

Road transport. For those who cannot afford to fly, or prefer not to, the public transport system and the horrendous state of the roads is a constant trial. However fast the roads are improved they deteriorate with equal speed, so the situation is unlikely to improve much.

A word of caution, too, about one aspect of the natural history. Although half of Madagascar's birds are endemic (with five families found nowhere else apart from the Comores) there are only 256 species, and none of these is abundant.

Whether Madagascar will work for you depends on your expectations and interests. Most of all, though, it depends on your sense of wonder. If that is intact, nothing should prevent you falling in love.

You were quite right: we LOVED it! A fabulous country, I can't wait to get back there.

Of our 15 days in Madagascar, 12 have been spent in and around Tana trying to get out.

In spite of being on my own I never felt lonely. The kindness and warmth of the people constantly took my breath away.

My impressions of Périnet seem to epitomise Madagascar. Mañana would indicate a sense of urgency – nothing seems to be being improved or even renovated... But I leave you with a final thought. Can a people who believe implicitly in 'razana' ever consider themselves in control of their own destiny?

Changes are a much talked about subject: hotel chains, private air lines... but, Dieu Merci, Madagascar has its own defence mechanism.

I could go on for pages – Madagascar is like nowhere else I've been. Our cosmopolitan group likened it to central Australia, Scotland, New Mexico, Peru, the Masai Mara... but it is unique.
One other good service your book did me. The urchins in Tana have become very persistent, dancing around and jostling and begging for 'monnaie, cadeaux, bon-bon'. I felt guiltily rich, yet irritated by their persistence. Later over delicious coffee in one of Tana's patisseries, I saw that my canvas handbag had been neatly split by razor slashes from below. As it happened, my ever-present Bradt was in the bottom of the bag, so nothing had dropped out, but I had been quite unaware of the episode and thought I had my bag safely over shoulder and under arm!

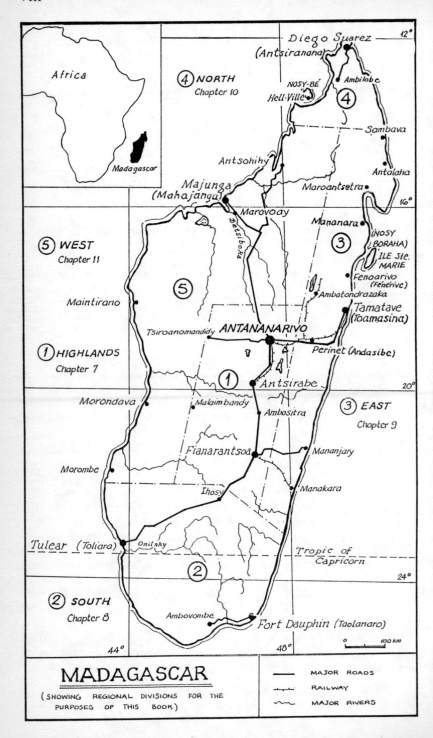

MADAGASCAR

(SHOWING REGIONAL DIVISIONS FOR THE PURPOSES OF THIS BOOK)

Contents

PART 2: MADAGASCAR

Chapter 1

The Country

FACTS AND FIGURES

Location
Madagascar, also known as the Malagasy Republic, lies some 250 miles (400 km) off the east coast of Africa, south of the equator. It is crossed by the Tropic of Capricorn near the southern town of Tuléar (Toliara). The incredible number of unique species of flora and fauna is due to the island's early separation from the mainland some 160 million years ago, and to the relatively recent arrival of man (around 500 AD).

Size
The world's fourth largest island (after Greenland, New Guinea and Borneo), 1,000 miles (1,580 km) long by 350 miles (570 km) at its widest point. Madagascar has an area of 227,760 square miles (590,000 square kilometres), two and a half times the size of Great Britain.

Topography
A chain of mountains runs like a spine down the east-centre of the island descending sharply to the Indian Ocean, leaving only a narrow coastal plain. These eastern mountain slopes bear the remains of the dense rain forest which once covered all of the eastern section of the island. The western plain is wider and the climate drier, supporting forests of deciduous trees and acres of savanna grassland. Madagascar's highest mountain is Tsaratanana (9,450 ft – 2,880 m), in the north of the island. In the south is the 'spiny forest' also known as the 'spiny desert'.

History
First sighted by Europeans in 1500 by the Portuguese, but there were Arab settlements from about the 9th Century. The name Madagascar comes from Marco Polo, who described (from

other travellers' imaginative accounts) a land where a giant bird, the Roc, picked up elephants with ease. United under one Malagasy monarch from the early 19th Century, a time of British influence through the London Missionary Society. Became a French colony in 1896 and gained independence in 1960.

Government

A Democratic Republic practising its own brand of Christian--Marxism. President Didier Ratsiraka assumed power in 1975 and has twice been re-elected for a further seven year term (most recently in 1989).

Population

The people of Madagascar, the Malagasy, are of Afro-Indonesian origin, divided into 18 'tribes' or clans. Other races include Indian/Pakistani, Chinese, and European. The population numbers approximately 11 million, over half of which are under the age of 20.

Language

The first language is Malagasy, which belongs to the Malayo-Polynesian family of languages. French is widely spoken in towns, and is the language of business. Some English is spoken in the capital and major tourist areas.

Place names

Since independence some towns bearing Colonial names have been renamed. Although they bear their new names on maps and pamphlets most people – including Air Madagascar – call them by the old one, and so have I: (old name first) Fort Dauphin = Taolañaro, Tuléar = Toliara or Toliary, Périnet = Andasibe, Île Sainte Marie = Nosy Boraha, Diego Suarez = Antsiranana. Antananarivo is often shortened to Tana.

Religion

Christianity is the dominant organised religion, with the Catholic church slightly stronger than other denominations. Islam and Hinduism are also practised, but to the majority of Malagasy their own unique form of ancestor worship is the most important influence in their lives.

Economy

Madagascar withdrew from the French Franc Zone in 1973 and set up its own central bank. It is a mainly agricultural country, exporting coffee, cloves and vanilla, along with some minerals. In the World Bank statistics of 1984, assessing poverty by Gross National Product per head of population, Madagascar came 183rd out of 203 countries.

Currency

The Malagasy Franc (Franc Malgache – FMG). In March 1990 the rate of exchange was: US$1 = 1,545 FMG; £1 = 2,461 FMG; 1 FF = 268 FMG; 1 DM = 806 FMG.

Climate

A tropical climate with rain falling in the hottest season – coinciding with the northern hemisphere winter. The amount of rainfall varies greatly by region, falling almost daily on the east coast (averaging 140 inches – 355 cm – annually in the wettest area) but only on an average of 51 days of the year (12 inches or 30 cm) in the arid south. Hot and humid near the coast, temperatures can drop to freezing in Tana (4,100ft – 1,250 m) and close to freezing in the extreme south during the coldest month of June.

Flora and fauna

A naturalist's paradise, most of the island's plants and animals are unique. 80% of the native plants are endemic, all of the mammals (excluding those introduced recently), half of the birds, and well over 90% of the reptiles. Much of this 'living laboratory' has yet to be scientifically classified.

LAMBAS

The colourful cotton wraps known as *lamba* (or, to be more precise, *lambarano* (cotton lamba), since *lamba* is the white shawl worn in the highlands) are worn by both men and women in Madagascar. In some rural parts of the country men wear their *lamba* as a kind of wraparound skirt, and women use it in a variety of ways, often as a baby- carrier. Even small shops in eastern Madagascar have a good selection of *lambas* which make attractive and versatile souvenirs. The designs are bright and cheerful and most *lambas* have a Malagasy slogan at the edge of the fabric; If you buy one, ask the shop manager to translate it for you.

The most important lambas are those of silk (*lambalandy*) and mostly used as *lambamena* (shrouds). Three villages near Fianar are centres for silk weaving: Andriana, Ambositra and Ambalavao. The Madagascar silkworm, *Brocera*, feeds only on the Tapia tree (*Napaca bojeri*), which grows in this area.

King Andrianampoinimerina (1745-1810).

A BRIEF HISTORY

Note: A more detailed regional history is given at the beginning of each chapter in Part 2.

The island was reached by the Portuguese in 1500, but hostility from the natives and disease prevented early attempts by Europeans to settle in Madagascar. Hence a remarkably homogeneous and united country was able to develop under its own rulers.

The first monarch to unite Madagascar was King Radama I who reigned from 1810 to 1828. Before then most regions had their own rulers, and empires rose and fell under monarchs with unpronounceable names such as Andrianalimbe, Andrianiveniarivo and Ratsimilaho (the son of an English pirate) who controlled much of the east coast. The powerful Merina kingdom was forged by Andrianampoinimerina (be thankful that this was a shortened version of his full name: Andrianampoinimerinandriantsimitoviaminandriampanjaka!) in 1794 when the various highland clans were conquered and united. It was his son who became Radama I and fulfilled his father's command to 'take the sea as frontier for your kingdom'. This king had a friendly relationship with the European powers, particularly Britain, and in 1817 and 1820 Britain signed treaties recognising Madagascar as an independent state.

To further strengthen ties between the two countries, the British Governor of Mauritius, which had recently been seized from the French, encouraged King Radama I to invite the London Missionary Society to send teachers. They were later followed by a number of craftsmen and the LMS had a strong influence in Madagascar during this period, culminating in the development of a written language using the Roman alphabet.

The next monarch was Queen Ranavalona I who ruled for 33 years and is remembered for her rejection of European influences which included Christianity. The missionaries, who had done so much for the country, were driven out and many Christians massacred. The Queen's xenophobia led to conflict with England and France and during this time (1841) France took possession of the island of Nosy Be.

It was during Queen Ranavalona's reign that an extraordinary Frenchman arrived in Madagascar: Jean Laborde who, building on the work of the British missionaries, introduced the island to many aspects of Western technology (see page 112).

After Queen Ranavalona I came King Radama II, a peace-loving and pro-European monarch. He didn't last long, being assassinated after a two-year reign. The monarchy was now in decline and power shifted to the prime minister. This man married the Queen but was overthrown by a brother who continued the tradition by marrying three successive queens and exercising all the power. During this period (1863 – 1896) the monarchs (in title only) were Queen Rasoherina, Queen Ranavalona II, and – the last one – Queen

Ranavalona III.

In 1883 France, using various pretexts, attacked and occupied the main ports of Madagascar and after a 30-month war imposed a harsh treaty including a form of French protectorate. The Prime Minister, hoping for British support, exploited ambiguities in the treaty to evade full acceptance of the protectorate; but after the British had recognised the protectorate in the Convention of Zanzibar, 1890, the French imposed their rule by invasion in 1895.

Madagascar became a colony in 1896, under the first Governor-General, Joseph Simon Galliéni. An able and relatively benign administrator, Galliéni set out to break the power of the Merina aristocracy and remove the British influence by banning the teaching of English. French became the official language. The monarchy continued, but with no power, and was finally abolished in 1897 when Queen Ranavalona III was exiled. There followed various insurrections, often put down very bloodily, and the spirit of nationalism grew. One French effort to quench the flames of independence was to eliminate references to the French Revolution in school history books. The First World War saw 46,000 Malagasy recruited for the allies and over 2,000 killed. France's defeat in 1940 and the overthrow of the Vichyist government of Madagascar by British troops in 1942 greatly weakened French prestige and encouraged nationalist hopes of independence. In 1947 came a major rebellion and an estimated 80,000 Malagasy were killed, many by Senegalese troops attached to the French Foreign Legion. The rebellion was finally suppressed a year later, after the bloodiest episode in Madagascar's history.

The Malagasy Republic was created in 1958, an autonomous but not independent state. Independence was granted by France in 1960.

The first president, Tsiranana, was pro-French and conservative. In 1972, student and worker strikes led to the assumption of power by General Ramanantsoa, head of the army, though Tsiranana remained President. However, after a referendum he stepped down. In the rising tide of socialism Ramanantsoa resigned in January 1975, handing over to the Minister of the Interior, Richard Ratsimandrava, who was assassinated a week later. A military junta stepped in, quashed an uprising, and in June 1975 Didier Ratsiraka, a naval captain, assumed power. President Ratsiraka embarked on a Malagasy brand of socialism and has twice been re-elected.

CLIMATE

Madagascar has a tropical climate divided into rainy and dry seasons. South-west trade winds drop their moisture on the eastern mountain slopes and blow hot and dry in the west. North and northwest 'monsoon' air currents bring heavy rain in summer, decreasing southward so that the rainfall in Fort Dauphin is half that of Tamatave. There are also considerable variations of temperature dictated by altitude and latitude. On the solstice of December 22 the sun is directly over the Tropic of Capricorn, and the weather is warm. Conversely, June is the coolest month.

As was noted in *Facts and Figures* rainfall varies enormously, but the rainy season is relatively consistent with some regional variations: the dry season is from April to October, and the rainy season from November to March.

The east of Madagascar frequently suffers from cyclones during February and March and these may hit other areas, particularly in the north.

Average midday temperatures in the dry season are 77°F (25°C) on the *hauts plateaux* and 86°F (30°C) on the coast. These statistics are misleading, however, since in June the night-time temperature can drop to freezing in Tana and close to freezing in the south, and the hot season is usually tempered by cool breezes on the coast.

The map and chart below give easy reference to the driest and wettest months and regions.

Rainfall chart

	Jan	Feb	Mar	Apr	May	Jun	Jul	Aug	Sep	Oct	Nov	Dec
WEST	▨	▨	▨	▨							▨	▨
CENTRAL	▨	▨	▨	▨		▦	▦	▦		▨	▨	▨
EAST	▨	▨	▨	▨	▨	▦	▦	▨	▨	▨	▨	▨
SOUTH-WEST						▦	▦	▦				
NORTH	▨	▨	▨	▨							▨	▨
NORTH-WEST (Sambirano)	▨	▨	▨	▨							▨	▨

Rain ▨   **Driest months** ☐   **Fine but cool** ▦

Climatic regions

West
Rainfall decreases from north to south.
Variation in day/night winter temperatures
increases from north to south.
Average number of dry months: 7 or 8.
Highest average annual rainfall within zone
(major town): Majunga, 152 cm.
Lowest: Tulear, 36 cm.

Central
Temperatures and rainfall
influenced by altitude. Day/
night temperatures in
Antananarivo vary 14° C. A
few days of rain in October are
known as *pluie des mangues* or
'mango rains' when that fruit is
ripening. The main rainy
season starts end of November.
Average number of dry
months: 7.
Highest average annual rainfall
within zone (major town):
Antsirabe, 140 cm.
Lowest recorded temperature:
− 8° C in Antsirabe

East
In the north and central areas there are no months (or weeks) entirely without
rain, but drier, more settled weather prevails in the south.
Reasonably dry months: May, September, October, November.
Possible months: April, December, January.
Impossible months (torrential rain and cyclones): February, March.
Highest annual rainfall (major town): Maroantsetra 410 cm.
Lowest: Fort Dauphin, 152 cm.

Southwest
The driest part of Madagascar. The extreme west may receive only 5 cm of rain
in a year, with precipitation increasing to around 34 cm in the east.

North
This could be included with the East zone were it not for the dry climate of the
Diego Suarez region, which receives only 92 cm per year, during a long and
fairly reliable dry season.

North-west (Sambirano)
Dominated by the country's highest mountain, Tsaratanana, this region
includes the island of Nosy Be and has a micro-climate with frequent heavy rain
alternating with clear skies. Nosy Be gets an average of 203 cm a year on 175
days.

Chapter 2

The People

THE MALAGASY PEOPLE TODAY
Origins

Most accounts agree that the first people in Madagascar arrived about 1,500 years ago from Indonesia/Malaya. While it is theoretically possible that they might have come directly across the Indian Ocean from Indonesia (and this was proved by a Kon-Tiki like expedition in 1985 – see next page) the great distance – 6,400 kilometres – makes this an unlikely route and most experts agree that the immigrants came in their outrigger canoes via Southern India and East Africa, where they established small Indonesian colonies. The strong African element in the coastal populations probably derived from later migrations from these colonies since their language is also essentially Malayo-Polynesian with only slightly more Bantu-Swahili words than elsewhere in the island.

Later arrivals, mainly on the east coast, from Arabia and elsewhere in the Indian Ocean, were also absorbed into the Malagasy-speaking population, while leaving their mark in certain local customs clearly derived from Islam.

The Merina people of the highlands retain remarkably Indonesian characteristics and may have arrived as recently as 500 – 600 years ago.

Beliefs and customs

The Afro-Asian origin of the Malagasy has produced a people with complicated and fascinating customs. Despite the various tribes or clans the country shares a common language and belief in the power of dead ancestors (*razana*). This cult of the dead, far from being a morbid preoccupation, is a celebration of life since the dead ancestors are considered to be potent forces that continue to share in family life. If they are remembered by the living, the Malagasy believe, they thrive in the spirit world and can be relied on to look after the living in a host of different ways.

The Malagasy believe in one God, *Andriamanitra* (which, interestingly, is also one of their words for silk, the material of shrouds) and Creator (*Zanahary*). This probably accounts for their ready acceptance of Christianity which is not at odds with their traditional

THE SARIMANOK EXPEDITION

By Sally Crook

The *Sarimanok* is a 60 foot double outrigger canoe constructed on the initiative and under the direction of Bob Hobman, a New Zealander, on the Philippine island of Tawi Tawi in the Sulu Sea, near to Borneo.

His intention was to construct a vessel of the kind that would have been used by the ancient island South-east Asians (linguistically closest to the people of modern Borneo) for their migrations to Madagascar, and to sail it directly across the Indian Ocean rather than following the coasts of India, Arabia and Africa. This safer coastal route is the one championed by most historians. Hobman, impressed by the courage and sailing prowess of modern day Indonesians, wanted to show that a traditional vessel made entirely of wood and bamboo, held together by rattan bindings with no contribution from metal nails, and propelled by wind in palm-weave sails, could weather the open ocean for long enough to reach Madagascar without other landfalls.

The food type, preservation techniques and cooking methods were also to be like those of 2500 years ago – the era in which he believes the migrations took place, though most consider the first millenium A.D. a more likely period – and the navigation was to be by readings of the positions of sun and stars.

The 'shakedown' voyage in 1984 from the Philippines to Bali was not performed with all the traditional elements, and an outboard motor had to be used to push against the wind. The voyage was eventful, however, with several stops on the coast of Sulawesi, Borneo and Java for repairs. Then Chico Hansen died of hepatitis shortly after the port town of Surabaya, Java, was reached. The loss was devastating to the crew, but preparations and improvements to the boat design continued the next year, and on 3rd June, 1985, the *Sarimanok*, now without motor, radio or sextant, set off across the Indian Ocean to be driven to Madagascar by the south-east trade winds.

Apart from a stop on the Cocos (Keeling) Islands to let off a sick member of the crew (eight men and one woman), the navigator, Bill McGrath, guided the vessel through high seas and unseasonal frequent rain directly to Diego Suarez on the northern tip of Madagascar. (An Argos satellite tracking device confirmed the accuracy of his calculation of the boat's position throughout the voyage to the tracking station in Toulouse, though the information was not accessible to the *Sarimanok* crew.)

Lack of help to land the unwieldy vessel resulted in the boat sailing on to Mayotte, the French island off the Comores where it was towed ashore. The *Sarimanok* finally landed at Nosy Be on 5th September 1985 to a warm welcome from the local people who were proud that their history had been relived by this seven week crossing of the Indian Ocean, and that the possibility that their revered ancestors had taken this more difficult and dangerous route had been vindicated.

Sally's account of her voyage will be published by Impact Books in 1990 under the title "Oceans Apart".

beliefs – the concept of resurrection is not so far from their veneration of ancestors. These ancestors wield enormous power, their 'wishes' dictating the behaviour of the family or community. Their property is respected, so great-grandfather's field may not be sold or changed to a different crop. Calamities are usually blamed on the anger of *razana*, and a zebu bull may be sacrificed in appeasement. Huge herds of zebu cattle are kept as a 'bank' of potential sacrificial offerings. As well as appeasing the ancestors, a sacrifice will do much to allay bad luck, as was demonstrated by the sacrifice of a zebu bull at the inaugural flight of Air Madagascar's first jumbo jet. The airline has an excellent safety record!

Fady

The dictates of the *razana* are obeyed in a complicated network of *fady* or taboos. These vary from family to family and community to community, and even from person to person. Perhaps the eating of pork is *fady*, or the killing of lemurs (most useful for conservation!). In Imerina it is *fady* to hand an egg directly to another person – it must first be put on the ground. Many villages have a *fady* against working in the rice-fields on Tuesdays and Thursdays, or consider it *fady* to dig a grave with a spade that does not have a loose handle since it is dangerous to have too firm a connection between the living and the dead. Other examples of regional *fady* are given in the *Ethnic groups* section.

Vintana

Along with *fady* goes an even more complex sense of destiny called *vintana*. Broadly speaking, *vintana* is to do with time – hours of the day, days of the week, etc, and *fady* involves actions or behaviour. Each day has its own *vintana* associated with a colour which makes it good or bad for certain festivals or activities.

The origin of *vintana* is the Arab-introduced lunar calendar, and this 'force of destiny' is believed to move round a house according to the phases of the moon. Houses are traditionally built north-south with their entrance on the west, and the first month of the year is the north east corner (sunrise). This is where special artifacts associated with the ancestors would be stored. People will be careful to move round their houses in the same direction as the *vintana* (clockwise) even if it means taking the long way round to enter the door.

In some respects *vintana* can be compared with astrology in that a person's destiny is tied up with the day and hour he or she was born; couples of opposing *vintana*, for instance, should not marry.

Healers and sorcerers

The Malagasy have a deep knowledge of herbal medicine and all markets display a variety of healing plants and artifacts. In large towns this is simply the 'chemist's shop' but in rural areas it will be presided over by the *ombiasy* or divine healer. As the name (*olona-be-hasina* –

person of much virtue) implies, their power is good. They do not just dispense herbal drugs but evoke the power of the ancestors to help effect a cure. In some areas they are also soothsayers. There are also witch doctors with an intimate knowledge of poison. These are the *mpamorika*.

Sorcerers are *mpisikidy* who use amulets, stones, and beads (*ody*) for their cures.

Mpanandro is an astrologer who has an intimate understanding of the vintana, and is thus a highly respected and sometimes feared member of a village. It is he who decrees the most auspicious day and time for family celebrations or major activities, such as *famadihana* (see below) or laying the foundations of a new house. He may also be at hand during a *tromba* – a trance-like state – to act as a medium for the ancestors.

After death

Burial, second burial, and 'bone turning' is an extremely important part of the Malagasy culture. Death is, after all, the most important part of a Malagasy's life, when he abandons his mortal form to become a much more powerful and significant ancestor. Burial practices among the different tribes are detailed in the *Ethnic groups* section and in regional chapters in Part 2.

Whatever method of burial is used, all tribes consider the fresh or decomposing body polluted, and must purify themselves with water after contact with it or its possessions. Objects laid on a tomb are there because they are polluted, and in some cases the house of the deceased is burnt down to prevent contamination. John Mack (*Madagascar: Island of the Ancestors*) reports one case of hospital patients burning all the bedding and medical equipment in the ward when someone died.

Bones, devoid of flesh, are the material presence of the ancestor, and the tomb his house. Exhumation is thus the logical way to collect these bones.

The southern tribes, who do not go in for second burial, carve commemorative wooden stelae, often depicting important scenes from the life of the deceased, and the tombs themselves are more elaborate and better built than any house in the area. A prodigous number of zebus will be killed for a rich man's funeral; 50 is not unusual.

In the highlands, among the Merina, *famadihana* (pronounced 'famad<u>ee</u>an') is still practised. The 'turning of the bones' ceremony is a time of great rejoicing, when the remains of a dead relative are wrapped in a fresh shroud (*lamba mena*) and paraded round the village before being returned to the family tomb. The corpse is treated as though it were alive – spoken to, shown new developments in the town and involved in the feasting.

The occasion for *famadihana* may be because an ancestor died elsewhere and his remains are being returned to the family tomb, or because a new tomb has been built, or because the *razana* decreed it was time for an outing (perhaps in a dream).

This is a family occasion in every way; the living relatives are gathered together (and will have contributed to the considerable cost of the *famadihana* feast) and the ancestors are grouped companionably together on their shelves in the tomb, thus increasing their power.

Famadihana is not just the custom of rural or more traditional Malagasy. Jane Wilson was lucky enough to be invited to a bone turning ceremony on the outskirts of Tana by a sophisticated and devoutly Christian family. She describes it below:

> When we arrived it looked as though the party had already been going on for some hours. We were given a drink and told to wait in the courtyard since the bones would soon be turned. There was a lot of activity in and around the tomb, and soon a group of six men came out carrying our hostess's great uncle. His bones, dusty and dry, were now held together in a polythene bag, the old *lamba mena* having disintegrated long ago. They brought him to a special shelter, wrapped him in a vastly expensive, beautifully embroidered new white *lamba mena* (*mena* means red, but the burial shroud is not always red) and laid him in the midst of the guests. Above his body hung a photograph of the man in his youth: with a waxed moustache and in the straw boater and fashionable clothes of the 1920s. The bones of his wife joined him on the little sheltered table and so did those of another relative.
>
> As a Catholic girls school choir began to sing, I studied the incongruous scene. There were around 200 guests, the men in their Sunday best and the women with their long, straight hair plaited into the traditional oval bun. They wore smart European clothes with fine embroidered *lambas* draped around their shoulders. A priest said some prayers and preached a short sermon before the Protestant girls choir took over, their faces glowing with pleasure as they harmonised.
>
> After the priest and choristers had dispersed our host showed us a room entirely filled with the butchered carcasses of perhaps 30 zebu cattle – there was going to be quite a feast! The bands were setting up their guitars and drums on the temporary stage and soon the room was throbbing with the sounds of rock music and everyone was disco dancing.
>
> Then I noticed that several more bodies were surreptitiously being taken out, quickly whisked around the tomb the required seven times (which makes it harder for death to re-emerge) and returned to their resting places. What was going on? The explanation was that the government taxes these *famadihana* parties according to the number of bodies turned. Our hosts were officially turning three ancestors and pulling a tax fiddle on the others. Or were they just pulling my leg!
>
> When we took our leave our hostess told us the party would continue for two or three days. 'But isn't it primitive?' she said.

Educated Malagasy may claim to be free of *fady* or other superstitions but it is quite likely that their lives are affected by these ancient traditions and beliefs, even if only by a sensitivity to the beliefs of older members of the family.

I have only touched on traditional Malagasy customs here. For more information you should read *Madagascar: Island of the Ancestors* (see *Bibliography*).

Ethnic groups

This section is mainly taken from 'A Glance at Madagascar' by kind permission of the author.

The Malagasy form one nation with one basic culture and language (though with many dialects), but there are eighteen different 'tribes' officially recognised by the government. This division is based more upon old 'kingdoms' than upon ethnic grouping. These tribes are listed individually below.

Antaifasy (People-of-the-sands)
Living in the south-east around Farafangana they cultivate rice, and fish in the lakes and rivers. Divided into three clans each with its own 'king' they generally have stricter moral codes than some tribes. They have large collective burial houses known as *kibory*, built of wood or stone and generally hidden in the forest away from the village.

Antaimoro (People-of-the-coast)
They are among the most recent arrivals and live in the south-east around Vohipeno and Manakara. They guard Islam tradition and Arab influence and still use a form of Arab writing known as *sorabe*. They use verses of the Koran as amulets. Their caste system includes 'untouchables'.

Antaisaka
Centred south of Farafangana on the south-east coast but now fairly widely spread throughout the island, they are an off-shoot of the Sakalava tribe. They cultivate coffee, bananas and rice – but only the women harvest the rice. There are strong marriage taboos amongst them. Often the houses may have a second door on the east side which is only used for taking out a corpse. They use the *kibory*, communal burial house, the corpse usually being dried out for two or three years before finally being put there.

Antankarana (Those-of-the-rocks)
Living in the north around Diego-Suarez they are fishers or cattle raisers whose rulers came from the Sakalava dynasty. Their houses are usually raised on stilts. Numerous *fady* exist amongst them governing relations between the sexes in the family, e.g. a girl may not wash her brother's clothes. The legs of a fowl are the father's portion, whereas amongst the Merina, for instance, they are given to the children.

Antambahoaka (Those-of-the-people)
The smallest tribe, of the same origin as the Antaimora, but with no caste system, and living around Mananjary on the south-east coast. They have some Arab traits and amulets are used. They bury in a *kibory*. Circumcision ceremonies are carried out every seven years (see page 176).

Antandroy (People-of-the-thorns)
They are mainly nomadic and live in the arid south around Ambovombe. A dark-skinned people, they wear little clothing and are frank and open, easily roused to either joy or anger. Their women occupy an inferior position. The villages are often surrounded by a hedge of cactus plants. They do not eat much rice but subsist mostly on millet, maize and cassava. They believe in the

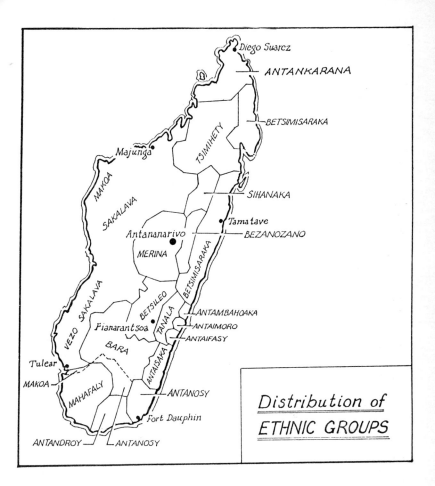

Distribution of ETHNIC GROUPS

THE VAZIMBA

Vazimba is the name given to the earliest inhabitants of Madagascar, especially in the centre, who were displaced or absorbed by later immigrants. Once thought to be pre-Indonesian aboriginals from Africa, it is now generally accepted that they were survivors of the earliest Malayo-Polynesian immigrants who were pushed inland by later arrivals.

Vazimba come into both legends and history of the Malagasy. Vazimba tombs are now places of pilgrimage where sacrifices are made for favours and cures. It is *fady* to step over such a tomb. Vazimba are also thought to haunt certain springs and rocks, and offerings may be made here. They are the ancestral guardians of the soil.

kokolampo – a spirit of either good or bad influence. Their tombs are similar to those of the Mahafaly tribe. Sometimes it is *fady* among them for a child to say his father's name, or to refer by name to parts of his father's body. Thus he may say *ni fandiany* (the-what-he-moves-with) for his feet; and *ny amboniny* (the-top-of-him) for his head.

Antanosy (People-of-the-island)

The island is a small one in the Fanjahira river. They live in the south-east principally around Fort-Dauphin. Their social structure is based on clans with a 'king' holding great authority over each clan. Many of them have emigrated to La Réunion and Mauritius. There are strict *fady* governing relationships in the family. For example, a brother may not sit on or step over his sister's mat. As with many other tribes there are numerous *fady* regarding pregnancy. A pregnant woman should not sit in the doorway of the house; she should not eat brains; she should not converse with men; people who have no children should not stay in her house overnight. Other *fady* are that relatives should not eat meat at a funeral and the diggers opening a tomb should not wear clothes. When digging holes for the corner posts of a new house it may be *fady* to stand up – and so one must sit down to do it.

Bara

Originally in the south-west near Tulear, they now live in the south central area around Ihosy and Betroka. Their name has no special meaning but it is reputed to derive from Bantu. They are nomadic and cattle raisers. They may be polygamous and women occupy an inferior position in their society. They attach importance to the *fatidra* or 'blood pact'. Cattle stealing is regarded as proof of manhood and courage, without which a man cannot expect to get a wife. So he must steal a few head of cattle before he can hope to get married! They are dancers and sculptors, a unique feature of their carved wooden figures being eyelashes of real hair set into the wood. They believe in the *helo* – a spirit that manifests itself at the foot of trees. Sometimes a whole village may move after somebody dies owing to the fear of ghosts. They use caves in the mountains for burial. It is the custom to shave the head on the death of a near relative.

Betsileo (The-many-invincible)

They are centred in the south of the High Plateau around Fianarantsoa but about 150,000 of them also live in the Betsiboka region. They are energetic and experts in the irrigation of terraced rice-fields. The soil is often prepared by chasing zebu cattle round and round to break the clods and soften it – a muddy, sticky job, but it is evidently great fun for the participants. The rice seedlings are planted by hand, the women being the experts at this work. The *famadihana* was introduced amongst them by the Merina at the time of Queen Ranavalona I. It is *fady* for the husband of a pregnant woman to wear a lamba thrown over his shoulder. It may be *fady* for the family to eat until the father is present or for anyone to pick up his fork until the most honourable person present has started to eat.

Betsimisaraka (The-many-inseparables)

They are the second largest tribe and live on the east coast in the Tamatave — Antalaha region. They have known some ancient European influence from pirates, etc. They cultivate rice and work on vanilla plantations. Their clothes are sometimes made from locally woven raffia. Originally their society included numerous local chiefs but they are not now important. The *Tangalamena* is the local official for religious rites and customs. They believe in *angatra* – ghosts; in *zazavavy an-drano* – mermaids; and in the *kalamoro* – which are little wild men of the woods, about 25 inches high with long flowing hair, who like to slip into houses and steal rice from the cooking pot. In the north coffins are generally placed under a shelter, in the south in tombs. Among the Betsimisaraka it may be *fady* for a brother to shake hands with his sister, or for a young man to wear shoes while his father is still living.

Bezanozano (Many-small-plaits)
The name refers to the way in which they do their hair. They were probably one of the first tribes to arrive, and live in an area between the Betsimisaraka lowlands and the Merina highlands. The *famadihana* is practised among them. As with most of the coastal tribes their funeral celebrations involve the consumption of considerable quantities of *toaka* – rum.

Mahafaly (those-who-make-taboos or Those-who-make- happy)
The etymology of the word is sometimes disputed but the former meaning is generally regarded as being correct. One of the least known tribes, they probably arrived about the 12th Century, and live in the south west desert area around Ampanihy and Ejeda. They are farmers, with maize, sorgho and sweet potatoes as their chief crops; cattle rearing occupies a secondary place. They kept their independence under their own local chiefs until the French occupation and still keep the bones of some of their old chiefs – this is the *jiny* cult. Their villages usually have a sacrificial post, the *hazo manga*, on the east of the village where sacrifices are made on various occasions. Some of the blood is generally put on the foreheads of the people attending.

The tombs of the Mahafaly always attract a great deal of interest (see page 132). They are big rectangular constructions of uncut stone rising some three feet above the ground and decorated with *aloalo* and the horns of the cattle slain at the funeral feast. The tomb of the Mahafaly king Tsiampody has the horns of 700 zebu on it. The *aloalo* are sculpted wooden posts set upright on the tomb, often depicting scenes from the person's life. The burial customs include waiting for the decomposition of the body before it is placed in the tomb. It is the practice for a person to be given a new name after death – generally beginning with 'Andria'.

The divorce rate is very high and it is not at all uncommon for a man to divorce and remarry six or seven times. It is very often *fady* for children to sleep in the same house as their parents. Their *rombo* (very similar to the *tromba* of the Sakalava) is the practice of contacting various spirits in order to obtain a cure for the sick. Amongst the spirits believed in are the *raza* who are not real ancestors and in some cases are even supposed to include *vazaha* (foreigners), and the *vorom-be* which is the spirit of a big bird.

Makoa
Spread along the north-west region many have moved south to the area of the Onilahy river. Descended from African slaves they are the most primitive tribe and the only true African negroid type in Madagascar.

Merina (People-of-the-Highlands)
They live on the High Plateau, which is the most developed area of the

The people of Madagascar are known as the Malagasy. Some English-speakers pronounce this as in the French *Malgâche* – Malgash. The French, however, have occasionally allowed the pun of *Malgâche* and *Mal gâche* – badly spoiled – to bring a derogatory slant to the name, so it is better to stick to the English pronunciation.

Aloalo *on a Mahafaly tomb.*

country, the capital being 95% Merina population. Approximately 175,000 of them live outside the province of Antananarivo. They are of Malayo-Polynesian origin and vary in colour from ivory to very dark, the women usually having long straight hair. They used to be divided into three castes – the *Andriana* (nobles), the *Hova* (free-men) and the *Andevo* (serfs) – and these were again sub-divided. In law these castes and divisions no longer exist. Most Merina houses are built of brick or mud, some only one room affairs, but the better ones are two storey where the people live mostly upstairs. Most villages of any size have a church – probably two, Catholic and Protestant. There is much rice cultivation by irrigation. The Merina were the first tribe to have any skill in architecture and metallurgy. The *famadihana* is essentially a Merina custom.

Sakalava (People-of-the-long-valleys)
They live in the west between Tulear and Majunga and are dark skinned with Polynesian features and short curly hair. They were at one time the largest and most powerful tribe but could not unite properly amongst themselves. They were ruled by their own kings and queens and certain relics remain – sometimes being kept in the north-east corner of a house. They are cattle raisers, and riches are reckoned by the number of cattle owned. There is a record of human sacrifice amongst them up to the year 1850 at some special occasion such as the death of a king. The *tromba* (trance state) is quite common. It is *fady* for pregnant women to eat fish or to sit in a doorway. Women hold a more important place amongst them than in most other tribes.

Sihanaka (People-of-the-swamps)
They live to the north-east of the old kingdom of Imerina around Lake Alaotra and have much in common with the Merina. They are fishers, rice growers and poultry raisers. Swamps have been drained to make vast rice-fields cultivated with modern machinery and methods. They have a special rotation of *fady* days.

Tanala (People-of-the-forest)
They live in the forest inland from Manakara, and are rice and coffee growers. They immigrated about 250 years ago and are the most recent tribe to arrive. Their houses are usually built on stilts. They are divided into two groups – the Ikongo in the south and the Menabe in the north. The Ikongo are an independent people and never submitted to Merina domination in contrast to the Menabe. Burial customs include keeping the corpse for up to a month. Coffins are made from large trees to which sacrifices are sometimes made when they are cut down. The Ikongo usually bury in the forest and may mark a tree to show the spot.

Tsimihety (Those-who-do-not-cut-their-hair)
They refused to cut their hair to show mourning on the death of a Sakalava king in order to demonstrate their independence. They are an energetic and vigorous people in the north central area and are spreading west. Amongst them the eldest maternal uncle occupies an important position. The most famous member of the tribe is Philibert Tsiranana – the first President of the Malagasy Republic.

These are the eighteen officially recognised tribes. Other groups or clans include:

Vezo

They are not generally recognised as a separate tribe but as a clan of the
Sakalava. They live on the coast in the region of Morondava in the west to
Faux Cap in the south. They are not rice cultivators but fishers. They use
little out-rigger canoes hollowed out from tree trunks and fitted with one
outrigger pole and a small rectangular sail. In these frail but stable craft they
go far out to sea. The Vezo are also noted for their tombs which are generally
well-hidden, some good examples being near Belo and Morondava. They are
graves dug into the ground surrounded by wooden palisades the main posts
of which are crowned by wooden carved figures of the most erotic kind. No
effort is made to keep them in repair as it is only when the palisades finally fall
into decay and ruin that the soul of the dead is fully released.

Zafimaniry

A clan of about 15,000 distributed in about 100 villages between the Betsileo
and Tanala south-east of Ambositra. It is a forest area and they are known for
their wood carvings and sculpture. They are descendants of people from the
High Plateau who went there early in the 19th Century and form an
important historic group as they continue the forms of housing and
decoration of past centuries. Their houses, which are made from vegetable
fibres and wood with bamboo walls and roofs, have no nails and can be taken
down and moved from one village to another.

St Marians

The population of Île Ste Marie (Nosy Boraha) is mixed. Although
Indonesian in origin there has been influence from both Arabs and
European pirates of different nationalities.

The tribes may differ in various ways but, as usual, the Malagasy have
suitable proverbs. *Tsihy be lambanana ny ambanilanitra* – 'All who live
under the sun are plaited together like one big mat'; *Ny olombelona toy ny
molo-bilany, ka iray mihodidina ihany* – 'Men are like the lip of the
cooking-pot which forms just one circle.'

Village life

The Malagasy have a strong sense of community which influences their
way of life. Just as the ancestors are laid in a communal tomb, so their
descendants share a communal way of life, and even children are almost
considered common property within their extended family
(*fianakaviana*).

The village community is based on the traditional *fokonolona*, or
council of elders, and it is they who make decisions on the day to day life
of the village.

Rural Malagasy houses generally have only one room and the
furniture is composed of mats (*tsihy*), often beautifully woven. These
are used for sitting and sleeping.

Part of the Malagasy culture is the art of oratory, *Kabary*. Even rural
leaders can speak for hours, using highly ornate language and many
proverbs. In a society that reached a high degree of sophistication
without a written language, *kabary* had an important communicative

role to play and it was through *kabary* that the early Merina kings inspired and controlled their people.

The description below by Sally Crook, will give you further insights into life in a southern village.

VILLAGE LIFE IN THE SOUTH

By Sally Crook

I was warmly welcomed into the Tandroy (Antandroy) village and soon found that visiting all the houses in the family compound was the purpose of life. Children went from one house to another and ate, talked, played or crawled onto a mat to sleep. All houses are home to them and it was difficult to work out the complex family structure, multiple marriages and frequent divorces resulting in aunts playing with nephews and nieces older than them, and divorcees greeting their husband's current wives.

Children do not have a family name but belong to the father and even the shaven-headed widow who lived with her three young children would have to give them up to a brother-in-law as soon as she married elsewhere.

Most Malagasy men seem to be orators and my arrival and departure brought forth semi formal speeches from Tokoembelo, the head of the compound. Talking among the men also resolves disputes and resolves problems. The divorce of a 17 year old girl from an unworthy husband was a long standing difficulty, and the feud with a neighbouring village suspected of stealing their goats was another which occupied the older men of the compound.

My lack of the language did not exempt me from the visiting circuit and I began at the house of Imaria, the younger current wife of Tokoembelo, who had invited me to watch her weave a mat from start to finish. My presence in her mat-lined house for a couple of hours each day allowed me to sit in on the chats and arguments of women and children who visited her. My efforts at conversation elicited smiles of encouragement or gales of laughter. I soon learnt key words and could guess the gist of the question since everyone was curious on the same points. The key word method was not foolproof, however, and a stunned silence, then guffaws of laughter followed any glaring errors. The women loved to tease me over my frequent *vazaha*-style use of the word for thankyou, *misaotra*, which is unnecessary among family members.

The children played the universal games of children without toys, a boisterous game of wheelbarrows ending with a tangled heap of children giggling on the ground. They sat around me whenever I read on a mat outside, or crowded around my door to look in.

'*Aiza taratasy misy ombiasy, Shallee?*' A request for the book with the picture of the soothsayer on the front and they would turn over pages poring over the pictures of familiar things.

My *sarintany* ('earth picture', or map) was often requested too and the children, most of whom could not read, would point with arms or lips in the direction of the villages or rivers I named from the local map since they knew their area well from walking through it, in company or alone, from a very early age. Lack of schooling and TV left them alert and questioning and I could not look upon it as a misfortune.

Malagasy give directions using the points of the compass and do not talk of right or left. I found this easy enough to follow in the compound since the rectangular houses are aligned with one door on the west and two on the north; sitting one day in my hut with a young visitor looking for page numbers in a book he suddenly exclaimed, 'There they are, to the east!' and they were.

When Tokoembelo's first wife, Talilie, had been wooed back by gifts from her father's village where she had returned after an argument, I began to visit her too, as careful as the husband to treat each wife equally. He spent alternate nights with each wife. As in the other homes, I was given *abobo*, curdled milk, from a gourd where it had been left to sour. Custom does not demand that the bowl be emptied but I always finished it because it was so good, and did so quickly because of the vast numbers of flies landing on it, the bane of people living so closely with their livestock.

Cattle are kept as wealth that is hoarded, traded, used to pay dowries, or guarded until the day of their sacrifice for the master's internment when their horns are placed on the tomb. They are rarely eaten on other occasions by this clan, the lowly goat providing meat for our New Year's Eve celebration, which, being a recently embraced foreign festival, is not important. Sparse meals of maize, cassava or sweet potatoes are more usual than the rice-based meals of elsewhere, eaten with *traka* (potato or cassava leaves). It is considered rude to watch people eating and it is prudent to keep hold of your spoon until you've finished, since putting it down results in the dish being whisked away. Eggs are not usually eaten since raising the chicks to adulthood is more sensible.

Keeping cattle is the real work of the Tandroy but cultivation is necessary for food. Work in the fields takes place in the morning after the cattle have been sorted out and assigned to the children to take out of the cactus-enclosed compound to graze. Wanting to try everything, I went out with the villagers one morning to their far and scattered fields. Tandroy people are proud of their liberty and he who takes the trouble to work a piece of land thereby lays claim to it.

My efforts at weeding – chopping horizontally at the unwanted plant roots with a hoe from a crouched position – were applauded but I was not allowed to do more than five minutes at a time before I was packed off to sit idly in the shade of a tree. I was not too sorry to be stopped since the accidental assassination of the legitimate inhabitants of the plots – maize, groundnut, melons, sweet potatoes and cassava – were too easy in fields planted with three different species together.

Barefoot teenagers and children came by with the cattle, lone herders sometimes singing to themselves at the top of their voices as they kept their charges away from unhedged fields. In the dry season the men set off with their spears (with hoe on one end for digging up roots) and take the zebu far afield for several months at a time to find enough grazing. They bivouac or build huts in a choice area, sometimes settling there permanently, happy to meet up with the Mahafaly to the west but not straying as far north as the Bara who are considered to be cattle thieves.

It was difficult for the family to understand what I considered interesting or unusual and I was called to look on only after a castration had been

Betsimisaraka woman near Sambava (the yellow mangary "paint" is used to improve the skin, rather than for decoration). (John R. Jones)

Mud-fishing in the Anjozorobe (Highlands) area. (John R. Jones)

Famadihana ("turning of the bones"). (John R. Jones)

Mahafaly tomb between Ampanihy and Ambovombe. (John R. Jones)

Zebu

*Zebu cow and herder.
(John R. Jones)*

Portable road warning. (John R. Jones)

Aloalo, Mahafaly country. (John R. Jones)

completed or a calf dropped which was already trying to get up on its weak legs for the first meal at the udder. I watched morning and evening milking in the cow pen. The cow's back legs were held loosely together with rope as she was milked by man and calf at the same time. Women are not allowed to milk into a container and men caught the twice daily half litre of milk in a calabash held in a hand.

Water is a problem even in the wet season. Most stream beds are dry and flow only occasionally when there is a heavy fall of rain on the hills feeding them. I was called down to the river one clear-skied evening to witness the torrent that the river had become from rain falling in the north, only to find next morning it had disappeared leaving newly contoured river banks and a muddy bed with pools of cloudy water stranded on the rocks. Holes are dug in the river bed for water and I was sent with a child who could choose the hole with the cleanest water that day or would dig a new one, the holes getting deeper and deeper until in the late dry season they would have to be several feet deep. My herding and farming companions did not carry water with them but dug a hole in the river bed when we reached it on the way home.

Pinde, cicadas, are caught for food by children in season while they are out herding or playing. These large bugs, whose stridulating makes the air ring in the heat of the day, are easy to locate and are pinned down by a thumb on a wing. I soon learnt to catch them too but did not play with them like the children who seem to have no concept of cruelty to non-human creatures. Divested of wings and legs, they are strung on a long piece of grass before cooking in a dry pot in the evening to make a crunchy, but tasty and nutritious snack. The ubiquitous termite hills are also broken open for chicks to feed on the insects. Creepy-crawlies are found all over the houses, many attracted in by the evening candlelight; and the sound of a large spider rattling its hurrying feet over the mat on which I was trying to sleep, ensured that I slept with a mosquito net each night, in spite of the puzzled enquiries as to why it was needed.

Visits to other compounds of this scattered village, as well as to other villages were also *de rigeur* and were always made with a precious bar of soap since whenever we came to running water in more secluded areas, we would take the opportunity for a proper bath. Honey was the ostensible object of one visit to a neighbouring compound. The split tree trunk hive was opened by an intrepid man brandishing burning grass, and puffing smoke from cigarettes to daze the insects. The owner of the hives claimed to be able to tell how much rain had fallen in his absence by the sweetness of the honey.

People are what matter in life and the old mother of the head man was treated kindly although it was clear she was senile. Mad people or those with epilepsy lived with their relatives and the blind young man from a nearby compound was often to be seen walking alone down the highway of the dry river bed, or picking his way down unknown paths apparently by the echo of his hand clapping from the obstacles in his path.

Old people are revered since they are closest to the ancestors. The most important man of the whole village was the *mpisoro* who makes the zebu sacrifices to the ancestors by the sacred posts in front of his house. I was taken to this man of 95-odd years to pay my respects. We entered his small wooden house through the north-west door, stooping and easing one shoulder in before the other through the tiny opening. The old man wore a traditional loin cloth with patterned edges which younger men sometimes wear over their western shorts. He was almost blind and I was invited to sit close as my visit was explained. He then took my right hand in his, putting his nose to it in a traditional greeting.

Our journey there took us over a scrubby landscape of hardy bushes and plants whose uses were explained to me. Tortoises making their pigeon-toed way over the thorn-strewn earth would suddenly retract into their shells or hiss if we touched them. The compound paths were strewn with ground nut shells as walking on these ensures a good harvest. A stroll across the river bed to another of the scattered village compounds took us to a young man who demonstrated the use of the leather sling that most herders carry over their shoulder, theoretically for self defence, soon gaining in accuracy and force as he sent stone after stone hurtling into a distant tree.

I was unfortunate that there were none of the elaborate funerals or other ceremonies while I was in the village. Bodies left to rot in their former home are removed through a hole broken in the east wall and placed in a massive wall-enclosed tomb, filled with stones and adorned with the horns of sacrificed zebu.

I especially wanted to hear the unique music of the area and on New Year's Day a fiddler and his wife who walk from one ceremony to another to work, came to sing for us. So many people crowded into Talilie's wooden house to hear them that she had to squat outside in the drizzle as the singer sat cross legged on the floor to bow his warped-neck fiddle. His wife used flint and stone to light his cigarettes of tobacco and maize leaf paper or sang almost listlessly beside him. He sang too or provided a song rhythm by a strange rasping breathing like that of a man dying of thirst. I had not heard this harsh sound in the guise of singing before.

Teenagers spend evenings in the river bed when the moon sheds enough light. There the girls sing and drum, and the boys wrestle. I asked the children to sing for me one day and found their style more African than Asian (as are most characteristics of this tribe) consisting of a hard chant without vibrato, often in harmony with others and with drum beat accompaniment. Young children were, as elsewhere, pot-bellied with worms and some had scabies. Frequent hair inspections resulted in the killing of legions of lice.

On Friday nights, before market day in the town a 2 hour walk away, hair was washed and greased with cow fat. Ragged everyday clothes were discarded for the shared market best, and the distance was covered on foot, with a stop to wash feet at the flowing stream near the town. During the three market days of my visit, on only one was there any food to buy but the villagers undertaking the trip that week enjoyed the day chatting in the shade, seeing and being seen before trudging home in the rain.

We waded over a wide flowing river to another, country, market where the 'car park' was full of lounging zebu and the *sarety* (wagons) they had lately been hauling. People socialised under the shade of a large tree or bartered in the market square, and the young men leaned on their long staffs wearing straw hats with colourful knitted bands with small pom-poms dangling over the brim. They acted like men-of-the-world as they eyed the girls before chatting them up.

Morals among this clan of the tribe are what Europeans would call 'loose', and as I sat on the *taxi-brousse* to leave the nearby town for the north, one of the young men of 'my' compound made me a public proposition, which I took from the evident amusement of other passengers to be an 'improper' invitation. It showed how well I had been accepted.

MAN AND NATURE: THE HUMAN PROBLEMS OF CONSERVATION

By Gordon and Merlin Munday

Man must satisfy certain fundamental needs for survival. Most primitively these are fulfilled by hunting and gathering or crop growing for food and barter, pasturing of domesticated animals, fuel for warmth and cooking, materials for shelter, and remedies for alleviating ailments. Man is here interacting with nature and enforcing his demands on the environment; in Madagascar as elsewhere, this along with the population growth, has led to deterioration on a grand scale.

Destruction of habitat with the consequent extinction of animal and plant species is irreversible and we would all wish to see it halted, but a narrowly ecological solution is unacceptable to the hungry and impoverished. So, in looking at Madagascar's problem the outsider should bear in mind the following: it has a population of nearly 11 million with a low population density; 16 inhabitants per square kilometre (compare 25 for the USA and 228 for the UK, according to 1985 United Nations estimates); but a more significant figure is the high population growth rate with a doubling time of 25 years.

Crop Production

It was long believed that forest originally covered the whole island and man, in the fifteen hundred years or so of his presence, was entirely responsible for its destruction and the consequent erosion. More recently another possible cause appears to be that a general extension of a drier climate (cf Sahel in Africa) has adversely affected the already delicate balance of a fragile vegetation, leading to widespread erosion. However all agree that the advent of man practising a shifting agriculture with a slash-and-burn technique (*tavy*) has great responsibility for loss of primary forest. The age-old technique is simple and devastating, forest is cleared of trees, burnt after drying for a few months, then mixed subsistence agriculture undertaken. The land may be used for a year or two before being left fallow, a new area then being cut down and the process repeated. The fallow period is about 10 years but during that time the rains erode and leach the soil on which a degraded vegetation, initially forest (*savoka*) but ultimately grass takes over. It has been estimated that 10 to 15 clearances are possible before the land is spent agriculturally but this picture is over optimistic since the richest and most productive soil is known to be that of virgin land. But the people must be fed. The main crops produced for local use are rice (the dietary mainstay of the population), cassava, sugar cane and sweet potatoes: the most important cash crops are coffee, vanilla and cloves. The government, conscious of certain deficiencies in earlier plans, aims to make the island self sufficient in rice production this year, 1988. Rice yields are low compared with more developed countries, consequently attempts have been and are being made both to increase the yield and put larger areas under cultivation.

Livestock

A significant contributor to the problems of land use is the zebu cattle (ten million; roughly the same as the population). They play a determinant role in most Malagasy lives, even in cultures that are not cattle-based, representing wealth for rural families and an outward sign of well-conducted lives; in short symbolising duty done towards ancestors and much that gives a meaning to existence. Even for rice-based cultures (Merina and Betsileo in the centre, Betsimisaraka, east coast) the zebu is at hand to prepare the paddies, pull carts etc. but its prime function is for sacrifice at the funeral.

In the cattle-based cultures, Mahafaly and Antandroy and much of the western region, where the zebu form the very basis not only of material wealth but aesthetic interest, spiritual beliefs, social structure such as family and kinship ties, and even language, the zebu unites them with ancestors and the hereafter. Large numbers of selected cattle become feast and sacrifice; afterwards the horns are placed on the tomb. Meat is rarely eaten apart from such symbolic meals.

Whilst it is true that zebu are well adapted to the climate, it is a beast that grows and matures slowly (edible yield 330-420 kg after 6-8 years); calf loss is about 32% and average milk yield only one litre per day; a general performance worse than that of other cattle developed in tropical areas. To maintain the cattle requires one hectare per head of pasture and in the dry season they suffer considerably despite great efforts to tide them over. Dry remains of grass are finally fired to hasten regrowth of young sprouts at the first rains; firing which is uncontrolled and often attacks forest edges.

Wood

In the cooler parts of the island people, at least part of the time, need fuel for warmth; everywhere fires are required for cooking (estimated at a little more than one kg of wood per person day). In a country with reputedly very little coal and without foreign currency to buy and equip itself with the products of the modern oil industry, wood is the only practical source of fuel. Should it cause surprise that forests have been cut down to provide wood for fuel? Put into numbers, 80% (1.2 million tonnes of fuel oil equivalent per year) of the total energy consumption in Madagascar goes in firewood: a problem preoccupying governments since the colonial era. Many of the local tree species grow slowly or very slowly, replacement has therefore been by faster growing foreign species, including *Acacia dealbata* and various species of pine and eucalyptus.

Medical

All countries and peoples have over the ages developed remedies from locally available materials for their ailments and disabilities. The study of plants for this purpose is known as ethnobotany. Although the pharmaceutical industry may have refined them, the origin of many useful drugs is the tropical forest rather than laboratory synthesis. It is estimated that one product in four in the pharmaceutical market is derived from wild plants and in 1985 the annual value of these medicines was worth at least £35 billion. The Madagascan Rosy Periwinkle (*Catharanthus roseus*) is the source of many alkaloids two of which are used with success to treat leukaemia: retail worldwide sales of these drugs was worth about $100 million in 1980. As the periwinkles are grown commercially in countries other than Madagascar the Malagasy have made no financial profit. Another species of *Catharanthus* (*C.coriaceus*) is included in the IUCN Plant Red Data Book (1978) as endangered as it is only known in a few localities where the forests in which is grows are threatened with fire; the genus, apart from its botanical interest is of pharmacological importance. Madagascar has a long record of ethnobotanical investigation as is shown by the number of publications in existence; a preliminary database has been compiled by WWF/IUCN. In 1977 the World Health Organisation adopted a resolution at its Assembly urging governments to promote research and interest in traditional medical systems; subsequently a Department of Ethnobotany was established at the National Pharmaceutical Research Centre (Antananarivo).

'But people must eat...' Mahafaly children with coua.

LANGUAGE

The Indonesian origin of the Malagasy people shows strongly in their language which is spoken, with regional variations of dialect, throughout the island. (Words for domestic animals, however, are derived from Kiswahili, indicating that the early settlers, sensibly enough, did not bring animals with them in their outrigger canoes.) Malagasy is a rich language, full of images and metaphors, and the art of oratory, *kabary*, is an important part of the culture. Literal translations of Malagasy words and phrases are often very poetic. Dusk is *Maizim-bava vilany*, 'Darken the mouth of the cooking pot'; two or three in the morning is *Misafo helika ny kary* – 'When the wild cat washes itself'.

Learning, or even using, the Malagasy language may seem a challenging prospect to the first time visitor. Place names may be fourteen or fifteen characters long (because they usually have a literal meaning, such as Ambohibao, The New Village), with erratic syllables stress. However, it is well worth taking the time to learn a few Malagasy words and phrases. English-speakers should remember that their noble efforts at communicating in French are not much use in villages where it is an equally alien language. If Malagasy seems difficult, thank the London Missionary Society that at least it is not still in Arabic script!

Some basic rules
Pronunciation
The Malagasy alphabet is made up of 21 letters. C, Q, U, W, and X are ommitted. Individual letters are pronounced as follows:

a: as in Father.
e: as in the a in Late.
g: as in Get.
h: almost silent.
i: as ee in Seen.
j: pronounced dz.
o: oo as in Too.
s: usually midway between sh and s but varies according to region.
z: as in Zoo.

Combinations of letters needing different pronunciations are:

ai: like y in My.
ao: like ow in Cow.
eo: pronounced ay-oo.

When k or g are preceded by i or y this vowel is also sounded *after* the consonant. For example *Alika* (dog) is pronounced *Aleekya*, and *Ary koa* (and also) is pronounced *ahreekewa*.

Stressed syllables.

Some syllables are stressed, others almost eliminated. This causes great problems with visitors trying to pronounce place names, and unfortunately – like English – the basic rules are frequently broken. Generally, the stress is on the penultimate syllable except in words ending in na, ka, and tra when it is generally on the last syllable but two. Words ending in e stress that vowel. Occasionally a word with the same spelling changes its meaning according to the stressed syllable, but in this case it is written with an accent. For example, *Tanana* means Hand, and *Tanána* means Town.

When a word ends in a vowel, this final syllable is pronounced so lightly it is often just a stressed last consonant. For instance the Sifaka lemur is pronounced – rudely, but memorably – as 'She-fuck'. Words derived from English, like *Hotely* and *Banky* are pronounced much the same as in English.

Vocabulary

The following basic travellers' vocabulary has kindly been provided by the author of *A Glance at Madagascar*. He has also written an excellent *English – Malagasy Vocabulary* which is sometimes available in Antananarivo. This is much better than *An elementary English – Malagasy Dictionary* which is aimed at the Malagasy student of English and gives definitions of English words rather than single-word translations.

A Malagasy phrase book has been published by Damien Tunnacliffe (a contributor to this book) and is available from Bradt Publications.

Stressed letters or syllables are underlined.

English	Malagasy
Sunday	*Alahady*
Monday	*Alatsinainy*
Tuesday	*Talata*
Wednesday	*Alarobia*
Thursday	*Alakamisy*
Friday	*Zoma*
Saturday	*Asabotsy*
Hello/How are you?	*Manao ahoana, Tompoko*.*
or,(on the coast)	*Salama, Tompoko.*
How is your health?	*Fahasalamango, Tompoko?*

* It is polite with many Malagasy expressions to add the word *Tompoko*, a form of address meaning roughly 'Sir' or 'Madam' but not so formal. A Malagasy will not reply just 'yes' or 'no' but will always add *Tompoko*.

I'm well	Salama tsara aho.
Good-bye	Veloma, Tompoko.
See you again	Mandra pihaona.
Yes	Eny, Tompoko.
No	Tsia, Tompoko.
Very good	Tsara tokoa.
Bad	Ratsy.
Thankyou	Misaotra, Tompoko
Excuse me	Aza fady, Tompoko
I don't understand	Tsy azoko, Tompoko
Give me...	Mba omeo ... aho.
I want...	Mila ... aho.
I'm looking for...	Mitady ... aho.
How much?...	Hoatrinona?.
Is there a place to sleep?	Misy ve toerana hatoriana?
I would like to buy some food/a meal	Te hividy hanina/sakafo aho.
Where is ...?	Aiza ...?
Is it far?	Lavitra ve izany?
Is there any ...?	Misy ve ...?
Please help me!	Mba ampio aho!
What's your name?	Iza no anaranao.
I'm hungry	Noana aho.
I'm thirsty	Mangetaheta aho.
I'm tired	Vizaka aho.
Village	Vohitra.
Countryside/Out in the country	Ambanivohitra.
House	Trano.
Food	Hanina (Safako – meal)
Water	Rano.
Rice	Vary.
Eggs	Atody.
Chicken	Akoho.
Bread	Mofo
(European-type bread	Mofo-dipaina).
Milk	Ronono
(Tinned milk	Nestle).
Road	Lalana.
Town	Tanana.
Newspaper	Gazety
Paper	Taratasy.
Hill	Tendrombohitra.
Valley	Lohasaha.
River (large)	Ony.
Stream	Riaka.
Ox/cow	Omby/Omby vavy.
Child/baby	Ankizy/zaza kely.
Man/woman	Lehilahy/Vehivavy.

Chapter 3

Natural History

INTRODUCTION

For most people it is the flora and fauna that draws them to Madagascar. This is 'nature's laboratory', where evolution took a different route.

The reason so many unique species evolved in Madagascar goes back to the dawn of history. It is thought that in the early Cretaceous era a huge land mass known as Gondwanaland began to break up and form the present continents of Africa and Madagascar, Asia, South America, and Australasia. The phenomenon of continental drift explains why some Malagasy plants and animals are found in South America and Asia but not Africa. The boa constrictor, for instance, occurs only in South America and Madagascar, and the urania moth and six plant families are also limited to these two places.

Madagascar broke away from Africa as much as 160 million years ago, when mammals were at a very early stage of evolution, so it is probable that the early lemurs, fossas and tenrecs were carried across the then narrower Mozambique channel on uprooted trees or rafts of vegetation. Once the channel widened, they had little need for evolutionary change since there were no large carnivores to threaten their existence and the thickly forested island provided food without competition. Thus the term 'living fossil' is appropriate here.

Man, however, arrived somewhere around the fifth century (although there is some speculation that it may have been considerably earlier) and quickly exterminated the largest animals. Up to that time eleven giant species of lemur swung through the branches or browsed on the forest floor; some were the size of gorillas. There were giant tortoises bigger than any today, and – largest of all – the *aepyornis*, or elephant bird, which stood ten feet high. Man was probably responsible for the extinction of all these animals, either by direct hunting or – more likely – by destroying their habitat.

Conservation has now become a government priority to halt the destruction of forests (reduced by half since 1950) which threatens Madagascar's amazing percentages of unique species: of the flora, 90% of all forest species are endemic (found only here); there are six unique families of plants. The eastern hardwood forests have 97 varieties of ebony; seven species of baobab flourish (there's one in Africa); all but

The rukh (roc), as visualised by an artist in 1595.

Elephant bird (Aepyornis) egg, in comparison with a hen's egg, Berenty museum. (Photo: Olivier Langrand.)

two of the 130 palm species are unique. Eight genera of fish are found only here; Madagascar contains two-thirds of the world's chameleons, and 225 of the 235 reptile species are endemic. There are 155 species of frog; apart from a few recently introduced animals all the land mammals are endemic: 34 genera and 66 species.

GEOLOGY

The main geological features of Madagascar are a precambrian basement (eastern two thirds of the island), overlaid with laterite, a sedimentary region along the west coast, and volcanic (mainly upper Cretaceous) outcrops.

There are no active volcanoes in Madagascar, but the Itasy region of the highlands shows craters and ashcones, and many hot springs.

Minerals mined include mica and titanium, but not in commercial quantities. Madagascar has an amazingly large number of mineral deposits, but none are large enough to add to the national wealth. The crystaline rock basement produces a fine variety of gemstones, sold in the market and near the places of origin. They include: petrified wood, rhodonite, agate, marble, labradorite (moonstone), amazonite and ammonite. There are many kinds of crystals (sometimes available in block or geode form) including quartz: smoky, rose, citrine, along with haematite, amethyst, celestite, and tourmaline. A beryl unique to Madagascar is the pink morganite.

GONDWANALAND AND THE FIT OF THE SOUTHERN CONTINENTS

THE DRONGO

One of the most recognisable birds in Madagascar is the drongo. Unmistakable in silhouette, with its deeply forked tail and silly crest, it is ubiquitous and fearless, and is said to be an excellent mimic. For the villagers near Maroantsetra it is *fady* to kill a drongo. Here's why:

Centuries ago the pirates who raided the east coast made incursions into the hills to pillage and take captives. At the warning that a pirate band was on its way the villagers would flee into the jungle.

One day in Ambinanitelo word came that a pirate band was approaching. The people scattered, but the women with young children could not keep up with the others and hid in a thicket. Just as the pirates were passing them a baby wailed. The pirates spun around and approached the source of the cry. They heard the baby again, but this time the cry came from the top of a tree. It was a drongo. Believing themselves duped by a bird, the pirates gave up and returned to their boats. And the drongo has been honoured in this valley ever since.

SCIENTIFIC CLASSIFICATION

Since many animals and plants in Madagascar have yet to be given English names, I have made much use of the Latin, or scientific name. For those not familiar with these and the associated terminology, here is a brief guide:

Having been separated into broad **classes** like mammals (mammalia), angiosperms (angiospermae) – flowering plants – etc., animals and plants are narrowed down into an **order**, such as Primates or Monocotyledons. The next division is **family**: Lemur (*Lemuridae*) and Orchid (*Orchidaceae*) continue the examples above. These are the general names that everyone knows, and you are quite safe to say 'in the lemur family' or 'a type of orchid'. There are also sub-families, such as the 'true lemurs' and 'the indri sub-family' which includes sifakas. Then come **genera** (**genus** in singular) followed by **species**, and the Latin names here will be less familiar-sounding. It is these two names that are combined in the scientific name precisely to identify the animal or plant. So *Lemur catta* and *Angraecum sesquipedale* will be recognisable whatever the nationality of the person you are talking to. We call them ring-tailed lemur and comet orchid, the French say maki and orchidée comète. With a scientific name up your sleeve there is no confusion.

FLORA

A glance at the statistics will warm a botanist's heart: Madagascar has around 10,000 species (estimates vary from some 7,000 to 12,000 but with so many still to be classified, the larger figure seems more realistic) whilst Great Britain has 1,750. The large number of species is due to the dramatically different climate zones, and around 80% of the flora is found nowhere else in the world. Unlike the fauna, however, which looks unique even to the unscientific eye, a large proportion of Madagascar's vegetation appears familiar to the non-botanist. Having worked out a successful blueprint in other parts of the world, Nature has come up with the same basic design to fit the different environments: water-retaining plants for arid zones and tall trees with buttress roots for the rainforest.

Descriptions of regional flora are given in respective chapters, particularly *Chapter 8: The South*. The account below is extracted from a more detailed survey of Madagascar's flora, kindly written by Gordon and Merlin Munday. You may order a full copy from Bradt Publications.

Flora – an overview

You may be surprised to discover that you already know a few Madagascar plants – many house or florists plants come from Madagascar. These include 'Crown of Thorns' (*Euphorbia millii*), with its bright red flowers and sharp spines, 'Flaming Katy' (*Kalanchoe blossfeldiana*) with brilliant red and long lasting flowers, 'Panda Plant' (*Kalanchoe tomentosa*), 'Madagascar Dragon Tree' (*Dracaena marginata*), 'Madagascar Jasmine' (*Stephanotis floribunda*) – the bridal bouquet with waxy, white, heavily scented flowers, the 'Polka Dot' plant (*Hypoestis phyllostachya*), and 'Velvet Leaf' (*Kalanchoe beharensis*). The most famous of all, however, is the poinsettia (*Poinsettia madagascariensis*), Madagascar's national flower.

Few of Madagascar's many unique species have been given English names, but one Malagasy plant name has made its way into English: raffia. The palm *Raphia pedunculata* grows in swampy ground to the east and has been a mainstay for craft workers and gardeners all over the world.

Estimates of the number of species of flora in Madagascar range from 7,370 to 12,000, making it one one of the richest botanical areas in the world. Of about 400 flowering plant families worldwide almost 200 are known to occur in Madagascar. There are eight endemic families and 18% of the genera and nearly 80% of the species are also endemic.

Evidence suggests that primitive flowering plants (Angiosperms) originated in the western part of Gondwanaland, probably in the early Cretaceous period, and that subsequently they spread north while diversifying, leading to the establishment of flora in the two large supercontinents. Africa has many genera in common with Madagascar, but individual species are quite distinct. For example, of the 300 African aloe species, not one is identical to the 60 found in Madagascar, and the 'succulent' euphorbias are here more woody than succulent. Africa has

MADAGASCAR
Types of vegetation

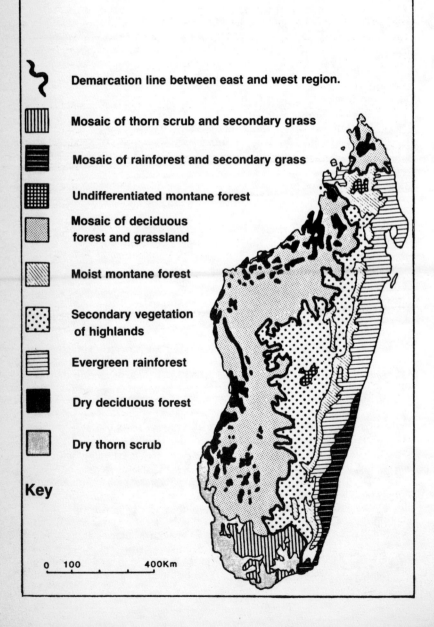

Key

- Demarcation line between east and west region.
- Mosaic of thorn scrub and secondary grass
- Mosaic of rainforest and secondary grass
- Undifferentiated montane forest
- Mosaic of deciduous forest and grassland
- Moist montane forest
- Secondary vegetation of highlands
- Evergreen rainforest
- Dry deciduous forest
- Dry thorn scrub

0   100   400Km

only a few hundred species of orchid, whilst Madagascar claims around a thousand. Nevertheless, many plants such as the African violet (*Viola abyssinica*) and *Cardamine africana* are widely distributed and identical in both places. Mangroves, as one would expect of water disseminated plants, are all identical with those found on the East African coast, whereas Madagascar's endemic palms – 13 genera – almost all show affinities with those of Asia and South America.

Regional flora and vegetation and where to see it

The island's vegetation falls naturally into two regions: east and west (see map). These are further divided into domains, giving a broad classification in terms of geography, climate and vegetation.

EASTERN REGION

This coincides with the climatic eastern region but includes the Sambirano domain and Nosy Be. The central domain is also included; this is the backbone of the region with erosion creating deep gullies, or *lavaka*. Heavy storms carry away the soil – thin clay over friable sedimentary layers – made vulnerable by tree clearance. Vegetation of the region is classified as evergreen forest, mosaic of rainforest and secondary grass, moist montane forest, secondary vegetation of the highlands, and montane bushland and scrub.

Evergreen forest   Occurs below 800 m. The rainfall is generally over 2,000 mm and in some places up to 3,500 mm. The vegetation is stratified in canopies, and the competition for light resulting in no undergrowth. Many trees have buttress roots or stilt-like aerial roots. Epiphytes, including orchids and ferns, are abundant.

The Madagascar rainforest is distinct from corresponding forests in Africa in having a higher species diversity, a lower main canopy and an absence of large emergent trees. Tree density is also three times greater than comparable rainforests in other continents. Families that form part of the upper canopy include Euphorbiaceae (nearly all with the milky latex sap), Sapindaceae (woody lianas), Rubiaceaae (including wild coffee), Ebenaceae, including the genus *Diospyros* (with 97 species, one of which is the true ebony), and palms.

Tourist-accessible evergreen forest can be seen in Lokobe (Nosy Be), the area round Maroantsetra, and Nosy Mangabe.

Île Ste Marie is botanically rewarding. Here you can see the spectacular comet orchid, *Angraecum sesquipedale*. The tubular nectary of this creamy-white flower is 38 cm (15 inches) long. When Charles Darwin was shown the orchid he predicted that a hawkmoth with a 15 inch tongue must exist in Madagascar to fertilise it. Sure enough; the moth is named *praedicta*, and the flower sometimes called Darwin's Orchid. Features of the coastal landscape on the island are large Barringtonia trees on the shoreline, with 'bishop's hat' fruits, and coconut palms leaning into the sea which disseminates their fruit.

Mosaic of rainforest and secondary grass   An outstanding example of a successful indigenous secondary forest tree is the Traveller's Palm

(*Ravenala madagascariensis*) the symbol of Madagascar and the logo of Air Madagascar. It gets its name from the relief it affords a thirsty traveller: water is stored in the base of its leaves and can be released with a panga blow. The fan arrangement of the leaves is extremely decorative. The Ravenala is, in fact, not a palm but is related to the *Strelitzia* or Bird of Paradise flower. It often occurs in combination with Pandanus (screw pine), which is somewhat like a palm, and Typhonodorum, which grows in or by water and has huge spinach-like leaves.

Other indigenous vegetation does less well in competition with introduced grasses, ferns and shrubs which take over after fire. Indigenous forest species able to colonise the edges of cut forests include some useful to man such as *Canarium*, a valuable all-purpose wood and a source of essential oils, *Croton*, from which drugs are derived, and two guavas, *Psiadia altissima* and *Haronga madagascariensis* which is also the source of a valuable drug, Harunganin, used for stomach disorders.

This type of vegetation (unfortunately) can be seen anywhere near inhabited places by the east coast, where the landscape is degraded as a result of fire, and dominated by grass. There are few trees.

Moist montane forest   Generally occurs between 800 m and 1,300 m but can go as high as 2,000 m if the conditions are right. The canopy is about 5 m lower than the lowland forest, and there is more undergrowth, including some temperate genera such as *Labiatae* and *Impatiens*. There are abundant epiphytes, ferns and mosses, and large lianas and bamboo. As the altitude increases, so the height of the canopy decreases, letting in more light and permitting the growth of epiphytes and shrubby, herbaceous undergrowth with an abundance of moss. Leaves become tougher, with a thicker cuticle to help retain water.

Trees at this altitude include *Dalbergia*, rosewood, and *Weinmannia*, a useful light timber; species of palm and tree fern grow in lower areas.

The most accessible example of medium altitude moist montane forest is Périnet. The upland variety can best be seen in Montagne d'Ambre National Park, and high altitude moist montane forest is best shown on the lower slopes of the Marojejy massif.

Highland vegetation (the central domain)   The forest that formerly covered the *hauts plateaux* has been replaced by grassland. These are relieved by granite outcrops which harbour succulents (Route National 7, between Ambalavao and Ihosy gives you good views of such rock formations). These hills are called 'Inselbergs'. *Pachypodium* occur in this environment, with, among others, aloes and euphorbia.

High altitude montane forest   Beginning at 1,300 m and extending to 2,300 m, the vegetation here is shaped by lower, more varied temperatures, wind, sun and rain. The forest resembles tall scrub with small, tough leaves. Moss and lichens clothe branches and cover the ground up to 30 cm, and provide anchorage for epiphytic ferns and orchids. Ericaceous species predominate in the undergrowth.

The massif of Marojejy provides the best example, along with the botanical reserve of Ambohitantely, 80 km north of Antananarivo.

Tapia forest This is the local name for the dominant species *Uapaca bojeri*, a tree with a thick, crevassed bark which is very fire resistant. The forest is on the western slopes of the central highlands, with a drier climate than eastern domains. The impenetrable vegetation appears similar to Mediterranean cork oak forests. There are few epiphytes or ground mosses.

Isalo National Park has Tapia groves and also various succulents on its sandstone outcrops.

Montane bushland and thicket Characterised by a single stratum, up to six metres, of impenetrable branching evergreen woody plants growing above 2,000 m, and interesting for trees belonging to the daisy family (*Compositae*).

None of Madagascar's high mountains is easily accessible. Probably Andringitra offers the best possibility.

THE WESTERN REGION

Dry deciduous forest The flora is extensive and varied but of lower density and less rich than in the moister eastern forests. Deciduous trees grow to a height of 12 to 15 m with some emergent trees up to 25 m. There are abundant lianas, and shrubby undergrowth, but no ferns, palms or mosses covering the forest floor, and few orchids.

Dry deciduous forest grows on clay or sandy soil. The latter includes the luxuriant gallery forests along rivers where tamarind trees predominate. Away from water, it is the baobabs that take precedence. A third environment, calcareous plateaux, produces a lower forest canopy with fewer lianas and evergreens. Trees and shrubs with swollen trunks or stems (*pachycauly*) are much in evidence.

The Forestry Station of Ampijoroa is an easily accessible area of dry deciduous forest. Harder to reach, but rewarding when you get there is the reserve of Tsingy de Namoroka, which has a dense combination of dry forest, savanna, and plants specially adapted to the pinnacles, or calcareous karst (*tsingy*), which gives the reserve its name.

Deciduous thicket ('spiny forest') Madagascar's most strikingly unique landscape comes into this category, where Didiereaceae, an endemic family are associated with tree Euphorbias. There are some evergreens here, probably because of sea mists bathing the plants. Heavy morning dews are a boon to the local people who collect the precious water with 'dew ladles'. Thickets vary in height from three to six metres, and with their thorns are impenetrable. Emergent trees are mostly baobab.

Didiereaceae show some resemblance to the Boojum cactus (Fouquieriaceae) of the south-west USA and Mexico. There are four genera, exclusive to the west and south of Madagascar: *Alluaudia* (six species), *Alluaudiopsis* (two species), Didierea (two species), and Decaryia (one species). Examples of the tree Euphorbia of the thicket are *E.stenoclada* (thorny, the latex used for caulking pirogues), *E. enterophora* (thornless, up to 20 metres), and *E. plagiantha*, also thornless, and characterised by peeling yellowish-brown bark.

Very conspicuous are the 'barrel' and 'bottle' trees with their massive trunks adapted for water storage. *Andanosia*, *Moringa*, and *Pachypodium* are the genera.

Leaf succulents are well represented, with several species of tall (3 – 4 metre) aloes. The shrivelled redundant leaves wrap the stem and give some resistance to fire. Look also for the genus *Kalanchoe*. One of the most interesting species, *K. beauverdii* (two to three metres long) forms buds around the leaf margins, each of which then becomes a tiny daughter plant, thus giving it great survival powers.

These are only a few examples of from well over a thousand species belonging to genera of widely different plant families, which nevertheless show much resemblance to one another in their methods of circumventing drought. After rain, leaves and flowers form fast and in some species the flowers even form before rain, thus giving maximum time for fruit formation and dispersal before the next drought.

The best place to view the spiny forest is near Tuléar, along the Fort Dauphin – Ambovombe road, and in Berenty reserve. Berenty is also an excellent example of gallery forest. Another nature reserve, but not as accessible, is Tsimanampetsotsa (partly a brackish lake) 100 km south of Tuléar.

Secondary grassland   After the excitement of the spiny forest this is inevitably a let down, but inescapable as about 80% of the western region is covered with secondary or wooded grassland, burnt yearly. Two species of palm, *Medemia nobilis* and *Borassus madagascariensis* (both riverside species) have settled in this habitat.

Mangrove   This is an environment of shrubs or small trees growing in muddy lagoons, river deltas, bays or shores, their roots washed by salt or brackish water. Mangroves are found mainly on the west coast and are characterised by stilt-like roots, some of which emerge above the water to take in oxygen. Some have another advantage because their seeds germinate in the fruit while remaining on the tree (viviparity), the fruit then dropping into the mud with its plantlet well on the way to independence. There are three families (nine species) in Madagascar. In the Tuléar region the contrast of spiny vegetation in land and a bright green band of mangroves is particularly striking. They are economically important to the people for various aspects of fish or shellfish farming. The wood is hard and very dense but not very durable, and is used for poles and planks and also firewood. The bark is good for tanning leather.

Apart from the Tuléar region, there is a population of *Avicennia marina* in the Betsiboka estuary and Nosy Be has the same species in a much smaller area.

THE BAOBAB

By Ed Fletcher

Baobabs occur in Africa and Madagascar: one species in Africa and seven in Madagascar. Many myths and folklore have been created about baobabs; it is commonly being called the upside-down-tree, the legend being that the devil plucked up the baobab, thrust its branches into the earth and left its roots in the air. It has been described as 'A Caliban of a tree, a grizzled distorted old goblin with a girth of a giant, the hide of a rhinoceros, twiggy fingers clutching at empty air.'

Baobabs can reach an age of several thousand years. Calculations have been carried out on mature baobabs in order to estimate their age using a formula of rate of growth, size and growing conditions in areas of low rainfall; some baobabs could be over 5,000 years old, which has caused theological arguments centred around the Great Flood destroying all animal and plant life. Michel Adanson, the botanist who first recorded the baobab in 1743, angered David Livingstone by his calculations of the age of some African specimens.

One of the most contentious issues surrounding the baobab is its classification as a tree. It could by definition be classed as a succulent, being able to store water in its trunk unlike other trees, temperate or tropical.

In Madagascar one of the common names for the baobab is the Bottle Tree. These are planted near the tombs of the Mahafaly tribe as a sacred vegetation.

The baobab has many traditional uses: bark fibre is used to make rope, baskets, snares, fibre cloth, musical instrument strings, and waterproof hats (one characteristic of the baobab, which other trees do not possess, is that stripping the bark will not kill the tree. The bark will regenerate). Wood pulp makes strong coarse paper, floats, trays and platters. The fresh leaves provide a vegetable similar to spinach and a beverage. Seeds are a source of food high in protein and oil content. The empty seed husks are used for various utensils, and the pulp makes a refreshing drink high in vitamin C.

Listed below are the species of baobab native to Madagascar:

Adansonia grandidieri   This is the largest. The trunk is cylindrical and very fat, with reddish bark. The flower is completely white and blossoms in March. The Sakalava regard the fruit as a valuable source of food, harvesting the fruit and edible seeds which produce a valuable fatty substance. The sheer vertical trunks are scaled by means of wooden spikes driven into the bark. The local name given is *Reniala*.

This baobab is rare, localised in the southern part of the Menabe area in the eastern region, particularly around Morondava.

Adansonia madagascariensis   One of the most beautiful of all the baobab species, its trunk generally has little swelling, being cylindrical or tapering from the base to the branches, ranging from 10 – 35 metres in height. The local names include *Za*, *Zabe*, *Renida*, and *Bozy* depending on the size and appearance and also on the tribes. The flower is red, and generally blossoms at the start of the rainy season in November and the fruit is ready for harvesting in the dry season. It has a wide distribution, being common on the western coast of Diego-Suarez (north) and Cap Sainte Marie (south), around the Ambongo-Boina area and around Manombo to the north of Tuléar.

Adansonia za   It varies in appearance. The trunk tapers from the base to the top, or is cylindrical and can be confused with a *Grandidier*. The height varies between 10 – 39 metres. The local names are *Za*, *Ringy* and *Boringy*. The flower is yellow tinged with red. It grows in regions where the climate is harsh, with little rainfall, in parts of Ambongo-Boina and

Sambirano in the west and north-west. This baobab is becoming rare since it is used to feed zebu in times of drought. After felling, the bark is peeled off to enable the cattle to feed on the water-saturated fibre.

Adansonia fony   It is of variable appearance, generally standing around 4 – 10 metres. The trunk can be swollen in various shapes, tapering from the base to the branches, or swollen in the middle, or cigar-shaped and constricted at the top. A truly remarkable tree. The local names are *Za*, *Ringy*, *Zamena*, *Boringy*. The flowers are yellowish, and blossom according to the rainfall which is irregular in the dry areas in which this species grows: the rocky regions in the southern park of Menabe, around Morondava, Mount Ambohibitsika (Basin of Mangoky), Marofondelia forest in the north of Morondava and the sandhills between Fiherena and Manombo.

Adansonia suarezensis   This species has a smooth trunk, usually tapered from the base, swelling at the branches. The height varies from 20 – 30 metres. The local names are not known. The flowers are large and deep red.

Adansonia perrieri   Only recently discovered (1960) in the region of Diego-Suarez on the plateau of Ankarana, it has a yellow flower. There is very little other information.

Adansonia alba   It has a swollen trunk, tapering gradually from the base to the top. The height varies from 10 – 15 metres. The local names are unknown. The flower is white, and the species is found to the north of Bezofo in dense wood and at an altitude of about 500 metres in an area where baobabs generally do not exist.

Adansonia digitata   This species is the one found on mainland Africa where it has a wide distribution. It has a large trunk up to 15 metres in diameter and can contain up to 30,000 gallons of water. The many local names include: *Sefo*, *Bontona* or *Vontona* (Swollen One), *Reniala* (Father or Mother of the Forest). The flower is white and large. It is often found in the central square of Sakalava villages, particularly the ports in the Ambongo-Boina area of the western region (there is a famous one in Majunga).

VANILLA

Not a native Madagascar species, vanilla is an orchid from Mexico. Because the insect necessary for pollination stayed behind in its native country, all vanilla in Madagascar must be pollinated by hand.

Vanilla is grown in the north and east of Madagascar; almost the entire crop goes to the United States for ice cream. The government sets the price for vanilla; in 1986 this was about £8 (7,500 FMG) per kilo.

FAUNA
Mammals

There are five orders of land mammals in the island: Primates (lemurs), Insectivora (tenrecs and shrews), Chiroptera (bats), Carnivora (carnivores, including the fossa), and Rodentia (rodents, such as the giant jumping rat). Of these it is the three families of lemur that get the most attention so it is worth describing them in some detail.

Once upon a time there were lemur-type animals all over the world, including North America. Known as prosimians, these creatures had evolved from the ancestral primate, father of all primates including ourselves. They had some monkey-like characteristics but retained the foxy face of their insectivorous forebears, the long nose being needed for a highly developed sense of smell. Lemurs have changed little since the Eocene period 58 – 36 million years ago. Other descendants of the ancestral primate evolved into monkeys; faced with competition from other mammals these developed a greater intelligence and better eyesight. Their sense of smell became less important so their noses lost their physical prominence.

Lemurs are the only surviving prosimians in the world apart from the bushbabies of Africa and the lorises of Asia. From their faces it's hard to believe they are our relatives, but quoting from *Defenders of Wildlife* magazine (April 1975) 'One needn't be a scientist to look at a lemur's hand ... and feel the thrill of recognition across a gap of 60 million years'.

The number of lemur species and sub-species known to science seems to grow yearly. When I wrote the first edition of this book there were 29 species; now there are 31, plus a thought-to-be-extinct species. For scientists to discover new species of primates is extremely rare. That this should happen three times in so many years is extraordinary, and demonstrates the vital importance of preserving habitats which no doubt harbour thousands of unclassified living things. The newcomers are the golden bamboo lemur, *Hapalemur aureus*, of Ranomafana (see page 127), the golden-crowned sifaka, *Propithecus tattersalli*, found in 1988 in Antsiranana province, and the endearingly named hairy-eared dwarf lemur, *Allocebus trichotis*, which was thought to be extinct but resurfaced near Mananara in 1989 to be identified by the indefatigable Bernhard Meier who discovered the golden bamboo lemur.

Only a handful of lemur species is diurnal, so easily seen. Dedicated lemur-watchers, however, can look for nocturnal species at night (see page 44) with the help of a headlamp. The diurnal lemurs that are common in certain nature reserves are described in those sections: ring-tails and sifakas in *Berenty*, indri in *Périnet* and black lemurs in *Nosy Be* but there are some generalities which are interesting. Diurnal lemurs live in troops where the females are dominant (which is rare in primates, where males are usually larger) and they sunbathe in the morning to raise the body temperature. Lemurs have slow metabol-

IDENTIFYING NOCTURNAL LEMURS. ———————

By R.W.Byrne

Seeing nocturnal lemurs isn't hard at all. They are far less shy than the often-hunted diurnal species and let you walk right underneath them in the trees, and their eyes have a silvery tapetum behind the retina which reflects the light, so 'eyeshine' is easily picked out with a torch. To see eyeshine, the axis of the torchlight has to be close to your own eyes so a strong headtorch is best. Then you can see a smallish, brown lemur... but what is it? Most illustrations are pretty confusing, but it's not hard to work out what genus it is. Notice if it sits upright, or along branches like a squirrel; whether the face is flattened or pointed; any markings or colour contrasts; the size; the tail. Then, assuming it's smaller than a brown lemur and brown or grey, use this key:

1. (a)   Face flattened, owl-like; body usually held upright, see 2.
    (b)   Face pointed, body usually held horizontally, see 3.
    (c)   Face blunt but not flat; body usually held horizontally; big, thick tail; short legs. Chiefly diurnal, no prominent dark marks (e.g. on face), no white marks = HAPALEMUR. *H. griseus*: rabbit sized, eating bamboo, greyish. *H. simus*: much bigger – size of brown lemur, greyish, nearly extinct. *H. aureus*: much bigger, size of brown lemur, orange-brown, nearly extinct, newly discovered in the forests of Ranomafana.

2. (a)   Tail invisible or curled up in front of body; pale underside or hind limbs show no stripe on thigh; ears tiny; yellowish and reddish colour. Sluggish, strictly nocturnal = AVAHI (*A. Laniger*).
    (b)   Tail quite easily seen; animal smaller (size of rabbit or less); no clear contrasts in colour, ears small or tiny. Nocturnal, may sleep in visible position, especially Nosy Be. = LEPILEMUR. (The best way of telling the seven species apart is by range).

3. (a)   Tiny, rapid running and leaping in branches; tail thin. Nocturnal = MICROCEBUS (mouse lemur. Either *M. murinus* or *M. rufus* – very hard to separate, range different).
    (a)   Medium small, contrasting pale underparts; black 'spectacles' and black ears and nose; long thick tail. Nocturnal = CHEIROGALEUS (dwarf lemur). *C. medius*: relatively small but tail very fat, greyish. *C. major*: relatively large, tail untapered and not flattened, brownish.

This key doesn't include *Microcebus coquereli*, which is very local and I suspect would look like a big edition of *M. rufus* and act like one, nor *Allocebus trichotis* which hasn't been seen for years, nor *Phaner furcifer* which is conspicuously marked and anyway very localised.

If what you've seen still doesn't fit, could it be a 'diurnal' lemur like brown lemur, which forages much of the night? And if it's hefty, has big bat-like ears, a bushy tail and sparse grey fur.... you hit the jackpot, it's an aye-aye!

ism, and need a bit of help from the sun for their daily quota of energy. Female dominance may be necessary because lemur young are dependent on their mother's milk for a long time so extra nutrition is needed for lactation.

One lemur that you are unlikely to see is the aye-aye, but its strangeness symbolises the uniqueness of Madagascar so it deserves a description. It took a while for scientists to decide that the aye-aye *is* a type of lemur, and it has a family of its own, *Daubentonia madagascariensis*. The aye-aye has been described as appearing to be assembled from the leftover parts of a variety of animals. It has the teeth of a rodent (they never stop growing), the ears of a bat, the tail of a fox, and the hands of no living creature since the middle finger is like that of a skeleton. It's this finger which so intrigues scientists as it shows the aye-aye's adaptation to its environment. In Madagascar it fills the ecological niche left empty by the absence of woodpeckers. The aye-aye uses its skeletal finger to hook grubs out of trees, having detected their movement with its bat-like ears and gnawed through the bark with its rodent's teeth. Its fingers are unique among lemurs in another way – it has claws not fingernails (except on the big toe).

This fascinating animal was long considered to be on the verge of extinction, but recently there have been encouraging signs that it is more widespread than previously supposed. Although destruction of habitat is the chief threat to its survival, it is also endangered because of its supposedly evil powers. Rural people believe it is the heralder of death. If one is seen near a settlement it must be killed, and even then the only salvation may be to burn down the village. A sorcerer can gain great powers if he has the courage to bite the aye-aye's skeleton finger from the living animal. The aye-aye is protected on the island reserve of Nosy Mangabe to which it was introduced in 1966, in Mananara, and has been sighted in Ranomafana and Périnet.

Aye-aye

Almost as strange as the aye-aye are the 21 species of tenrec. These insectivores are considered by some zoologists to be the most primitive of all mammals, and the most prolific. A female may give birth to 32 young! Many tenrec species have prickles and resemble miniature European hedgehogs, and the tiny striped tenrec (*Hemicentetes*) has rows of specialised spines which it can vibrate and strike together, producing a sound (inaudible to humans) which is used to call the young when they scatter to feed. Not all tenrecs have prickles. Some are furry, resembling mice or shrews. Spines seem to be the favoured form of defence, however, and even the furry species often have a few prickles hidden in the fur. Tenrecs are commonly eaten by the Malagasy, especially the largest species, known as the tail-less tenrec, which is the size of a rabbit. There is also an aquatic tenrec which is hunted in the fast-flowing rivers of the eastern rainforest.

Some species of tenrec gestivate (i.e. go into a torpor) during the dry season when food is scarce.

Not all the 26 bat species in Madagascar are endemic (evidently they could fly across the Mozambique Channel), but 13 live only here. Very few studies have been done on them. The most visible are the fruit bats or flying foxes (*Pteropus rufus*), an endemic species closely related to those of Asia and seen in Berenty. They are much sought after for food.

The seven species of Malagasy carnivore all belong to the family Viverridae, and are related to the mongoose, civet and genet of Africa. The largest is the puma-like fossa, (also spelt fosa to avoid confusion with the smaller nocturnal *Fossa fossana* or fanaloka). The fossa's scientific name is *Cryptoprocta ferox* and although rarely seen it is not uncommon. The fossa is an expert tree climber, and the only serious predator (apart from hawks) of lemurs. It has reddish fur, short strong jaws, retractable claws, a long tail, and is roughly the size of a labrador. More often seen are the four species of mongoose-like *Galidia*. Quite common is *Galidia elegans* which is chestnut brown with a stripy tail and frequents the east and northern rain forest.

None of the rodents is the same as ours (although mice and rats have been introduced and the latter seem very at home in cheaper hotels). There are seven genera of which the giant jumping rat is the most interesting: it leaps like a wallaby amongst the baobabs near Morondava, where it now has a reserve.

'Nature seems to have retreated there into a private sanctuary, where she could work on different models from any she has used elsewhere. There, you meet bizarre and marvellous forms at every step.'

Philibert Commerson, 1771. French Naturalist.

Amphibians and reptiles

Madagascar is particularly rich in this group of fauna – there are 144 species of frogs (the only amphibians here – there are no toads, newts or salamanders) most of which are treefrogs, and 257 reptiles. Many species have only recently been discovered so the number will almost certainly be increased as more studies are made.

Of the many types of lizards in Madagascar, chameleons deserve special mention because they are easily seen and handled. Most people think they know one thing about chameleons – that they change colour to match their surroundings. In fact this is not really true: chameleons do have a remarkable ability to change colour but emotional factors play a much more important part than environment. A green chameleon crossing a brown road remains green, but when confronted with another chameleon it will break out into spots and stripes of rage. Chameleons turn darker in the sun and lighter during the night. They can and do vary their normal colour to blend with their surroundings, but rely more on slow movements and concealment behind branches to render them inconspicuous. Chameleons are only found in the Old World, and 'chameleons' sold as pets in the U.S.A. are actually anolis lizards. Although they share the true chameleon's colour-changing abilities, there are many important differences: chameleons can move their eyes independently, looking forward and back at the same time; their feet are adapted for grasping branches, and their tongues can shoot out to a length exceeding their body to catch insects.

There are two genera of chameleon, *Chamaeleo* and the tiny *Brookesia*. Madagascar is the home of two thirds (51 species) of the world's chameleons, including the smallest and the largest.

Chameleons may be good at camouflage, but the real masters of the art are the fringed geckos (also called leaf-tailed lizard) of the *Uroplatus* genus. These reptiles blend so perfectly into the bark of the trees on which they spend the day, that when I pointed one out on Nosy Mangabe (particularly rewarding for *Uroplatus*) my companions failed to see it until I had encouraged it to gape in self defence. Not only does the lizard's skin perfectly match the bark, but its sides are fringed so no shadow appears on the tree; even its eye is flecked like bark. It is truly almost invisible.

None of Madagascar's 60 species of snake is venomous; or to be accurate, since they are all back-fanged they cannot inflict a venomous bite (there are, in fact, six genera of poisonous snakes). The most commonly seen snake is the *do*, or boa constrictor, whose nearest relative is in South America.

It is interesting that despite the harmlessness of the island's snakes, the local population still hold them in fear and myths abound. It is thought, for instance, that the long, slim *fandrefiala* snake can spear a zebu by dropping down from a tree, tail first. They say this devilish creature measures its aim by dropping a couple of leaves first. The Malagasy name *Kapilangidro* means 'lemur's plate' and describes *Sanzinia madagascariensis*. They say that this snake will coil itself into a bowl from which lemurs drink. Nice!

There are several species of tortoise, but 80% of these reptiles are thought to have been killed off by introduced animals. The radiated and plow-share tortoise are the most attractive and also in danger of extinction. A successful breeding programme for the latter has been established in Ampijoroa.

Butterflies

Madagascar has over 300 species of butterfly and moth, of which 233 are endemic. Since Madagascar probably became separated from Africa before the evolution of butterflies, the forefathers of these butterflies probably flew – or were blown– over from East Africa, where they show most affinity. However, there is a swallowtail, *Atrophaneura antenor*, whose nearest relative is in India, and the Urania moth *Chrysiridea madagascariensis* is very similar to the one found in South America.

The most spectacular moth is the comet (*Argema mittrei*), one of the largest in the world, with a beautiful silver cocoon. They are still relatively common but large numbers are collected for the tourist trade.

Birds

Compared with mainland Africa Madagascar is poor in birds. There are 256 species, of which 211 are resident and 115 endemic. Endemic families comprise mesites (similar to rails), ground-rollers, cuckoo-rollers, asitys, vangas, and couas. A striking group are the couas (10 species) which, with their long broad tails, resemble the African touraco. The insect–eating vanga family (14 species) is also conspicuous, particularly the grotesque helmet bird with its oversized blue beak. It is very rare, however. More easily seen is the distinctive sicklebill, and also the hook-billed vanga.

The Berenty section has more details on birds, including a check list.

Parson's chameleon

Sickle-billed vanga

Books and field guides

There are now some good books on the natural history and nature reserves of Madagascar (see *Bibliography*). The long-awaited *Field Guide to the Birds of Madagascar* by Olivier Langrand is due to be published by Yale University Press early in 1991. Until then, the best available combination for serious ornithologists is *The Endemic Birds of Madagascar* published by the ICBP and Collins' *Field Guide to the Birds of East Africa*. The former has no illustrations but gives scientific data about every species and its habitat, which narrows down the choice, and the Collins guide is helpful with non-endemics. Otherwise *Madagascar* (*Key Environments*) is the best bet, with good black and white illustrations of several endemic species. *Madagascar: Un Sanctuaire de Nature* has some good colour illustrations, taken from the massive *Faune de Madagascar*.

Also in preparation is the *Field Guide to the mammals of Madagascar* by Martin Nicoll and Russell Mittermeier. With luck this will be available in 1991.

CONSERVATION IN MADAGASCAR: THE PAST AND THE FUTURE

By Alison Richard

Introduction

In the eastern rain forests of Madagascar it is told how once upon a time there lived an animal called the *babakoto* who ate the leaves and fruit of the trees and led an easy, carefree existence. The *babakoto* had four children. Two grew up and lived off the fruit and leaves of the forest as their ancestors had done. Two left the forest and set to work cultivating the land. These were the first ancestors of the Malagasy people, and this is why today it is forbidden, or *fady*, to hunt or kill the *babakoto* or *Indri indri*.

This traditional tale is but one of many still to be heard throughout rural Madagascar, each one explaining why a particular animal or plant should be protected or, at least, left unharmed. At what point in Madagascar's history *fady* became widely applied, particularly to the island's species, we do not know. There is mounting evidence that hunting by the first settlers contributed to the extinction of the largest animals and it would be misleading to suggest that Madagascar's remaining animals are all protected by this belief system today. To the contrary, as traditional beliefs break down, as people become hungrier, as migrant labourers move into areas containing species unknown to them and to which their own *fady* do not apply, the protection afforded by the system of *fady* is incomplete and perilous. Even so, the national government's recent and mounting concern with the conservation of the island's natural heritage finds echoes in the tradional beliefs of people living alongside and, sometimes, quite literally in the midst of this natural heritage. This fact alone provides some hope that the government's efforts, coupled with increasing assistance from the international community, will have a chance of succeeding.

Integrating conservation and development

By establishing a national strategy for conservation and sustainable development in 1984, the government of Madagascar became one of the first in the world to give formal recognition to the importance of integrating these activities. Searching for ways of implementing the strategy, late in 1985 the government hosted a major international conference on conservation for development and many collaborative efforts, large and small, are now underway as a result. The Ministry of Animal Production (Fisheries, Husbandry), Waters and Forests – abbreviated as MPAEF – which administers the reserve system, has entered into a series of partnerships with international organisations ranging from the World Bank to the World Wide Fund for Nature. Diverse as these organisations may be in their scale and mode of operation, they share with the MPAEF a commitment to slow down and eventually halt encroachment into and exploitation of the reserves, by protecting them better and, in particular, by providing people living around them with economically viable alternatives. The MPAEF's activities with the World Wildlife Fund are a good example of these efforts.

The first step in the joint MPAEF/WWF programme which began in 1986 was to do a thorough evaluation of all protected areas in the country to find out which were the most severely threatened and to formulate preliminary proposals for their future management. Now these efforts have focused on Andringitra (Reserve No.5) in the south-east, Andohahela (Reserve No.11) in the south, Marojejy (Reserve No.12) in the north-east, and the Montagne d'Ambre National Park in the north. In the conventional conservationist tradition, staffs in these reserves are being increased in size and provided with uniforms and the transportation needed to patrol effectively. Scholarships enable the heads of reserves to seek further training in natural resource management. Reserve boundaries are themselves gradually being delineated better and posted with signs. These are all essential activities that the government of Madagascar has been unable to undertake in the past for want of funds and perhaps also because only recently has a real sense of urgency set in. What is particularly exciting and just as essential as these traditional measures, however, is the new effort being made to coordinate them with activities initiated by organisations concerned with economic development. In this context, the emphasis is upon enhancing agricultural practices or techniques of livestock management, increasing fuelwood production, instituting or improving soil conservation measures, and so on. The specific activity varies according to local needs but the goal is the same: to ensure that conservation efforts focusing on the reserves go hand in hand with, rather than at the expense of, economic development in the areas surrounding them.

The success of this programme, and others like it, will ultimately depend on the support and participation of the people most immediately affected. Accordingly, a serious effort is being made to find out what people living around the reserves consider to be their greatest problems and needs, and to include these people in the planning process rather than simply to impose conservation measures and development schemes upon them. Public awareness and education are also important components of the overall effort, and a mobile unit equipped with audio-visual aids and a trained staff is now travelling to villages around the reserves to explain the magnitude of the environmental problems and to discuss ways of alleviating or solving them.

At the Special Reserve of Beza Mahafaly in the south-west, another level of education is also being promoted. With the enthusiastic support of people living in the area, Beza Mahafaly was established as a university reserve in 1977 by the University of Madagascar and two American universities (Washington University and Yale). Financial support was provided by the World Wide Fund for Nature. Remote, relatively inaccessible and just 600 ha. in area, the Beza Mahafaly reserve helps protect what satellite images suggest is the only significant patch of riverine forest left in south-west Madagascar, as well as the ecological gradient from this habitat type to the dry, spiny forest characteristic of much of the south. Ring-tailed lemurs (*lemur catta*) and sifakas (*Propithecus verreauxi*) are abundant and approachable in the reserve, and at night the mouse lemur (*Microcebus murinus*) and sportive lemur (*Lepilemur mustelinus*) can be seen. Among the other wildlife forms present are more than 65 species of birds, and a large population of the highly endangered radiated tortoise (*Geochelone radiata*).

The Beza Mahafaly reserve was founded to promote conservation in the south-west and to serve as a testing ground for ideas about ways of making the survival of Madagascar's natural heritage compatible with the economic needs of its people. Activities connected with these goals are in full swing today. But it was also intended to serve as a training ground for students at the University of Madagascar's School of Agronomy: from the ranks of these students will come the next generation of managers and administrators in whose hands the future of the island's natural resources will lie. A field school, held twice yearly at Beza Mahafaly, has gradually been developed to expose these students to the practical aspects of conservation biology, to 'get their feet wet', as it were, and simply enhance their knowledge of the unique and diverse plants and animals for which they will soon be responsible. Each year Beza Mahafaly also accommodates a small number of students for longer periods to do research on the vegetation, wildlife and socio-economic problems of the area.

If the possibility of drawing upon traditional beliefs protecting some plants and animals provides grounds for cautious optimism about the future survival of Madagascar's natural riches, so too do the developments of the last few years. For instance, when the Beza Mahafaly project began in 1977, small in scale as it was, it was nonetheless the only project of its kind in Madagascar. Ten years later, it is but one of a growing number of efforts to transform the ideal of conservation into a practical reality. The threats are real, and great. But so too, increasingly, are the resolve and wherewithal with which to combat them.

Since Alison wrote this piece in 1988, the WWF has successfully continued its work in surveying the protected areas. Their findings have been published in Madagascar: Review de la conservation et des aires protégées. *The WWF recommend that 14 new reserves be established; these would include coral reefs, offshore islands, mangroves and inland wetlands since none of these ecosystems is covered by existing reserves. They would also like to see 11 existing or proposed areas included in the integrated conservation and development projects, to be added to the five already underway.*

VISITING THE NATIONAL PARKS AND RESERVES

There are six categories of protected area, of which the first three have been established to protect natural ecosystems or threatened species:
1.   Réserves Naturelles Intégrales (Strict Nature Reserves).
2.   Parcs Nationaux (National Parks).
3.   Réserves Spéciales (Special Reserves).
4.   Réserves de Chasse (Hunting Reserves).
5.   Forêts Classées (Classified Forests).
6.   Perimètres de Reboisement et de Restauration (Reafforestation Zones).

1.   There are 11 reserves in this category, four of which are described in this book: Tsingy de Namoroka, Tsimanampetsotsa, Andringitra, Marojejy, and Lokobe.
   These reserves protect representative ecosystems, and strictly speaking are open only to authorised scientific research.

2.   As in other countries, National Parks protect ecosystems and areas of natural beauty, and are open to the public (with permits). There are only two National Parks, Montagne d'Ambre, which is popular, and Isalo, which receives relatively few visitors.

3.   There are 23 Special Reserves, of which Ankarana, Périnet-Analamazaotra, and Nosy Mangabe are described here. These reserves are for the protection of ecosystems or threatened species. Not all are supervised. Access may be limited to authorised scientific research.

4.   Four lakes (including Kinkony and Ihotry) are duck hunting preserves.

5 and 6.   The 158 Classified Forests and 77 Reafforestation areas conserve forests and watersheds using accepted forestry principles.

There are also some private reserves, the most famous of which is Berenty. Permits are not required for these, the cost of admission being decided by the owner.

The WWF intend to include 'ecotourism' in their development plan for certain parks and reserves. Tourist visits are now, or soon will be, encouraged in the following: Montagne d'Ambre, Ankarana, and to a limited extent in Andringitra. Planned facilities are the creation of access roads, nature trails, accommodation, education and visitor centres. Other reserves receiving special attention are Marojejy, Manongarivo, Nosy-Mangabe, Zahamena and Tsingy de Bemaraha. Three new national parks are planned: Ranomafana, Mananara-Nord, and Masoala Peninsula. They would also like to extend

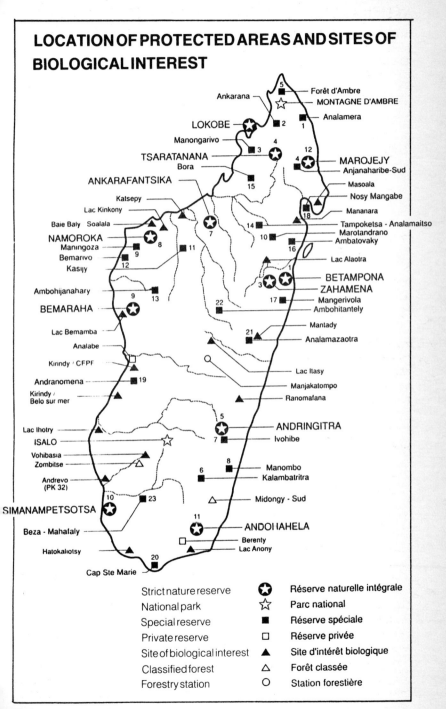

LOCATION OF PROTECTED AREAS AND SITES OF BIOLOGICAL INTEREST

Ankarana
Forêt d'Ambre
MONTAGNE D'AMBRE
Analamera
LOKOBE
Manongarivo
TSARATANANA
Bora
ANKARAFANTSIKA
MAROJEJY
Anjanaharibe-Sud
Masoala
Nosy Mangabe
Katsepy
Lac Kinkony
Mananara
Baie Baly Soalala
Tampoketsa - Analamaitso
Marotandrano
NAMOROKA
Maningoza
Ambatovaky
Bemarivo
Kasijy
Lac Alaotra
Ambohijanahary
BETAMPONA
ZAHAMENA
Mangerivola
Ambohitantely
BEMARAHA
Lac Bemamba
Mantady
Analabe
Analamazaotra
Kirindy / CFPF
Lac Itasy
Andranomena
Manjakatompo
Kirindy /
Belo sur mer
Ranomafana
Lac Ihotry
ANDRINGITRA
ISALO
Ivohibe
Vohibasia
Zombitse
Manombo
Andrevo
(PK 32)
Kalambatritra
Midongy - Sud
SIMANAMPETSOTSA
Beza - Mahafaly
ANDOHAHELA
Berenty
Hatokaliotsy
Lac Anony
Cap Ste Marie

Strict nature reserve ⊕	Réserve naturelle intégrale
National park ☆	Parc national
Special reserve ■	Réserve spéciale
Private reserve □	Réserve privée
Site of biological interest ▲	Site d'intérêt biologique
Classified forest △	Forêt classée
Forestry station ○	Station forestière

Map reproduced from *Madagascar: Revue de la conservation et des aires protégées* by kind permission of the WWF, Switzerland.

Analamazaotra-Périnet (popularly known as Périnet) into the Parc National de Mantady.

It is often possible to visit reserves not mentioned in this book, but access may be difficult or permission denied.

Permits to visit the reserves and parks used to be free, but now cost foreigners 20,000 FMG per person per reserve. At the current rate of exchange this is about £8.00 or $12. The money is used for conservation so each visitor is playing his or her part. Groups will have this paperwork done for them, but independent travellers must apply in person at the Départment des Eaux et Forêts in Antananarivo. The office is in the Nanisana district, best reached by taxi although buses numbered 1, 2 and 3 take you in the general direction. It is open from 8.00 to 12.00, and 14.00 to 18.00. The 'autorisation d'accès' is often available on the spot, but it is safer to apply in the morning with a view to returning in the afternoon. If you are planning to stay overnight in any of the reserves make sure you mention it since a separate permit may be needed. Have your itinerary worked out – you will need to give approximate dates.

Hiring guides

In the early days of tourism, boys would offer to be your guide in the more popular reserves and be delighted with a modest tip afterwards. The blossoming of tourism brought the blossoming of the Big Tippers (by Malagasy standards) and the end result in one reserve was tragedy (see *Bedo*, page 93).

The WWF recommends that 'you do not tip your guide but give a daily salary of 2,500 FMG – 3,000 FMG'. £1 for a day's work will seem incredibly mean, but you must balance it against the monthly minimum wage of 40,000 FMG (about £18). To encourage the emergence of merit rather than greed, it would be sensible to encourage the guides to keep a book of recommendation (it wouldn't hurt to buy a cheap exercise book for that purpose) in which tourists can praise a job well done (or the contrary). If the guide has been exceptional, by all means add a tip or present to the salary, but do not feel that it is obligatory.

Further information

Serious naturalists and expedition planners are advised to buy a copy of *Madagascar: Revue de la conservation et des aires protégées* (see *Bibliography*). A similar book – and in English, but not as up to date – is *Madagascar – an environmental profile* from the IUCN. Due mid-1990, from the same organisation, is a Red Data book on *The Lemurs of Madagascar*.

Keen botanists can contact Alfred Razafindratsira, one of Madagascar's experts on succulents, orchids and palms. B.P.198, Antananarivo 101. Tel: 261-10, 448-21.

CONSERVATION ORGANISATIONS

Madagascar needs all the financial help it can get. If you can spare some money to help save the rainforests and improve the lot of the Malagasy themselves, the following agencies will welcome donations:

World Wide Fund for Nature (UK)
Panda House, Weyside Park, Godalming, Surrey GU7 IXR.

Friends of the Earth
377 City Rd, London EC1V INA.

Living Earth
10 Upper Grosvenor Street, London W1X 9PA.
Working specifically to protect the world's rainforests.

Money for Madagascar
29 Queen's Rd, Sketty, Swansea SA2 0SB.
A small charitable trust working with rural communities and funding village agricultural projects. In the three years that the charity has been running, £120,000 has been raised which, amongst other programmes, has funded a small irrigation scheme and six tree-nurseries. The current project is to raise the standard of living in villages in the Betampona area, north of Tamatave, to help reduce pressure on the nearby rainforest reserve.

56

Madagascar

See the wildlife,

the scenery,

the people.

WILDERNESS TRAVEL

Our carefully planned 18 day itinerary is the result of many years of running wildlife tours to Madagascar. Led by Hilary Bradt, small groups (maximum 15) travel in comfortable minibus through the spectacular scenery of the highlands and the spiny desert of the south. We also visit Berenty Reserve, the island of Nosy Be (and Nosy Tanikely with its fabulous snorkeling), Montagne d'Ambre National Park, and take the exciting train journey to Tamatave, stopping at Perinet reserve.

Special itineraries may also be set up for private groups – minimum two people.

For a Madagascar Trip Itinerary and the current trip schedule (outlining tours to all five continents) send for a color catalog.

801 Allston Way, Berkeley, CA 94710, USA
(415) 548-0420 – (800) 247-6700 (toll free, US only). Telex 671-3481.

Chapter 4

Planning and preparations

RED TAPE
Visas

A visa is required by everyone except citizens of Malawi and Lesotho and is valid for a stay of one month, within six months of the date of issue. Applications from some professions, such as journalists, may have to be referred to Head Office before a visa will be granted. Forms must be completed in quintuplicate but most embassies have a photocopier. You will need five photos. You may be asked to show evidence of a return ticket; a letter from the travel agent dealing with your flights is sufficient.

Embassy and consulate addresses (Democratic Republic of Madagascar)

Great Britain

Honorary Consulate; 16 Lanark Mansions, Pennard Rd, London W12 8DT. Tel: 081 746 0133. Fax: 081 746 0134. Hours 9.00 – 1.00. Visas supplied immediately; very helpful. £30 (single entry) tourist visa. £45 business visa.

France

Embassy. 4 Ave Raphael, 75016 Paris. Tel: 145 046211. Takes three days. Costs 70 FF.

Italy

Embassy. Via Riccardo Zandonai 84/A, Roma. Tel: 327 7797 & 327 5183.

Belgium

Embassy. 276 Ave de Tervueren, 1150 Bruxelles. Tel: 770 1726 & 770 1774.

West Germany

Consulate. Rolandstrasse 48, 5300 Bonn Bad Godesberg (Postfach 188). Tel: 228 331057/58.

Austria

Consulate. Potzleindorferstr. 94-96, A-1184 Wien. Tel: 47 41 92 & 47 12 73.

Switzerland

Birkenstr. 5, 6000 Lucerne. Tel: 01 211 2721.

United States

Embassy. 2374 Massachusetts Ave N.W., Washington D.C. 20008. Tel: (202) 265 5525.
(Visas also available from the Permanent Mission of Madagascar to the United Nations, 801 Second Ave, Room 404, New York, N.Y. 10017. Tel: (212) 986 9491.)

Honorary Consulate. 19th floor Fidelity, 123 South Broad St, Philadelphia, PA 19109. Tel: (215) 893 3067.

Honorary Consulate. 867 Garland Drive, Palo Alto, CA 94303. Tel: (415) 323 7113. Gives far more than just a visa: advice, enthusiasm, and an information leaflet. Visas cost $22.50.

Canada

Honorary Consulate. C X Tranchemontagne Cie Lte, 459 St Sulpice, Montreal 125, Quebec. Tel: (514) 844 4427.

Honorary Consul. 335 Watson Ave., Oakville B.P. L6J 3V5 Toronto. Tel: (418) 845 8914.

Australia

Consulate. Suite 2, 4th Floor, 92 Pitt St, Sydney, NSW 2000. Tel: 221 3007. Hours 9.00 to 12.00, 14.00 to 15.00. Helpful.

Tanzania

Embassy. Magoret St 135, Dar es Salaam. (P.O. Box 5254.) Tel: 29 442.

Kenya

Consulate. Nairobi Hilton. (P.O. Box 41723.) Tel: 25206/26494.

Mauritius

Embassy. Ave Queen Mary, Port Louis. Tel: 6 50 15 & 6 50 16.

Réunion

Consulate. 39 Angle Rues Mac Aulife et Juliette Dodu, 97461 Saint Denis. Tel: 21 05 21.

Extending your visa

It is not difficult to extend your visa in Madagascar for one month. If you plan to stay more than two months you must make your arrangements before you leave home, or briefly leave the country by flying to Réunion.

Applications for visa extensions (*prolongation*) must be made at the Ministry of the Interior, near the Hilton Hotel in Antananarivo. You will need: three photos, a photocopy of your currency declaration, a typewritten declaration (best done at home) of why you want to stay longer, your passport, and a certain amount of patience.

Raniero Leto reports, however, that if your extension is only for a few weeks, it can be done quickly and simply at any police station.

Scientific study

Many naturalists want to visit this 'living laboratory' for scientific research; since the formula for getting permission keeps changing, British readers should contact the Expedition Advisory Centre at the Royal Geographical Society. They will be abreast of the situation and will be able to help in many other ways as well. 1 Kensington Gore, London SW7 2AR, Tel: 071 581 2057.

GETTING THERE

From Europe

The cheapest way of getting to Madagascar from Britain is via Aeroflot. It's 3 hours to Moscow where you have a 3 hour stop ('dinner' pass provided) then another dawn stop in Aden. There are all sorts of disadvantages: they are notorious for changing their flight dates at the last minute, losing luggage, and being booked up months in advance. That said, the fare is almost half that of Air France/Air Madagascar so for those on a tight budget there is no choice. Besides, Aeroflot puts you in the right frame of mind for Madagascar – anything can happen, and the airline is a great source of humour. 'In the entertainment stakes, lift-off on Aeroflot was a resounding success. The dishes in the kitchen galley all came crashing down... The senior stewardess, in the course of yet another lifejacket demonstration, attempted to blow the whistle. Its feeble tone was none too encouraging. The humorous interlude was shortlived; the rest of the leg was served with unremitting surliness by two matrons whose disdain was delicious to behold.' (Tim Cross). Perhaps *glasnost* will change things. Talking of which, one of the advantages of flying Aeroflot is the 14 hour stop-over in Moscow on the way back. You can join a city tour, but several readers warn that you should start queuing well before the stated sign-on time: there is apparently only one bus.

Harry Sutherland-Hawes claims that happy travel on Aeroflot is all a question of being prepared: 'On most flights the first five rows of seats to the right of the door have more room than most airlines' business class (behind those they have less room than most charter flights). You have to push and shove to get those (no numbered boarding passes!) but it's well worth it'. Take something to drink and some snacks (the food provided is not too bad, but the beverages are very sweet).

The plane leaves London on Sundays, around 12.00 noon, and arrives in Antananarivo at 12.00 noon local time (3 hours later than GMT). Don't try to book direct through Aeroflot, but use one of their agents, such as Wexas (see below) or Sam Travel, 14 Broadwick St, London, W1V 1FH (Tel: 071 636 2521 or 071 434 9561). Their price is currently (March 1990) £430 (low season) and £490 high season.

The alternative to Aeroflot is the much more comfortable and gourmet Air Madagascar/Air France, although even they have some quirky features. Air Mad is the only airline I know where free-range white poodles enjoy the same privileges as passengers, and the Emergency literature can be read for sheer entertainment value. 'Beside a picture of a girl escaping via a chute: "Sit one the thrush, and skid feet first". It still baffles us.' (Robert Stewart).

Bookings in Britain are currently made through Air France or Air Mauritius (071 434 4379), but it is rumoured that Air Madagascar is opening an office in London. Discounted fares (from an agency, see below) are around £770 return, via Paris.

At the same time as arranging your international flight, you should reserve the key internal ones which can be heavily booked in the peak season, especially to the south and Île Ste Marie. In the past you could buy the Air Tourist Pass, giving you unlimited internal travel, but this was discontinued in 1990.

Two excellent British companies do discounted flights (through Air France) to Madagascar: Wexas International (071 584 8116), and Trailfinders (071 938 3366). Wexas also do Aeroflot (and Sam Travel, who does Aeroflot, also has an Air France special fare).

British (and other European) travellers may want to make their travel arrangements in France. The visa price is less than a quarter of what you pay in London (but takes three days), and Eric Bruand, a French reader, reports an Air France fare of 6,000 FF (about £600). He got it from Forum Voyage, 1 rue Cassette, Paris 14e, or Avenue de l'Opéra, Paris. The latter is near Air Madagascar's Paris office, at 7 Avenue de l'Opera, Paris 75001. Tel: 42 60 30 51.

Air Madagascar/Air France flights depart Mondays (leaving Charles de Gaulle airport, Paris, at 19.40, via Jeddah, arriving Antananarivo 09.15), Wednesdays (leaving 14.35, via Djibouti, arriving 05.50), and Saturdays (leaving 18.15, via Zurich and Nairobi, arriving 09.15). A Thursday flight is being introduced in June 1990, and will run at least until October. Departs Paris 18.30, arrive Antananarivo 8.10 Friday.

Apart from Paris, other European agencies for Air Madagascar are: Air Madagascar, c/o ATASH Sa, 34, Neumuhlequai, 8006 Zurich, Switzerland, Tel: (0)1 362 72 40 (English spoken); and Air Madagascar, Herzog-Rudolf-Strasse 3, 8000 München 22, West Germany. Tel: 089 2318 0113. Very efficient and English–speaking.

For those willing to be creative over flights, there are alternative ways of getting to Madagascar. Perhaps the best bet is to get a cheap charter to Nairobi then buy a 21 day excursion for £235 to Antananarivo (more than 21 days is £390). Air Madagascar or Air Mauritius planes leave Nairobi three times a week, Sunday, Tuesday, and Friday. It's best to avoid the Sunday flight which is a 747 originating in Paris; there are more passengers to be processed on arrival and they are often overbooked so tend to 'bump' those joining the plane in Nairobi. Other flights are often full but I have successfully gone standby.

You can also get a charter flight to Réunion with the French companies Le Point – tel: 89 42 4451 (Mulhouse) or 42 96 6363 (Paris) – or Nouvelle Frontière – tel: 42 73 1064 (Paris). From Réunion there are flights (£177) five times a week to Antananarivo. Flights from Mauritius are £210 but there are no cheap flights to Mauritius from the UK.

If you make your travel arrangements through North-South Travel Ltd (Tel: 0245 492882; Fax 0245 356612) you will be directly benefiting the Third World since all profits go toward aid projects. See page 94 for more information.

From North America

The normal fare from New York is from $2,109 (low season) to $2,426 (high season) and from Los Angeles $2,349 to $2,756. But Americans are lucky. They have a specialist tour operator who ties in cheap flights (Air France) with individualised land arrangements and a knowledge and love of Madagascar. You won't find better in the USA: Monique Rodriguez, Cortez Travel Services, 117 Lomas Santa Fe Dr., Solano Beach, CA 92075; Tel: 619 755 5136, Fax: 619 481 7474. (Californians get all the breaks – they also have the marvellous Jean-Marie de la Beaujardière, the honorary consul at Palo Alto.)

Australia

Air Madagascar has an office in the same building as the Sydney Consulate, but they do not sell airline tickets. The nearest Air Madagascar gateway to Australia is Mauritius.

WHAT TO BRING

Luggage

A sturdy canvas duffle bag or backpack with internal frame is more practical than a suitcase. Backpackers should consider buying a rucksack with a zipped compartment to enclose the straps when using them on airlines. Those made by Mountaincraft (UK) are good. Bring a light folding nylon bag for taking purchases home, and the largest permissible bag to take as hand baggage on the plane. Pack this with everything you need for the first four or so days, especially if travelling by Aeroflot. Then, if they lose your luggage, you won't be too inconvenienced.

Clothes

You will be meeting every temperature, from cool/cold in the highlands to very hot by the coast. Layers of clothing – tee shirt, sweatshirt, light sweater – are warm and versatile, and take less room than a heavy sweater. I am a devotee of Rohan Bags (30, Maryland Rd, Tongwell, Milton Keynes, Bucks MK15 8HN. Tel: 0908 618888). They are lightweight, dry overnight whatever the humidity, and have an inside zipped pocket for security. Their jackets are equally good. You will need a showerproof jacket and rain cape and perhaps a small umbrella. If you are planning to spend much time in the rainforests, take good waterproof clothing (including rain-trousers) and light rubber boots. The highlands (and also Périnet) get very cold on winter evenings (June/July) as does the southern desert; a fibre-pile jacket or bodywarmer are practical. A light cotton jacket is always useful for breezy evenings by the coast.

Good outdoor clothing and other travel supplies can be bought from the excellent YHA shops; phone 0784 458625 for the address of your nearest branch.

The most versatile footwear are trainers (running shoes) and sandals. Hiking boots will be needed if you are planning a lot of walking but are not necessary for the main tourist circuits.

Give some thought to beachwear if you enjoy snorkelling. In addition to a swim suit you'll need an old pair of sneakers (or similar) to protect your feet from the coral (or – better – buy a pair of plastic sandals in the market) and teeshirt and shorts or even long trousers to wear while in the water. The underwater world is so absorbing it is very easy to get badly sunburnt, especially on the shoulders and back of thighs.

Toiletries

Not so long ago it was impossible even to buy soap in Madagascar. Happily those days are over, but it is still safer to bring everything you need. One thing you can't buy is decent toilet paper. Good hotels do provide paper, but it is the sort favoured by the rural French – more like tree-bark than anything you want to bring in repeated contact with your skin. This is awkward for those planning a long stay; one traveller, pointing out that you can't bring enough toilet paper to last the trip, recommends wetting the local stuff to make it less abrasive – and cooler. If you normally blow your nose on loo paper you'd better bring a handkerchief. And while on the subject, if you're flying Aeroflot bring some toilet paper for your stopover in Moscow where it is very rare.

Women should bring enough tampons to last the trip. The brands without an applicator take up less luggage space.

Some toilet articles have several uses: dental floss is excellent for repairs as well as for teeth, and a nail brush gets clothes clean as well.

Don't take up valuable space with a bath towel – a hand towel is perfectly adequate.

Protection against mosquitoes

With malaria on the increase, it is vital to be properly protected against mosquitoes. There are a lot of new products on the market, one of the most useful being Buzz-Bands (made by Traveller International Products). These slip over the wrists and ankles (mosquitoes' favourite area) and really do the job. The same company makes Buzz-Off, a tablet vaporiser which works as a plug-in mosquito coil (pyrethrum coils, which burn slowly through the night, are available all over Madagascar and are very effective). If you use the plug-in variety you'll need to know that voltage in Madagascar varies (it would!): 110v or 220v.

If you expect to be using C category hotels, it is essential to have a mosquito net, and a self-standing one at that since there is rarely anywhere to hang the other sort. Two companies make suitable ones: Long Road, USA (see advert overleaf) whose Indoor Travel Tent is sturdy enough to use outdoors, and has a built-in groundsheet giving protection from bed bugs and fleas as well as mosquitoes, and Mosquito Nets International, 45 Lismore Place, Glasgow G77 6UQ, Tel: 041 639 8443, whose Protector-Net stands conveniently over a bed. A variety of mosquito nets is also available from Clothtec, 92 Par Green, Par, Cornwall, PL24 2AG, Tel: 0726 813602. With the tent design you will need to bring a sheet sleeping bag and you may prefer to buy your own blanket in the market rather than use those supplied by the hotel.

Rough travel equipment

Basic camping gear gives you the freedom to travel adventurously and can add a considerable degree of comfort to overland journeys.

The most important item is your backpack: this should *not* have an external frame which is antisocial on the very crowded vehicles that serve as public transport, and anyway will get stomped on and broken. Invest in a good pack with an internal frame and plenty of pockets. Protect it from oil, dirt, and the effluent of young or furry/feathered passengers with a canvas sack or similar adapted covering.

A light sleeping bag will keep you warm in cheap hotels with inadequate bedding, and on night stops on – or off – 'buses'. Add a sheet sleeping bag for hot nights, and when the hotel linen is missing or grubby.

An air-mattress or pillow pads your bum on hard seats as well as your hips when sleeping out. One of those horseshoe-shaped travel

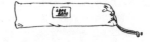

pillows lets you sleep sitting up.

A lightweight tent allows you to strike out on your own and stay in nature reserves, on deserted beaches and so forth. It will need to have a separate rain fly and be well-ventilated.

To complete your independence you will need a stove. Camping Gaz cylinders are sometimes available, but you would be safer to bring a meths burning stove. This fuel is called *alcohol à brûler* and can usually be bought in general stores. Since a stove without fuel is useless, however, one that burns petrol (gasoline) or paraffin (kerosene) would be preferable. Outdoor shops such as the YHA chain have a good selection.

Since you'll be eating in *hotelys* much of the time, bring a tube of flavoursome sauce; it will help those mounds of sticky rice. Marmite (or Vegemite for Australians) will keep addicts happy and has the side effect of discouraging mosquitoes (it contains vitamin B12). Bring your own mug and spoon (and carry them with you always). That way you can enjoy roadside coffee without the risk of a cup rinsed in filthy water, and market yoghurt without someone else's germs on the spoon.

Finally, here's an idea: how about bringing puncture-repair patches for those desperate taxi-brousse drivers? If that doesn't get you a front seat, nothing will!

Miscellaneous

Now that most guides are willing to take you on a nocturnal lemur hunt, a headlight with lots of spare batteries should be added to your list (these are used by mountaineers, so shops like the YHA chain are the best bet). It's convenient for other purposes too, like reading in your tent at night, since it leaves your hands free.

Here is a suggested checklist:

Small torch (flashlight) with spare batteries and bulb, or headlamp, travel alarm clock (or alarm wristwatch), penknife, sewing kit, scissors, tweezers, safety pins, sellotape (Scotchtape), Magic Marker or felt-tipped pen, ballpoint pens, a small notebook, a large notebook for diary and letters home, plastic bags (all sizes, sturdy; Zip-loc are particularly useful), universal plug for baths and sinks, elastic clothes line or cord and pegs, concentrated detergent (available in tubes in camping stores), ear plugs (a godsend in noisy hotels and taxi-brousses), insect repellent, sunscreen, lipsalve, spare glasses or contact lenses, sun glasses, medical and dental kit (see *Health*), a water container, water purifying tablets or other sterilising agent (see *Health*).

Compact binoculars, camera, plenty of film (twice as much as you think you'll need), books, miniature cards, Scrabble/pocket chess set.

Goods for presents, sale or trade

I now feel so strongly about the selfishness of giving presents (see *Responsible Tourism*, page 92) that I nearly took out this heading. However, I do admit that there are times that presents are an appropriate way of showing your gratitude. In rural areas these should take the form of show and tell items that will increase you interaction with the people: postcards from home, picture books (read Sally Crook's account of her stay in a southern village on page 21 to see how popular familiar pictures are), paper and skill at origami, string and a knowledge of cat's cradles. Photos of your family (or, failing that, the Royal Family) will be pored over gratifyingly. Frisbees, balls, or ... dare I say it after the story on page 93, balloons, all add to the fun.

Always consider what you are introducing into the culture and be very wary of giving an appetite for hitherto unwanted consumer goods.

In urban areas or with the more sophisticated Malagasy people, presents are a very good way of showing your appreciation for kindness or extra good service. Calendars showing scenes of your country are good small presents or 'Teach yourself English' books for the many Malagasy keen to improve their language skills. High class toiletries are appreciated and it's always worth bringing your allowance of duty-free whisky and cigarettes. Clothes, especially jeans, are often requested by those with an appetite for the 'western' look, and you will always find a home for running shoes.

Money

How much money to take is covered in Chapter 6, but give some thought to *how* to take it.

Bring your money in US dollars or pounds sterling. These days sterling is as easy to change as dollars, and travellers cheques can be changed in most hotels. I always take a supply of French francs (cash) for those occasions when I cannot change travellers cheques or do not have my passport with me. Since hard currency prices are usually quoted in French francs it is useful to start thinking in that currency.

The large hotels and Air Madagascar accept credit cards, but only American Express is widely accepted. Master Cards is the next best; one traveller reports that Visa (apart from Carte Bleue) is 'totally useless'.

If you will need to have money sent out to you, see page 91

WHEN TO GO

Read the section on climate before deciding when to travel. Broadly speaking, the dry months are between April and September, but rainfall varies enormously in different areas. The months to avoid are August, when popular places are crowded, and January, February and

March (the cyclone season) when it will rain. However, if you stick to the west and south this off-peak season can be rewarding, with cheaper international airfares and very few other tourists.

September is nice, but very windy in the South. My favourite months are October and November, when the weather is fine but not too hot, the jacarandas are in flower, the lemurs have babies, and the markets are full of fruit.

PACKAGE TOUR OR INDEPENDENT TRAVEL?

Even the most diehard independent travellers should consider a package tour in Madagascar, at least for part of their trip. Unless you have plenty of time and a good command of French, it is difficult to see the most interesting parts of the country on your own. The great advantage of a tour is that you get ground transport laid on, so can stop and look at scenery, tombs, birds, villagers... Public transport tends to be so crowded that even looking out of the window (if there *is* a window) may be impossible. Special interest groups (botany, ornithology) would be particularly advised to go with a group organised in their own country, to be sure of having an expert guide as well as the necessary transport to reach remote areas.

Package tours

A growing number of tour operators do trips to Madagascar. When choosing a tour do not be over-influenced by price – find out how long the company has been running trips to Madagascar since it takes a few years to iron out the problems, and check that the leader actually knows the country.

Britain Twickers World (081 892 7606), Hann Overland (071 834 7337), Guerba Expeditions (0373 826689), Silk Cut Travel (0730 65211), Swan Hellenic (071 831 1515), Ramblers Holidays (0707 331133), Indian Ocean Hideaways (071 930 5551) – who will do a taylor-made package, Voyages Jules Verne (071 486 8080); Ornitholidays (0243 821230) – birdwatching, David Sayers Travel (081 995 3642) – botany, and Alfred Gregory (0742 29428) – photographic.

U.S.A. Wilderness Travel (415 548-0420 or 800 247- 6700) – see page 56, Questers (212 673-3120), International Expeditions (205 870-5550), Cortez Travel Services (619 755-5136) – taylor-made tours.

Tour operators in Madagascar

Madagascar Airtours, Hilton Hotel, Antananarivo. B.P. 3874. Tel: 341-92. Telex: 222-32 AIR MAD MG.

By far the most experienced agency, running a wide variety of tours including natural history, ornithology, speleology, trekking, mineralogy, river trips, sailing, etc.

Liounis Voyages, Immeuble COROI, Antsahavola, Antananarivo. B.P. 425. Tel: 238-26. Telex: 22214 COROI MG.

Operate in conjunction with Cortez Travel of California to produce off-beat packages as well as conventional. The manager, Christophe de Comarmond, seems able to achieve just about anything!

Julia Voyage, 7 Rue P.Lumumba, Antananarivo. B.P. 3179. Tel: 330-06/304-98.

Julia (see page 129) has started a Minerals Circuit, which will visit mineral deposits in the south of Madagascar.

Other tour operators, who may be just as good but I know nothing about them, are:

Transcontinents, 10 Ave de l'Indépendance, Antananarivo. B.P. 541, Tel: 223-98. Telex 22259 ZODIAC.

Voyages Bourdon, 15 Rue P.Lumumba, Antananarivo. Tel: 296-96. Telex 22557 YOYDON MG.

Trans 7, 11 Ave de l'Indépendance, Antananarivo. B.P. 7117. Tel: 248-38. Telex 22381.

Touring Fima, 41 Rue Ratsimilaho, Antananarivo. B.P. 6073. Tel: 222-30. Telex: 22464.

Tourisma, 15 Ave de l'Indépendance, Antananarivo. B.P. 3997. Tel: 287-57 & 289-11.

Independent travel – suggested circuits

One of the hardest decisions facing the first-time visitor to a country as diverse as Madagascar is where to go. Even a month is not long enough to see everything so itineraries must be planned according to interests. Here are some suggestions for tours lasting three to four weeks.

The comfort circuit

This includes all the most interesting places which have comfortable accommodation (categories A and B) and are accessible by air. Most organised tours cover the same ground.

Antananarivo – Fort Dauphin and Berenty – Antananarivo – Péirinet (by train or road) – Tamatave – Diego Suarez – Nosy Be – Antananarivo.

The rough explorer

For those on a limited budget, their own sleeping bag, etc., and a willingness to exchange comfort for Amazing Experiences. (A month would be needed for each full circuit here.)

Antananarivo – Antsirabe (by train) – Fianarantsoa (by road) – side trip to Ranomafana (road) – Manakara (by train) and back – Fianarantsoa – Fort Dauphin (by road) – Tuléar (by road or plane) – Antananarivo.

Alternatively or in addition (if no time limit):

Antananarivo – Majunga (by road or plane) – Nosy Be (by road or plane) – Diego Suarez (by road) – Sambava or Maroantsetra (plane) – Tamatave (plane) – Île Ste Marie – Antananarivo. Or Île Ste Marie – Tamatave – Périnet (train) – Antananarivo.

You could vary this by going from Tamatave to Fénérive and thence by boat to Île Ste Marie.

The naturalist
A three to four week tour could take in the following:

Antananarivo – Fort Dauphin and Berenty – Antananarivo – Majunga (Ampijoroa) – Nosy Be (Lokobe) – Diego Suarez (Montagne d'Ambre) – Maroantsetra (Nosy Mangabe) or Mananara – Tamatave – Périnet – Antananarivo. Or skip the east coast to see Ranomafana.

Ethno-tour (tombs and things)
Antananarivo and area (for Merina tombs) – Fianarantsoa (with excursions to Ambositra and Ambalavao) – Tuléar (excursion through Mahafaly country) – Fort Dauphin (Berenty and visit to Antanosy tombs) – Antananarivo – Tamatave and east coast (Betsimisaraka graves) – Antananarivo.

History
Antananarivo – Ambohimanga – Fort Dauphin – Antananarivo – Île Ste Marie – Tamatave – Mahavelona (fort) – Tamatave – Antananarivo.

Remember   The east coast should be excluded from these tours in the rainy season (December to March). If you want to avoid other travellers and see the parts unaffected by tourism there are plenty of interesting places mentioned in this book and not on the circuits above. And hundreds of other places not mentioned in the book. Madagascar is a large country: make it your oyster!

Stop press: In April 1990 Air Madagascar raised their international fares by 3% and are rumoured to be considering a 50% rise on domestic airfares!

Chameleon. (J.R.J.)

Radiated tortoise. (J.R.J.)

Uroplatus.

Striped tenrec.

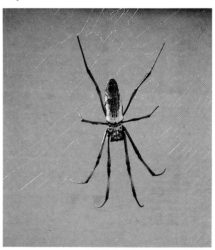

Nephilia madagascariensis.

Boa.

Lemurs

Sifaka.

Female black lemur.

Lepilemur. (J.R.J.)

Brown lemur.

Horse-drawn bus. Antananarivo.

Pousse-pousses waiting for customers. (John R. Jones)

Taxi-brousse. (John R. Jones)

Chapter 5

Health and safety

HEALTH

By Dr Jane Wilson

Staying healthy in Madagascar, as in other developing countries, is a matter of good preparation and common sense.

Before you go

Malaria

Madagascar boasts three species of malaria and drug (chloroquine) resistance is now becoming a problem. Since one form of the disease, cerebral malaria, is dangerous it is worth getting up to date advice on malaria prophylaxis. This is available from the Malaria Reference Laboratory in London, Tel: 071 636 7921 (a continuous loop tape giving general information – Madagascar is not mentioned specifically but is lumped in with Africa) or 071 636 3924 from 9.30 – 10.30 and 14.00 – 15.00, Mondays to Fridays, for specific advice.

At the time of writing two chloroquine (Nivaquine) weekly and two proguanil (Paludrine) daily was recommended. These drugs are best absorbed after food and when taken after a meal are less likely to cause the side effect of nausea which troubles some people. You should start taking malaria prophylaxis one week before leaving for Madagascar and continue six weeks after returning home. It is safe to take Chloroquine during pregnancy and breast feeding. Proguanil is generally thought to be safe to take in pregnancy, but some experts suggest taking a Folate with it. Fansidar is *not* a safe drug to take as prophylaxis and should not be taken in pregnancy as prophylaxis or cure.

Even if you have been taking your malaria prophylaxis carefully there is a slight chance of contracting malaria. You should therefore consult a doctor (mentioning that you have been abroad) if you get a flu-like illness within a month or so of getting home.

Immunisations

Disease patterns and international health regulations change so it is worth taking special advice. It would be sensible to have up-to-date immunisations for polio, tetanus, typhoid and cholera and probably gamma globulin against hepatitis. It is also worth having a Schick Test to check that your childhood immunisation for diphtheria is still protective. An 'ordinary' intramuscular shot against rabies is now available and may be worth arranging if you think you are at risk. The disease is a problem in Madagascar because of the quantity of semi-feral dogs in many parts of the island, but lemurs are not carriers.

Remember that 'live' vaccines cannot be taken within a fortnight of each other, so plan well ahead. There is a list of vaccination centres at the end of this section.

If you are coming from Africa you will be required to show an International Vaccination Certificate showing that you are up to date with yellow fever and cholera vaccinations; these are not required for passengers arriving from Europe or the USA.

Teeth   Have a dental check-up before you go. There is now a Dental Emergency Kit on the market (if you can't get it at Boots ask your dentist). Amongst other things it contains emergency fillings.

Insurance

Make sure you have insurance covering the cost of treatment in Madagascar and a flight home or to Réunion or Nairobi which offer more sophisticated medical facilities than are available in Madagascar.

In Madagascar

Local medical facilities

The local medical services are excellent considering the constraints imposed by poor communications, lack of drugs and facilities. Malagasy doctors are knowledgeable and well trained and all I met seemed reliable, trustworthy and friendly. Many of the younger doctors speak English.

Insects and insect-borne diseases

The only known Trypanosome organism (sleeping sickness) which exists in Madagascar affects only chameleons! The African forms of sleeping sickness do not exist in Madagascar as there is no tsetse vector to spread it. However, there are plenty of mosquitoes which spread malaria, elephantiasis and viral diseases. It is worth avoiding being bitten to prevent contracting these diseases but also to avoid the itching bites which so easily become infected later. So cover up, keep insect repellent handy, and use a mosquito net in poorly screened hotels.

Once bitten, calamine lotion or calamine-based creams seem best to stop the itching.

Other nasty animals

Malagasy land-snakes are back-fanged so are effectively non-venomous. Sea-snakes, however, are dangerous but being brightly coloured are easy to see and unaggressive. They breathe air, so the only time you may be at risk is when you are swimming or snorkelling over them when they decide to surface for air.

Particularly when in the forest it is wise to be wary of scorpions and centipedes. Neither is fatal but are very unpleasant. Scorpions are nocturnal but often come out after rain; they like hiding in small crevices during the day. If you are camping in the forest it is not unusual to find they have crept into the pocket of a rucksack – even if you have taken the sensible precaution of suspending it from a tree. Scorpion stings are very painful for about 24 hours but are not life-threatening. After a sting on the finger I had an excruciatingly painful hand and arm for several days. The pain was only eased with morphine. My finger had no feeling for a month and still has an abnormal nerve supply three years later.

Centipedes are probably the best fighting machine ever designed. They bite at one end, sting at the other and each leg is capable of inflicting a small wound. Madagascar has some very large (15 cm) species which are best avoided. The large spiders can be dangerous and the (over-rated!) black widow occurs in Madagascar. The large navy digger wasps have an unpleasant sting. In my experience, however, it is only the scorpions which cause problems because they can be very common in the dry forests and because they favour hiding in places where one might plunge a hand without looking. If you wish to sleep on the ground, in forest areas, it would be prudent to isolate yourself from these creatures – mat, hammock or tent with sewn-in ground sheet.

Leeches can be a nuisance in the rainforest but they are only revolting, not dangerous. These are best avoided by covering up, again tucking trousers into socks and applying insect repellent (even under the socks and on shoes – but beware, Deet dissolves plastics). Once leeches have become attached they should not be forcibly removed. Either wait until they have finished feeding (when they will fall off) or encourage them to let go by applying a lit cigarette or salt. A film canister is a convenient salt container. The wound left by a leech bleeds a great deal and may become secondarily infected if not kept clean.

Beware of strolling barefoot on damp, sandy river beds. This is the way to pick up jigger. These are female sand fleas, which resemble maggots and burrow into your toes to feed on your blood while incubating their eggs. Dig them out with a sterilised needle, and disinfect the wound thoroughly to prevent infection.

Plants

Madagascar has quite a few plants which cause local skin irritation.

The worst one I have encountered is a climbing legume which has pea-pod like fruits which look furry. This 'fur' penetrates the skin as thousands of tiny needles which must be painstakingly extracted with tweezers. Relief from secretions of other irritating plants is often obtained by bathing. Sometimes it is best to wash your clothes as well and immersion fully clothed may be the last resort!

Some travellers' diseases

Traveller's diarrhoea, etc. Most people suffer gastro- intestinal upsets at some stage, and this is more likely if you are new to tropical travel. The best foods to eat to ensure illness are, in descending order of danger: ice cream, ice, water, salads, uncooked foods, cooked food which has been hanging around or has been inadequately reheated. Street sellers' foods may be safe if they are sizzling hot. There is a high prevalence of tapeworm in cattle, so I would recommend eating your steaks (which are usually excellent in Madagascar) well done.

The best treatment for traveller's diarrhoea is 24-48 hours starvation: no solid food but plenty of clear fluids. Only resort to antidiarrhoeal drugs if you really must (e.g. when travelling) since they delay recovery by slowing the natural expulsion of toxic products. Should the diarrhoea be associated with passing blood, treatment may be advisable but as long as you drink plenty no harm will be done by waiting a couple of days. I would try Metronidazole (Flagyl) first. This is also a useful antibiotic if the upset is associated with production of *a lot* of sulphurous wind. If in doubt starve for 48 hours and in most cases you'll start feeling better.

Sometimes the gut alternates between mild diarrhoea and constipation. Constipation is made worse by dehydration (a problem in the heat) and bananas. Other fruits will help relieve it.

Some people believe in having a stool check-up when they return home. Personally I would only bother if I had symptoms.

Bilharzia This is a nasty debilitating disease which is a problem in much of Madagascar. It is caught by swimming or paddling in clean, still water (not fast-flowing rivers) but takes 10 – 15 minutes to penetrate the skin where it causes 'swimmer's Itch'. A quick wade across a river (as long as you dry off quickly) should not put you at risk of infection. It is now easily cured with a single dose of Praziquantel.

Sexually transmitted diseases There are plenty in Madagascar, and although Aids still seems to be limited to a few prostitutes. If you enjoy nightlife, condoms will make encounters less risky.

Medical kit

You can't take all the medicants you may need when you are travelling, and apart from personal medication taken on a regular basis it is unnecessary to weigh yourself down with a comprehensive medical

kit as many of your requirements will be met by the pharmacies.
The list below is for the 'ordinary' tourist/traveller. Expeditions or
very adventurous travellers should contact MASTA (*Useful addresses*,
below).

Malaria tablets, lots of plasters (Band-aids) to cover broken skin,
infected insect bites, etc. Antiseptic such as Dettol (salt in boiled water
is also excellent), small pieces of sterile gauze (Melonin dressing) and
sticky plaster, soluble aspirin – good for fevers, aches, and for gargling
when you have a sore throat. Lanosil or some kind of soothing cream for
sore anus (post diarrhoea), Canestan for thrush and athletes foot. A
course of Flagyl, a course of Amoxyl or similar antibiotic – good for
chest infections, skin infections and cystitis, Cicatrin antibiotic powder
for infected bites, etc., antibiotic eye drops, anti-histamine cream or
tablets. Tweezers for extracting splinters, small thorns and coral.

Useful addresses

Thomas Cook Vaccination Centre, 45 Berkeley Square, London W.1.
(near Green Park tube station). Tel: 071 499 4000.

British Airways Travel Clinic (vaccination service), 9 Little Newport
St, London WC2H 7JJ. Tel: 071 287 2255/3366. They also sell
travellers' supplies.
   These travel clinics are being set up all over Britain.

The Ross Institute of Tropical Hygiene, London School of Hygiene
and Tropical Medicine, Gower Street, London, WC1E 7HT. Tel: 071
636 8636. The Malarial Reference Laboratory is located here.

An excellent service for travellers is MASTA (Medical Advisory
Service for Travellers). For £12.50 they will provide an individually
tailored Personal Health Brief (£7.00 for the standard one). The
Personal one gives up to date information on how to stay healthy in
Madagascar (or any country you specify) and includes malaria, inoculations, and what to bring. For expeditions they offer a Comprehensive Health Brief for £25.00. Forms for ordering your Health Brief are
available from Boots or other chemists, or ring 071 631 4408. MASTA
also sells basic tropical supplies, and a Medical Equipment Pack with
sterile syringes, etc. The latter is available by mail (cash with order) for
£9.80 from MASTA, Keppel St, London WC1E 7HT.

*Dr Wilson has led two expeditions to Ankarana. In addition to studies
on the natural history of the reserve, she investigated Bilharzia in the
surrounding villages.*

Water sterilisation

By drinking Eau Vive or mineral water, you will cut down the risk of water-borne diseases but this is not always available and can be quite expensive. It's often better to purify your own tap water.

The most convenient and effective sterilising agent is iodine (preferable to chlorine because it kills amoebic cysts) which is available in liquid or tablet form. To make treated water more palatable bring packets of powdered drink.

An alternative is a water filter such as the Travel-Well. It gives safe water with no unpleasant flavour, but is too slow for most people's thirst. Another possibility is a plug-in immersion heater so you can boil your water; this is the most effective form of sterilisation there is and has the by-product of a nice hot cuppa (if you bring teabags).

A miscellany of health and comfort tips

Rehydration therapy is increasingly being used in the Third World as a treatment for infant diarrhoea. It works well for adult travellers, too, replacing the lost minerals and preventing dehydration. Reader J.M.Layman sent this recipe: 'At its simplest, rehydration medication is one teaspoon of salt and eight teaspoons of sugar to a litre of water (bottles of *Eau Vive* are 750ml and 1500ml; I assumed they were one and two litres before actually measuring them). If clean or purified water is not available, remember that coconut water is not only sterile (if taken direct from the nut) but has about the correct concentration of sugar present. Half a teaspoon of salt should be about the right amount to add to the water of an average coconut.'

Evelyn Horn Wootton sent the following tried-and-tested tips: 'Anti-malarial tablets make many people feel nauseous when taken without food, yet it wasn't always convenient to take them with breakfast (and easy to forget). I took mine first thing in the morning, by "padding" my stomach with Metamucil (psyllium hydrophilic mucilloid) which is a natural bulk laxative. One teaspoon in a glass of water is enough.

'Over the years I have found Medicinal Spirits of Ammonia (smelling salts) very useful. One half teaspoon in a glass of Coca Cola, sipped slowly, is an almost instant cure for nausea, when one is travelling and desperate. I have also found that it stops the itch of insect bites.

'My skin is sensitive to sun-screen and I have to use Zinc Oxide instead. A dab of white Zinc Oxide on the nose of a sixteen year old in a bikini can be quite fetching, but I am 66 years old. If I'd used it in Madagascar they might have wrapped me in a lamba, run me around a tomb a few times, and shoved me in! I tinted the Zinc Oxide with make-up base (one that I'm not sensitive to) and it worked beautifully! Still on the subject of sensitive skin, I find that packets of Wash and Dry, which contain alcohol, burn if I have to use them on my face. Johnson's Baby Wipes are much more soothing, as well as being a generous size. To keep them moist and portable I repackaged them in Zip-loc bags'.

SAFETY

Only in the capital, Antananarivo, are you in real danger of being robbed. Thursday evening and Friday (market day) are particularly bad, and the area around the station is the worst. It pays to be paranoid. Tamatave is also risky, with at least one report of violent robbery.

There are bandits and cattle thieves in the south, but I have yet to hear of tourists being involved. Sadly though, increasing tourism is almost bound to bring an increase of thieves in all popular areas, so be sensible. Here are some ways of protecting your valuables:

Carry your cash in a money belt or neck pouch and divide up traveller's cheques so they are not all in one place. Keep a note of the numbers of your travellers cheques, passport, credit cards, plane ticket, insurance, etc. in your money belt. Keep a copy in your luggage.

Keep a photocopy of the first page of your passport and of your Madagascar visa. Guard your currency declaration as carefully as your passport.

Bring a combination lock that can be used on your hotel door (in cheap hotels in cities).

In posh hotels leave your valuables in a security box.

Be very careful of handbag slashers in the market or on crowded buses. They use a razor and are very skilful (I was thoroughly and competently robbed this way in the local bus to Ivato airport; I was sure that my handbag was out of harm's way, but the side was accessible to the thief and his accomplice who had helped me into the bus and companionably got in beside me). Consider making your own bag out of slash-proof material (and at least carry this book at the bottom (see page IX)!

Do not wear gold chains or jewellery of any sort.

Avoid leaving your clothes on the beach while you go swimming (in areas where they are used to tourists).

If you are robbed, go to the police. They will write down all the details then send you to the chief of police for a signature. It takes hours, but you will need the certificate for your insurance.

Women travellers

In my experience, and in that of the women contributors to this book (all of whom travelled very adventurously), Madagascar is one of the safest and most enjoyable countries in the world for a lone woman traveller. Of course, in a country where there are many prostitutes it is sensible to dress modestly and make it clear through your general demeanour that you are not soliciting custom.

My only experience that comes remotely close to what one has come to expect in more 'hot-blooded' countries was when a small man sidled up to me in Hell-ville harbour and asked – in English – 'Have you ever tasted Malagasy man?'.

Useful books

Travellers' Health Dr Richard Dawood.
O.U.P., £5.95. Detailed and up to date.

The Traveller's Health Guide Dr Anthony Turner.
Roger Lascelles, £4.95. Clearly written and straightforward.

MOSQUITOES AND MALARIA

In October 1988 *The Economist* reported that 100,000 Malagasy had died in the Highlands from malaria, in 'an area without immunity to the disease, or means of coping with it'. The WHO links the outbreak with two causes: the reappearance of the mosquito *Anopheles funestus* which was almost eradicated under the French, and the warming of the climate, due either to the 'greenhouse effect' or to deforestation, which favours the lifecycle of the mosquito. The highland paddy fields make ideal breeding grounds.

A Swiss aid programme has made some inroads into treatment and prevention, but the disease is there to stay.

If you take no other medication, follow the malaria prophylaxis routine rigidly, following the guidelines of the Malaria Reference Laboratory. Make every effort not to get bitten and at the last resort follow this reader's advice: 'Since one researcher suggested that mosquitoes are attracted to carbon dioxide, maybe the best prevention is not to talk!'

Chapter 6

In Madagascar

COST OF LIVING/TRAVELLING

Compared with the Third World in general, Madagascar is not a cheap country. Because good hotels and first class travel (rail and all air) must be paid for in hard currency, those looking for a degree of comfort – and wishing to see the best of Madagascar – cannot take advantage of local prices. Visits to Madagascar's most rewarding accessible area, Fort Dauphin and Berenty, are monopolised by one private landowner whose prices are very high. If you plan on taking a few internal flights (as you must if time is limited), visiting Berenty, and staying in mid-range hotels you can expect to spend at least £30 a day (average). The 1990 airfare from Antananarivo to Fort Dauphin is 360 FF (about £36/$60) and an overnight visit to Berenty (in late 1989) cost 780 FF (£78/$128) all in. Budget travellers willing to suffer (though excellent meals are always affordable) can hold to a daily expenditure of about £10/$16; they will see the Real Madagascar but only a small part of it unless they have plenty of time. However, be warned: the rate of exchange has hardly changed over the past two years but prices certainly have. Most hotels now cost twice as much.

In Madagascar a couple can travel almost as cheaply as one, since most rooms have double beds and are charged as such.

Malagasy Francs

Madagascar's unit of currency is the Franc Malgache (FMG). With recent inflation one rarely sees the small lower denomination coins of 5, 10, and 20 francs, but thoroughly to confuse you there are also large silver coins which look, at face value, to be for 10 and 20 francs. Closer inspection show that they are *ariary* (one ariary is 5 francs) so they are worth 50 and 100 francs respectively.

The March 1990 rates of exchange were 2,461 FMG to the pound, 1,545 FMG to the dollar, 806 FMG to the DM, and 268 FMG to the French Franc.

Note: I give prices in FF (if the service must be paid for in hard currency) or FMG. These are bound to change but you should soon learn what multiplying factor is needed to bring the quoted prices to current levels.

'The Good Old Days'. The filanzana *was used to transport high officials until the 1940s. This tomb carving shows a pith-helmeted* Vazaha *so bored with the journey that he is reading a book.*

TRANSPORT

There are three ways of getting around Madagascar: rail, road and air. Whichever method you use, you'd better learn the meaning of *en panne*; it is engine trouble/break down.

Rail

There are only four railway lines in Madagascar, by far the most popular (with tourists) being the Antananarivo to Tamatave route which is described on pages 000 and 000. The first class fare works out at 1p per mile – a wonderful bargain! 2nd class can get very crowded, but is worth trying once for the experience of being crammed in with dozens of good natured Malagasy. Note that the windows in first class are higher than most trains; short travellers should bring something to sit on so they can see the view.

The other railway lines are Moramanga to Ambatondrazaka, Antananarivo to Antsirabe, and Fianarantsoa to Manakara.

A railway treat available only to groups is the **Micheline**, a beautiful white bus-cum-train which carries 19 passengers and runs on rubber wheels. The smooth ride is matched by the luxurious interior which includes a bar.

To book the Micheline apply, in writing and 20 days in advance, to Monsieur le Directeur Général de Réeau National de Chemins de Fer Malgache, BP 259, 101 Antananarivo. Tel: 205 21. Your application must include the date and time of departure, place of departure, destination, time of return. The maximum lease is five days. Rates (hard currency only – Feb 1990): 8.28 FF per kilometre (£.86/$2.61) single, and 14.54 FF return. On board service as requested.

Road

In Madagascar public transport is anything on wheels, even zebu carts and rickshaws

Taxi-brousse, **car-brousse**, and **taxi- be** are all varieties of 'bush taxi' which run between major towns. I doubt if there is any country offering more crowded transport. If you think you're a well-seasoned traveller, wait until you try Madagascar! Taxi-brousses are generally minibuses or Citroen vans with seats facing each other so no good view out of the window (a *baché* is a small van with a canvas top). More comfortable are the Peugeot 404s or 504s known as taxi-be (although some people call the 25-seater buses taxi-be) designed to take 9 people, but often packed with 14. A car- brousse is any sort of vehicle sturdy enough to cope with bad roads. Being sturdy it is usually excessively uncomfortable. Madagascar has a problem with its public transport because there is so little hard currency to pay for spare parts, and the bad roads shake them to bits anyway. If this situation improves the vehicles will also improve.

Vehicles leave from a *gare routière* on the side of town closest to their destination. You should try to go there a day or two ahead of your planned departure and buy a ticket in advance (there is always some sort of kiosk selling tickets). It is also wise to arrive early to claim your seat, since they are usually allocated on a first come first served basis. Be prepared for the vehicle to leave hours later than scheduled. On short journeys vehicles simply leave as soon as they fill up.

There is no set rate per kilometre; fares are calculated on the roughness of the road and the time the journey takes. A sample of taxi-be (bus) rates (Feb 1990): Tana to Tuléar – 22,000 FMG (about £9.00/$15.00), Tana to Fort Dauphin – 32,000 FMG, Tana to Majunga – 13,000 FMG.

Drivers usually stop to eat and sleep, but they may drive all night. During night stops most passengers stay in the vehicle or sleep on the road outside, but there is often a hotel – of sorts – nearby.

There is much that a committed overland traveller can do to soften his/her experiences on taxi-brousses – see *What to bring* on page 63. In addition to basic camping equipment, bring a good book, cards, Scrabble, etc, as well as snacks and drink, to pass the time during inevitable breakdowns and delays. If you're prepared for the realities, an overland journey can be very enjoyable (one traveller told me that the trip to Fort Dauphin was one of his best memories of Madagascar) and gives you a unique chance to get to know the Malagasy. But you'd better read the journey descriptions by Robert Stewart (page 120) and Tim Cross (page 197) before committing yourself to this form of transport.

Car hire

With public transport so unreliable, more visitors have been renting cars in recent years. You would need to be a competent mechanic to hire a self-drive car in Madagascar, but most agencies also have chauffeurs available. Try Madagascar Airtours, Aventour, and Société Auto Express, Route Circulaire Ampahibe. Tel: 210 60.

A recommended company is Rahariseta, B.P. 3779, Antananarivo (located next to Lake Behoririka); Tel: 257 70, Telex: 225 17 MG, Tax: 261 2 224 47. Their prices in February 1990, per day/per kilometre, range from Renault 4 – 10,000/280 FMG to Toyota 4 X 4 (7 places) or Merc minibus (12 places) – 27,000/680 FMG. Tax is 15%. A driver costs 2,500 FMG a day, and insurance 3,500 FMG a day.

Mountain bike

Last year I met a Dutch couple who'd brought their own mountain bikes to Madagascar, experienced no trouble transporting them on planes, and had had a marvellous time (they cycled from Tana to Tamatave and then flew to Ste Marie). This would seem the perfect form of transport for Madagascar's roads and what better way of meeting the people?

Transport within cities

There are **taxis** in all cities. Their rates are reasonable – usually a fixed price for the centre of town – and they will pick up other passengers. They have no meters, so set the price before you get in. Taxi drivers in Madagascar have no tradition of cheating tourists so strenuous bargaining is seldom necessary. Some major cities (Tana, Majunga, Diego Suarez) have good new **buses** (Japanese).

Rickshaws, known as *pousse-pousse* ('push-push' – said to originate from the time they operated in the capital and needed one man behind to push up the steep hills), are a Madagascar speciality and provide transport in Antsirabe, Majunga, and Tamatave. Occasionally you see them in Antananarivo, but they are mostly used for transporting goods.

Many western visitors are reluctant to sit in comfort behind a running, ragged, bare-foot man and no-one with a heart can fail to feel compassion for the *pousse-pousse* drivers. However, this is another case of needing to abandon our own cultural hang-ups. These men want work. Most rickshaws are owned by Indians to whom the 'drivers' must pay a daily fee. If they take no passengers they will be out of pocket – and there's precious little *in* their pockets. I square my conscience by taking a *pousse-pousse* whenever possible, bargaining them down to the normal 500 FMG (25p) or so, then giving them a good – and unexpected – tip at the end of the ride. But *do* bargain hard (before you get in); *pousse-pousse* drivers have recently become quite cunning in their dealings with tourists.

Air travel

Air Madagascar started its life in 1962 as Madair but understandably changed its name after a few years of jokes. It now serves 59 destinations, making it by far the best way – and for some people the only way – of seeing the country. Foreigners must pay their fares in hard currency. Here are some sample prices from Antananarivo: Tamatave 350 FF; Nosy Be 885 FF; Diego Suarez 995 FF; others are given in the relevant chapters.

The **Air Tourist Pass** which formerly gave you unlimited flights for a month was discontinued in 1990.

The recent rise in tourism in Madagascar has brought more passengers than Air Mad can cope with, particularly in July and August. You are strongly advised to make your key bookings in advance. I had a sad letter recently from someone who'd spent most of his two week holiday at Antananarivo airport trying to get on a flight – any flight, anywhere. If you are doing your bookings once you arrive, avoid the crush by getting to the Air Mad office when it opens at 8.00. Often flights which are said to be fully booked in Tana are found to have seats when you reapply at the town of departure. In any case, you should reconfirm your next flight as soon as you arrive at your destination (at the Air Mad office in town). You can very often get on

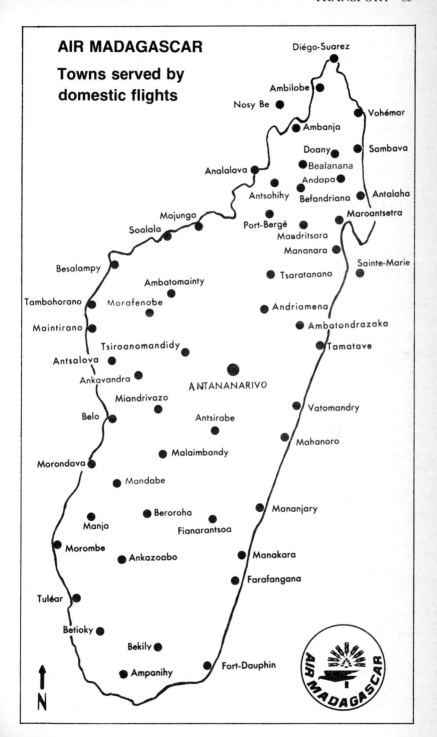

AIR MADAGASCAR

Towns served by domestic flights

fully booked flights if you go standby.

There are no numbered seats or refreshments on internal flights.

It is useful to know that *Enregistrement Bagages* is the check-in counter and *Livraison Bagages* is luggage arrival.

Schedules are reviewed annually at the end of March, but are subject to change at any time and without notice.

Air Madagascar have the following planes: Boeing 747 (jumbo) on the Paris to Tana route, Boeing 737 (flying to the larger cities and Nosy Be), the smaller Hawker Siddeley 748, and the very small and erratic Twin Otter and Piper which serve the smaller towns.

With a shortage of planes and pilots, planes often get delayed or cancelled, but Air Mad is basically safe and reliable.

Private charters

For a small group this is a viable option and not as expensive as you may think. TAM (Travaux Aeriens De Madagascar) have the following planes and prices. Cessna 402 8 (wide cabin) 6 seats: daily hire rate $165 plus $220 per flying hour; Piper PA 23 250 (5 seater) is a similar price, and the 3 seater Piper PA 28 180 is $36 daily, $80 per flying hour. There's an additional $20 for miscellaneous expenses and pilot's expenses – hotel, meals etc) are also payable. The advantages are obvious – you can get where you want when you want.

TAM, 31 Avenue de l'Indépendance, Antananarivo. Tel: 222 22. They also have an operations office at the Hilton Hotel, Tel: 296 91.

ACCOMMODATION

Hotels in Madagascar are classified by a national star system – five star being the highest, but in my experience this designates price, not quality. In this book I have used three categories: A, B and C. Often B, being less pretentious, are the better hotels. Beach bungalows, which come into all three categories, are usually excellent value. Five and four star hotels must be paid for in hard currency.

Category A   Up to international standard in Antananarivo, Tamatave, Tuléar, Fort Dauphin and Nosy Be, but usually large and impersonal. Often overpriced and very run down in other less-visited towns. Prices range from 150 FF (£15/$24) to 785 FF (£78/$128) double.

Category B   These can be just as clean and comfortable with the added attraction (if you have the right attitude) of a certain amount of wildlife in the rooms. Geckos, in particular, seem to enjoy hotel bathrooms, perhaps because of the prolific insect life found there. Most hotels in this category have a basin and bidet in the room, and comfortable beds although hard, French-style bolsters take the place of pillows. They are often family-run and very friendly. The average price is £8/$14.

Category C   Exhilaratingly ghastly at times but quite charming at others, these are not for the squeamish. There may be rats, cockroaches, and other such creatures sharing your room. The pillows are filled with sisal, and the double beds can be quite amazingly uncomfortable with lumpy mattresses sagging like hammocks so that couples are thrown companionably together in the centre, or thin coverings over slats.

Some hotels have basins in the room, and occasionally they are clean and excellent value, only earning the C because of their price. In an out of the way place you will pay as little as £1 for the most basic room, although £3 or £4 would be more usual.

Many B and C hotels will do your washing for you at a very reasonable price.

Sally Crook points out: '*Toilette* means shower or bathroom, at least in northern Madagascar, so to prevent accidents ask for the W.C. ('dooble vay say'). I only found it by the smell in one small overnight hotel after asking repeatedly for the wrong thing.'

Note: The Malagasy word *Hotely* usually means a restaurant/snackbar rather than accommodation.

There are no organised campsites in Madagascar. You used to be able to camp anywhere, but sadly tent-slashers have made an appearance in some resorts. In out of the way places you will be in no danger.

FOOD AND DRINK
Food
Eating well is one of the delights of Madagascar, and even the fussiest tourists are usually happy with the food served at better hotels and restaurants. International hotels serve international food, usually with a French bias and often do special Malagasy dishes (such as the Hilton on Thursdays). Lodges and smaller hotels serve local food which can also be excellent, particularly on the coast where lobster, shell fish and other sea food predominates. Meat lovers will enjoy the succulent zebu steaks. Outside the capital, most hotels offer a set menu (*table d'hôte*) to their guests. Where the menu is *à la carte* it is a great help to have a French dictionary, preferably one with a food section.

Chinese and Indian food are common in many towns, and almost always good and reasonably priced. *Soupe Chinoise* is found almost everywhere, and is filling and tasty. The Malagasy eat a lot of rice (see Box, page 114) so most dishes are accompanied by a sticky mound of the stuff. It's bland and flavourless, but sops up the tasty sauces (or, for places where the accompanying slops look anything but tasty, bring your own flavouring).

Dairy products, which used to be unobtainable, can now be found in larger towns. There's usually a good selection of fruit in the markets and fruit is served in most restaurants, along with raw vegetables or *crudités*. From June to August the fruit is largely limited to citrus and bananas, but from September there are strawberries, mangoes, lichees, pineapples, citrus fruit, bananas and loquats. Slices of coconut are sold everywhere, but especially on the coast, where coconut milk is a popular and safe drink, and toffee-coconut nibbles are sold on the street, often wrapped in paper from school exercise books.

Drink

The Malagasy 'Three Horses' beer is very good as is the new 'Beeks Brau'. The price goes up according to the surroundings: twice as much in the Hilton as in a *hotely* and there is always a hefty deposit payable on the bottles.

Madagascar produces its own wine in the Fianarantsoa region, and some are rather good. L'azani Betsileo (costing around 8,000 FMG) is recommended.

Rum, *toaka gasy*, is very cheap and plentiful, especially in sugar-growing areas such as Nosy Be, and fermented sugar cane juice, *betsabetsa* (east coast) or fermented coconut milk, *trembo* (north), make a change. The best drink of all is *punch au coco*, with a coconut milk base, which is a speciality of Île Ste Marie but is found in other coastal areas.

Soft drinks are limited to a good but rather expensive spring water, 'Eau Vive' and, of course, Coca-Cola. The locally produced *limonady* sadly bears no resemblance to lemons.

Malagasy food

After a year of living in Madagascar and travelling in remote areas, David Curl described the standard Malagasy dishes as: 'skin and rice, gristle and rice, fat and rice, and bones and rice', these being chicken, beef, pork and fish respectively. A sometimes true summary for the smaller villages, where basic menus are chalked up on a blackboard outside *hotelys*:

Henan-omby (or *Hen'omby*) – beef.
Henam-borona (or *Hen'akoho*) – chicken.
Henan-kisoa – pork.
Henan-drano (or *Hazan-drano*) – fish.

The menu may add Mazotoa homana. This is not a dish, it means *Bon appétit!*.

Along with the meat or fish and inevitable mound of rice (*vary*) comes a bowl of stock. This is spooned over the rice, or drunk as a soup.

Thirst is quenched with *ranovola*, or rice water, obtained by boiling water in the pan in which the rice was cooked. It has a slight flavour of burnt rice, and since it has been boiled for several minutes it is safe to drink. (Indeed, it is actually therapeutic: the WHO recommends 'barley water' as rehydration therapy, since starch (as found in rice and barley) is a more easily absorbed source of energy than sugar. All you need is to add a little salt to your *ranovola* and your diarrhoea treatment is perfected!)

In smarter restaurants Malagasy food can be very good indeed, and all visitors should at least sample the most popular dish, *Romazava*, a meat and vegetable stew, spiced with ginger. This is usually served with *brèdes* (pronounced 'bread'), a variety of greens which often have a pleasant peppery taste. Another good local dish is *ravitoto*, shredded manioc leaves with fried pork.

HANDICRAFTS AND WHAT TO BUY

You can buy just about everything in the handicrafts line in Madagascar. Most typical of the country are wood carvings, raffia work (in amazing variety), crocheted and embroidered table-cloths and clothes, semi-precious stones, carved zebu horn, Antaimoro paper (with embedded dried flowers), mounted butterflies, shells, and so on. The choice is almost limitless.

The luggage weight limit when leaving Madagascar is 20 kg (30 kg if you are going non-stop to Paris which manages to count as a 'national' flight!). Bear this in mind when doing your shopping.

Other local products which make good presents are vanilla pods (although strictly speaking you are limited to 100 grammes), pepper corns, saffron and other spices, and honey.

Do not buy products from endangered species. That includes tortoiseshell, crocodile skins, and, of course, live or stuffed lemurs and other animals. Also prohibited are endemic plants and any genuine article of funerary art.

To help stamp out the sale of endangered animal products, tourists should make their feelings – and the law – known. If, for instance, you are offered a tortoise or turtle shell, tell the vendor it is *prohibé* and to push the point home you can say it is *fady* for you to buy such a thing.

Permits

Some purchases need, in theory, an export permit, but the rule is seldom enforced with tourists – indeed, looking at the official list, which contains every item tourists are likely to buy, it would be impossible to enforce it. Check, if possible, with a local tour operator and use your judgement: if you are planning to take home a rosewood wardrobe or a stuffed Aepiornis you'd do well to get the paperwork; if it's a carved bookend, I wouldn't bother.

Export permits for craft items are obtained from Ministère

de l'Art et de la Culture Révolutionnaire, Galerie 6, Avenue de l'Indépendance, Analakely. You will need to list your purchases and have receipts. Leave the list in the morning and pick up your permits in the afternoon. For animal products such as mounted butterflies, or large wooden items apply to room 42 or the 4th floor of the Départment des Eaux et Forêts in Nanisana.

MISCELLANEOUS

Electrical equipment
The voltage in Madagascar is 110 or 220. Outlets (where they exist) take 2-pin round plugs.

Transferring funds
If you are likely to need to have money sent from home, it's best to arrange it before-hand. The best bank for this is Banque Malgache de l'Ocean Indien, Place de l'Indepéndance, Antaninarenina. Its corresponding bank in the UK is Banque Nationale de Paris, King William St, London.

Communication with home
In 1990 a three minute phone call to England cost 6,555 FMG (9,840 FMG from a hotel).

If you want to receive mail, have your correspondent address the envelope with your initial only, your surname in block capitals, and send it to you c/o Poste Restante in whichever town you will be. It will be held at the main post office.

Note: The area called Antaninarenina in some addresses is the Upper Town, around the Hotel Colbert.
   B.P. in an address is *Boîte Postale* – the same as P.O. Box...

PUBLIC HOLIDAYS

January 1 New Years Day	June 26 National Day
March 29 Commemoration of 1947 rebellion	August 15 Feast of the Assumption
Easter Monday (movable)	November 1 All Saints Day
May 1 Labour Day	December 25 Christmas Day
Ascension Day (movable)	December 30 Republic Day
Whit Monday (movable)	

When these holidays fall on a Thursday, Friday will also be a weekend. Note that banks always close at 12.00 the day before a holiday.

VILLAGE ETIQUETTE

Travellers venturing well off the beaten path will want to do their utmost to avoid offending or frightening the local people, who are usually extremely warm and hospitable. Unfortunately, with the many *fady* prohibitions varying from area to area and village to village, it is impossible to know exactly how to behave; all you can do is watch the villagers and do as they do, and if possible take a local guide. *Vazahas* (white foreigners) and other outsiders are exempt from the consequences of infringing a local *fady*, but of course may inadvertently cause the community to make expensive sacrifices to propitiate the offended *razana*.

On arrival at a village, ask for the 'Ray aman'dreny' (mother and father) of the village. This will be the village elder(s). Another person to introduce yourself to is the *Président du Fokontany* or head of the People's Executive Committee. He will show you where you can sleep (sometimes a hut is kept free for guests, often someone will be moved out for you). You will usually be provided with food, and as an honoured guest may even receive meat (in rural villages the day to day diet is rice and *brèdes*). To suggest paying for your board and lodging would be considered an insult, but a small present would be appropriate.

The above applies to very remote areas, inaccessible by vehicle and unaccustomed to foreigners. In other communities you should still make contact with the *Président du Fokontany* but may be expected to pay for your lodging. You should certainly offer to do so.

RESPONSIBLE TOURISM

The ethics of tourism have only recently been given any attention, but tourism in 'undeveloped' countries has a profound effect on the inhabitants, some good, much bad. Madagascar seems to me a special case – more than any other country I've visited it inspires a special devotion and an awareness of its fragility, both animal and human. Wildlife is definitely profiting from the attention recently given it, and in this respect I see responsible tourism (or ecotourism, as the WWF prefers it to be called) as a benefit. For the people, however, the blessings are very mixed: some able Malagasy have found jobs in the tourist industry, but many are in the process of losing their cultural identity, their dignity and their integrity.

Think before you give

Cultural sensitivity is not easy to acquire, and is particularly difficult for visitors from industrialised countries who are only too aware of their wealth in relation to the extreme poverty they see around them. Their reaction is to give – money or gifts. Children are usually the recipients – because they are endearing, not because they are needy – and the giver is unaware that the beggar he has just created will seem

Balloons

Eight years ago, when Madagascar tourism was in its infancy, I was escorting an American couple from Fort Dauphin to Berenty. Passing one of the sparse collection of huts that make up a Antanosy village we saw that something important was happening: there were drums and dancing. At our request the driver got out to ask what was going on, and we learned that a village woman had become possessed of an evil spirit and the dance was the first stage in a three day exorcism process which would culminate with the sacrifice of a goat. We arranged with our driver to leave Berenty in time to see the closing stages. Two days later the dance had become a shuffle, but still a remarkably energetic shuffle. Permission was asked, and graciously given, for us to stay and even to take photos. We were objects of mild curiosity but the onlookers were much too involved in the goings on in front of the houses to give us much attention.

After an hour the tourists began to get restless. It was very hot and nothing new had happened for some time. No sacrifice, no escaping evil spirit. Suddenly I heard a commotion: one of them had produced a packet of balloons and was busy blowing them up and distributing them to the children. 'Kids always love these things' he chuckled. They did indeed love them. We were soon surrounded by first a pleading, then irate group of mothers and wailing children who either had not received a balloon, or whose ephemeral new toy had burst. The exorcism was still going on, but most onlookers had now turned their attention to us. The mood was broken, a private and solemn occasion turned into a public squabble.

Bedo

Anyone with an interest in natural history who visited Périnet in the 1980s knew Bedo. He was 12 when I first met him, the son of the warden; an undersized, spindly child who looked years younger than his age but who exuded enthusiasm for the creatures which lived in his forest. Instead of subjecting them to some mild torture, as would other boys, he watched and learned – a Malagasy Gerald Durrell who could spot a *Uroplatus* pressed invisibly against the bark of a tree, who knew where the Indri would be calling and invariably found them, and who could recognise all the birds by their song.

In those early days most of Périnet's visitors were naturalists, photographers or film-makers. They started to teach Bedo the scientific names of the animals, and after weeks of filming or study they naturally gave him a tip. Bedo's exceptional intelligence and aptitude made him a quick learner, and through the years he not only increased his knowledge of natural history but he learned enough French, English and German to be the most sought after guide in Madagascar. The tips became bigger, and he started presenting invoices to make sure they stayed that way.

By the time he was 19 Bedo was, by Malagasy standards, a wealthy young man. Yet he still lived in a small village where the only thing to spend his money on was alcohol. Naturalists who had known him for years complained that he was becoming unreliable; certainly this rich kid was becoming unpopular with his contemporaries.

In July 1989 he got into a fight with two youths; some say he won and went down to the river to wash, others say he was chased down to the river. The two youths hurled a rock at him from the bank which struck him on the head. He fell into the river and was drowned.

less appealing to the next *vazaha* who comes along. And the little pest that will not take no for an answer will learn – perhaps for the first time – what it feels like to be shouted at by an angry adult. Thus the cultural gap is widened. Not much thought is needed to see that children should not be given pens, money, sweets... all the goodies that tourists have, by habit, lavished on them.

The dark side of generosity is further illustrated by the two stories opposite.

Organisations and publications

There are at least two small organisations addressing themselves to the problems of tourism. They need support, and I am sure that anyone who has seen a much-loved country or area fall to the blight of mass tourism will want to become involved. Remember to include a stamped addressed envelope with your enquiry. I would like to hear of similar organisations in the USA and other parts of the world.

Tourism Concern, c/o Alison Stancliffe, 8 St Mary's Terrace, Ryton, Tyne and Wear, NE40 3AL, England.

With the slogan 'putting people back in the picture', Tourism Concern is now publishing a quarterly newsletter. Their £10 membership fee keeps you abreast of relevant events and publications.

CART (Centre for the Advancement of Responsive Travel); Director Dr Roger Millman, 70 Dry Hill Park Rd, Tonbridge, Kent TN10 3BX, England.

CART has published an excellent leaflet titled *Credo for the Caring Traveller* with 11 pointers for those wishing to reduce their impact on the host country.

North-South Travel Ltd, Moulsham Mill Centre, Parkway, Chelmsford, Essex CM2 7PX. Tel: 0245 492882; Fax 0245 356612.

The only travel agency to give its profits to aid projects in the developing world.

The UK and Third World Tourism, Ten Publications (Third World Tourism European Ecumenical Network).

A thoroughly researched and unemotional analysis, available for £5.00 from CART (address above).

Tourism: Environment and Development Perspectives by Peter Mason.

Sponsored by the WWF and aimed at students of Tourism, this book stresses the impact of tourism on the economy, society, culture and environment of all countries. Available for £9.95 from the WWF, Weyside Park, Catteshall Lane, Godalming, Surrey GU7 1XR.

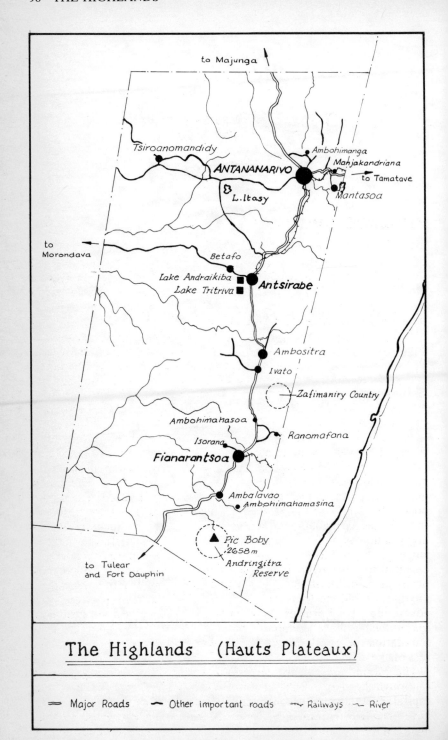

The Highlands   (Hauts Plateaux)

= Major Roads   — Other important roads   ⊶ Railways   ⌇ River

Chapter 7

The Highlands

(Hauts Plateaux)

INTRODUCTION

The kingdom of Imerina was born in the highlands. Recorded history of the Merina people (also known as the Hova), who are characterised by their Indonesian appearance and exhumation practices (*famadihana*) begins in the 1400s with a chief called Andriandraviravina. He is widely thought to have started the dynasty that became the most powerful in Madagascar, eventually conquering much of the country.

Key monarchs in the rise of the Merina include Andrianjaka, who conquered a Vazimba town called Analamanga built on a great rock thrusting above the surrounding plains. He renamed it Antananarivo and ordered his palace to be built on its highest point. With its surrounding marshland, ideal for rice production, and the security afforded by its high position, this was the perfect site for a Merina capital city.

In the 18th century there were two centres for the Merina kingdom, Antananarivo and Ambohimanga. The latter became the more important and around 1787 Ramboasalama was proclaimed king of Ambohimanga and took the name of Andrianampoinimerina. The name means 'the prince in the heart of Imerina' which was more than an idle boast: this king was the Malagasy counterpart of the great Peruvian Inca Tupac Yupanqui, expanding his empire as much by skilful organisation as by force, and doing it without the benefit of a written language (history seems to demonstrate that orders in triplicate are not essential to efficiency). By his death in 1810 the central plateau was firmly in control of the Merina and ably administered through a mixture of old customs and new. Each conquered territory was governed by local princes, answerable to the King, and the system of *fokonolona* (village communities) was established. From this firm foundation the new king, Radama I, was able to conquer most of the rest of the island.

The Merina are still the most influential of the Malagasy peoples (although President Ratsiraka is Betsimisaraka) and dominate the capital. Further south, the highlands are occupied by the Betsileo, who have been heavily influenced by the Merina and also practise *famadihana*. Since the mid 19th century Merina houses have been built of brick or red mud (laterite), often with roofs supported on slender pillars. These typical houses are a feature of the city and its surroundings. Invariably they are of less sturdy construction than the cement tombs that can be seen on the outskirts of town, the dead being considered more important than the living.

There is some splendid scenery on the *Hauts Plateaux*. Route Nationale 7, which runs to Tuléar, passes dramatic granite domes and grassy hills, and always the mosaic of paddy fields add colour and pattern to a land journey. These patterns are best appreciated from the air, from where the old defence ditches, *tamboho*, forming circles around villages or estates can be seen. I never tire of staring down as the plane circles before landing at Ivato airport. The aerial view is as exotically different as Madagascar itself.

ANTANANARIVO
History
The city founded by Andrianjaka was called Antananarivo which means 'City of the Thousand', supposedly because a thousand warriors protected it. By the end of the eighteenth century, Andrianampoinimerina had taken Antananarivo from his rebellious kinsman and moved his base there from Ambohimanga. From that time until the French conquest in 1895 Madagascar's history centred around the royal palace or *rova*, the modest houses built for Andrianjaka and Andrianampoinimerina giving way to the splendid palace designed for Queen Ranavalona by Jean Laborde and James Cameron. The rock cliffs near the palace became known as Ampamarinana, 'the place of the hurling' as Christian martyrs met their fate at the command of the Queen.

There was no reason for the French to move the capital elsewhere: its pleasant climate made it an agreeable place to live, and plenty of French money and planning went into the city we see today.

Arriving and leaving
Airport formalities
In its red tape heyday, getting from the aircraft to taxi or bus could take a couple of hours, although the actual process was conducted with a courtesy and patience that some leading airports (Kennedy, are you listening?) could copy. The process has now been streamlined, and though visitors still find themselves milling around the arrivals area in confusion, there are giggling women in green uniforms to hand you immigration forms and currency declaration forms (you need two of each) and to direct you to the right queue. Proceed as follows:

1. Police. Have your passport checked and stamped.
2. Douane. Fill in your currency declaration form. Make quite sure it tallies with the amount of money and travellers cheques you have

(make a note of the total *before* you get to the airport); the officials may count your money (rare these days but have it handy). If you have a video camera, or other expensive photographic equipment, you will be asked to declare it.

3. Santé (Health). You may need your vaccination card here showing that you are up to date with necessary inoculations.

4. After a final document check you descend some stairs and are in the main airport

While waiting for luggage to arrive, change money. There are two banks: on the right at the bottom of the stairs and facing the stairs. Remember to have your currency declaration handy (and at all times when you change money).

Uniformed baggage handlers help you to retrieve your luggage (in the good old Marxist days they did not expect to be tipped) and you then take it into the customs area for checking (these days tourists are rarely asked to open luggage) and there you are.

Leaving is also much easier these days. I felt almost let down in 1989 when it took a mere 30 minutes and only mild bruising to get into the departure lounge!

Flights are often overbooked so it's as well to get to the airport three hours before departure. Join the queue and shuffle forward with your luggage to pass through customs where your bag may be opened to make sure you are not exporting prohibited items (see page 00). Then comes Police who will collect your completed departure form and currency declaration. Now you can check in and get your boarding pass, and finally seat assignments when you pay the airport tax (currently set at 1,500 FMG, but almost sure to change so check before you spend all your local money). Remember you may not change FMG back to hard currency.

Ivaty has a very good restaurant (waiter service, slow). Worth booking in advance if you are expecting a long stopover at the airport.

Transport into the city centre (12 km)

There is a good airport bus service, Air Routes Service, which costs 1,500 FMG. Or you can take a posh taxi, cheap taxi, or local bus (although the new-found capitalist spirit of the baggage-handlers may make it almost impossible to make your own choice here).

Posh taxis meet you *in* the airport, and hustle you and your luggage to their vehicle outside. The fare is about 12,000 FMG.

Walk across the road to the car-park where lurk the cheap taxis (understandably they are none too popular with the posh guys). These can be bargained down to about 7,000 FMG.

Bare-bones budget backpackers can walk to the nearby town of Ivato – or the road junction (½ km) and get the local bus or taxi-brousse for 250 FMG.

Antananarivo today

One of the most attractive capitals anywhere, Antananarivo (popularly known as Tana) has the quality of a child's picture book. Brightly coloured houses are stacked up the hillsides, and there are very few of the modern skyscrapers that deface most capitals. Rice paddies are tended right up to the edge of the city, clothes are laid out on the river bank to dry, and ox-carts rumble along the roads on the outskirts of town. It's all deliciously foreign, and can hardly fail to impress the first-time visitor as he or she comes in from the airport. The good impression is helped by the climate – during the dry season the sun is hot but the air pleasantly cool (the altitude is between 1,245 m and 1,469 m).

The city is built on two ridges which combine in a V. Down the central valley runs a broad boulevard, Avenue de l'Indépendance (sometimes called by its Malagasy name Fahaleovantena), which terminates at the station. It narrows at the other end to become Avenue du 26 Juin, then dives through a tunnel to reach lake Anosy and the Hilton Hotel (pedestrians make their way breathlessly up and down flights of stairs). The Avenues Indépendance and 26 Juin are the focal point of the Lower Town, lined with shops, offices, hotels, and crammed with market stalls and lower class bustle, but the 'centre of town' could just as easily refer to the Upper Town where the president's palace (now – or soon to be – a museum), the Hotel Colbert, the main post office and other assorted offices are located. This is where you will find the most expensive boutiques and best jewellers' shops.

It is all very confusing, and made worse by streets being unnamed, changing name several times within a few hundred metres, or going by two different names (when reading street names it's worth knowing that *Lalana* means street and *Arabe* avenue). Fortunately you can never really be lost since this is a town for wanderers – you are just seeing a new area. As a rough wandering guide, however, I would recommend that lots of time be spent in the Upper Town – and on the opposite side, above the market – but don't venture beyond the station where distances are long and streets dreary.

Sightseeing

As if to emphasise how different it is to other capitals, Tana has very little in the way of conventional sightseeing. It doesn't even have a Tourist Office as such, although the Department of Tourism is at Tsimbazaza, on the left as you go down the hill to the park.

President's Palace (exhibition of Malagasy culture)

I'm jumping the gun a bit here, since until 1990 you dared not go near the President's Palace in the Upper Town because heavily-armed guards would warn you away. Now, John Mack tells me, his wonderful exhibition from the Museum of Mankind and New York's Natural

History Museum will be on permanent display here. Don't miss it, but don't elbow your way past armed guards, either.

The Queen's Palace (Rova)
Standing high above the city, this miscellany of mausoleums and palace dominates the skyline (especially when viewed from lake Anosy or the Hilton Hotel).

The energetic can walk there – it's a breathtaking (in both senses of the word) climb which takes about half an hour from the Colbert, but is well worth it for the views and scenes en route. Start at Lalana Ratsimilaho and when in doubt take the uphill road. The entrance to the *Rova* is topped by a very European-looking eagle; King Radama I had his stronghold here guarded by elite troops known as The Eagles. The Queen's Palace, originally built in wood by Jean Laborde at the request of Queen Ranavalona I, is enclosed in a stone structure, designed by James Cameron in 1873 during the reign of Queen Ranavalona II. Laborde's building is perfectly in harmony with Madagascar, Cameron's would be more in keeping with Edinburgh. The main palace, *manjakamiadana* ('where it is pleasant to reign') was for years closed for renovations, but the ground floor is finally open so you can see the 39 metre high rosewood pillar, said to have been brought from the eastern forests by ten thousand slaves, and the throne itself. Other rooms should be opened before too long.

On entering the compound you will see on the left what appears to be two attractive wooden chalets. These are *tranomanara*, sacred houses, over the Tomb of the Queens, where the remains of four Queens are interred, and the Tomb of the Kings which houses three Kings. Their bodies lie seven metres below the ground.

Another building contains paintings of the monarchs as well as James Hastie, Radama I's advisor, Sir Robert Farquhar, governor of Mauritius, and a fascinating early photo of Jean Laborde.

The reconstruction of Andrianampoinimerina's little palm-thatched house is interesting. The King's bed is high on a platform in the north-east corner, opposite a much wider shelf on which slept eleven of his twelve wives. The lucky twelfth spent one week in the royal bed, no doubt in acts of procreation. A tall column rises to the roof by the King's bed. We are told that on hearing the approach of a stranger, his highness would scramble up this pillar (there are tiny handholds) and if the visitor was welcome he would inform whichever wife was tending the cooking pots beneath the pillar by dropping a pebble on her head. Or so we are told.

Andrianampoinimerina's sedan chair, borne by eight men, is here, and an accompanying litter for his luggage. He travelled widely in his kingdom, exhorting the peasants to greater labours by replacing their worn out agricultural tools.

The *Besakana* contains the litter that carried the bodies of Ranavalona I and II. The royal initials RM stand for Ranavalona Manjaka

The white parasols of the Zoma line Avenue de l'Indepéndance

(the rough equivalent of Regina).

Also in the royal compound is a church in the Wren-classical style built in stone for Ranavalona II by the British missionary - architect, William Poole. (Other churches built by British missionaries on sites of Christian martyrdoms are also worth a visit, especially Ampamarinana ('the place of the hurling') just below the palace, and Ambohipotsy at the south end of the ridge with spectacular views to the Ankaratra mountains to the south - west).

The *rova* is open weekdays 10.00 to 12.00, 13.00 to 17.30, Saturdays 14.00 to 17.00, Sundays 9.00 to 12.00, 14.00 to 1700. You are not permitted to take photos within the compound (cameras are checked in at the gate). However, you can apply for a photo permit (it takes 24 hours) and come back with your camera the next day.

Tsimbazaza

Rather a good museum (natural history and ethnology), botanical garden and zoo. The park is open on Thursdays, Saturdays, Sundays and holidays, from 8.00 to 11.00, and 14.00 to 17.00. On other days, however, although not open to the general public, tourists will usually be admitted on request (if possible arrange this beforehand).

Some international conservation efforts have gone into improving the zoo, and establishing educational programmes and as more money is made available this trend will no doubt continue. There is a good collection of lemurs, including the recently discovered golden bamboo lemur (see page 127) and an island of cheerful ring-tails, and a lake with hundreds of egrets nesting in the trees. The excellent vivarium is open only in the afternoons but the helpful attendants will sometimes show you round in the morning. It has a well-displayed collection of reptiles and small mammals.

The botanical garden is spacious and well laid out, and also displays some reproduction Sakalava graves. It is the museum, however, that attracts the most interest for its selection of skeletons of now extinct animals, including several species of giant lemur and the famous 'elephant bird' or *Aepyornis* which may only have become extinct after the arrival of the first Europeans. It is displayed next to the skeleton of an ostrich, so its massive size can be appreciated. Another room displays stuffed animals, but the efforts of the taxidermist have left little to likeness and a lot to the imagination. It's worth taking a close look at the aye-aye, however, to study its remarkable hands (I have a soft spot for that particular creature – I saw it in its previous existence when, during my first visit in 1976, the keeper woke it up for us; it reacted as you would if someone pulled back the bedclothes at 3 am).

The museum also has a good ethnological section.

Tsimbazaza is about 4 km from the city centre. There are buses from Avenue de l'Indépendance (no 15), but it is easier to take a taxi there and bus or taxi-be back.

Zoma

No-one should visit Tana without going to the market. *Zoma* means Friday and this is the day when the whole of Avenue de l'Indépendance erupts into a rash of white umbrellas. The market runs the length of the street and up the hillsides, filling every available space with an amazing variety of goods. There are stands selling nothing but bottles, or spare parts, or years-old French magazines; there are men who repair watches, or umbrellas or bicycles; there are flowers and fruit and animals (including cats) and herbal medicines and charms; and there are dozens of varieties of handicrafts, from embroidery to wood carvings, semi-precious stones, raffia goods, and so on.

Bring lots of small change, and nothing else – the *zoma* is notorious for thieves. Carry larger sums of money in a money belt. The best time to visit is between 12.00 and 2.00 when most people are having lunch.

Although the *Zoma* proper is on Fridays, there is always a market in Tana, always some white umbrellas shading fruit and vegetables opposite the stairs leading to the upper town, and some handicraft stalls down each side of the avenue towards the station. It is interesting to wander around on Thursday nights, watching stalls being set up and goods unpacked under the flickering light of paraffin lamps. This is the one bustling evening: Tana is usually very quiet after dark.

Antananarivo Centre – Key

1. Station   2. Restaurant Grand Orient   3. Hotel Terminus
4. Hotel la Muraille de Chine   5. Institut de Hygiène Social
6. Bank   7. Hotel Bolidor Lapasoa   8. Travel Agent
9. Hotel Mellis   10. Hotel de France   11. Hotel Anjary   12. Hotel Nishate
13. French Embassy   14. Air Madagascar   15. Hotel Glacier
16. Zoma (Market)   17. Patisserie Suisse   18. Prisunic Supermarket
19. Place de l'Indépendance   20. Main Post Office   21. Restaurant Grand Île
22. President's Palace   23. Hotel Colbert   24. Aeroflot
25. Youth Hostel   26. Hotel Hilton, Madagascar Airtours

In a 1989 survey of tourists leaving Madagascar, the 'niceness of the people' was most often cited as their favourite memory of the island. Natural history came second.

HELP! ... see page 227

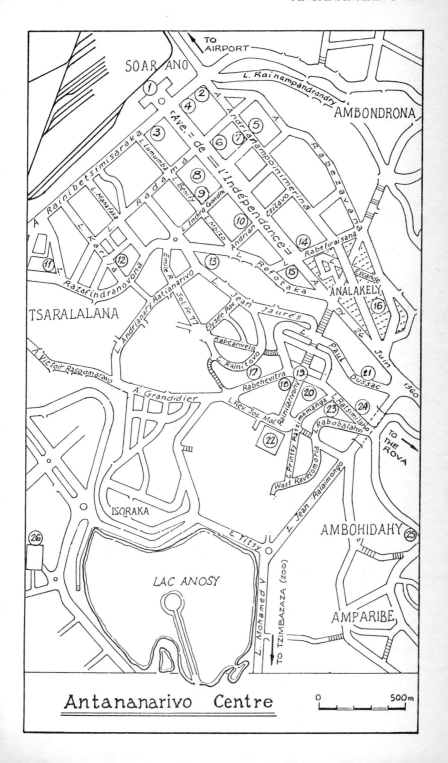

Antananarivo Centre

0   500m

Where to stay

Category A

Hilton Hotel. Near lake Anosy. Tel: 260 60. One of Tana's skyscrapers (as you'd expect), very comfortable with good meals. Its advantages are that Madagascar Airtours has its office in the building (and there are many other convenient offices and shops), and it has a swimming pool. In the pleasantly hot sun of the dry season this is a real bonus. The disadvantage is that it is not in the centre of town (although the walk in is enjoyable). 1990 rates: 851 FF doublé, 782 FF single.

Hotel Colbert. Lalana Printsy Ratsimamanga. Tel: 202 02. Very French, usually full, my choice of the posh Tana hotels for its excellent location in the Upper Town, superb food, and lively atmosphere. 1990 rates: 420 FF per room (single or double).

Hotel de France. The only first class hotel on Avenue Indépendance. 350 FF. Ask for an inside room – 59, 60, 61, among others. Convenient for those staying only briefly in Tana, and currently being renovated and expanded. Very good meals (but single men be warned – you'll be hassled by the bar-girls!), and a super patisserie with pain au chocolat (great for a breakfast splurge if you're sleeping cheap); very useful for Zoma zombies!

Solimotel, near Lac Anosy. Tel: 250 40. Said to be very good, with swimming pool. 180 FF.

Category B

Castello Hotel. Near the airport with great views of Tana. New, quiet.

Le Relais des Pistards. Bungalows on L. Fernand Kasanga (same road as Tsimbazaza), about 1 km beyond the zoo. Owned by Florent and Jocelyne Colney who can organise tours for their guests. Mid price range. Recommended.

L'Etape Hotel. 5 minutes walk from Tsimbazaza. Recently opened, clean, English spoken.

Hotel Mellis, Rue Indira Gandhi (off Avenue de l'Indépendance). Tel: 234 25. Popular, but its prices have risen a lot in the last year, and there is no restaurant. 14,000 FMG.

Muraille de Chine, Avenue de l'Indépendance, near the railway station. Convenient, and considered by some to be the best bet in this category. 12,000 FMG – 14,000 FMG.

Select Hotel, Avenue de l'Indépendance. Seedy. Poor value.

Hotel Terminus, Avenue de l'Indépendance (near the railway station). Tel: 203 76. A popular hotel with *vazahas* but the area is frequented by thieves.

Auberge du Cheval Blanc, near Ivato. Very convenient when you have a late arrival and early departure the following morning. Efficiently run with excellent food. 14,000 FMG single, 17,000 FMG double; breakfast 2,000 FMG, other meals 4,500 to 5,500 FMG.

Category C
Hotel Glacier, Avenue de l'Indépendance. Rooms around 9,000 FMG. Formerly a *vazaha* hangout and conveniently central, but is becoming increasingly sleazy with some dubious goings-on. Probably worth it only if you get rooms 9 or 10 which overlook the street for marvellous zoma-views.

Hotel Lapasoa du Bolidor, Ave Andrianampoinimerina. Near the station. Friendly. Reports conflict on whether it's dirty or clean; certainly it's not dull. Tim Cross writes: 'I barely slept that night for the squeaking of bed joints and groans and whispers of what I thought was an astonishing example of metronomic love-making next door.' 7,500 FMG double.

Hotel Anjary, Lalana Razafimahandry and Dr Ranaivo. Clean, large, secure. Hot water. Friendly and helpful. 10,000 FMG (in Annexe) to 14,000 FMG. Recommended.

Hotel Indira, in the same area; clean and friendly. 8,000 FMG. Next door is the Hotel Nishate, 9,000 FMG.

Auberge de Jeunesse (youth hostel), 76, Rue Ratsimilaho, Ambatona-kanga. (Past the Aeroflot office in the Upper Town near the Hotel Colbert.) Very clean and reasonably priced, but usually full. Meals provided, and no YHA membership needed.

Where to eat

All the big hotels, Colbert, Hilton, France, serve good food. The 'all you can eat' Sunday buffet at the Colbert costs about 10,000 FMG and is good value if you are hungry. A set menu is 14,500 FMG. Bring your French dictionary – menus are rarely translated. The Hilton does a whole series of buffets – each lunchtime there is a 'businessman's buffet' for 11,800 FMG, with a 'gourmet buffet' on Sundays. For an evening blow-out try the Chinese buffet (Sundays, 15,580 FMG) or Malagasy (Thursdays, 12,800 FMG).

The best two independent restaurants are under the same management: l'Aquarium (sea food, tel: 222 66) at Mahavoky, Besarety (take

L'Étape Hôtel

BP: 380   Tel: 307.79

- Tsarafaritra Tsimbazaza ANTANANARIVO -

Near the Zoo at Tsimbazaza (opposite SOLIMA service station).
Half board 20,000 FMG or full board 26,000 FMG (1990 prices)
European/Malagasy cuisine
Managers Mr and Mrs Rakotomanga

大東
GRAND ORIENT
cuisine chinoise
TANANARIVE   TEL 202 88
MADAGASCAR

lettres et lumiere

a taxi), and La Rotonde (French, everything but seafood), 19, rue Besarety, tel: 207 88.

Villa Mahatehotia, Ambohidraserika/Mahazoarivo. Tel: 203 59. Menu 9,000 FMG. Special Malagasy meals (and musicians) on request for 4 to 12 people. Transport can be provided.

Restaurant Grand Orient (tel: 202 88) near the station. One of Tana's oldest restaurants, serving sea food Chinese style and Hong Kong style fondu. 'Nice atmosphere and a pianist who played all evening and was happy to do requests.' (Ceinwen Sinclair)

Restaurant de la Grande Ile, beyond the market (away from the station) a little way up Rue Paul-Dussac to the right. Very good Chinese meals, but it's been losing favour recently.

Restaurant Fiadanana. 12, Ave Andrianampoinimerina. Probably the best for Malagasy food. Very good value but tiny portions, so order two of everything!

Restaurant Rivière Parfums. Same street, good Malagasy food.

Le Pavé, Route des Hydrocarbures. New steak house with Italian specialities. Highly recommended.

Au Bol Pekinois. 'An excellent Chinese restaurant. Five minutes by taxi from the station – the drivers know where to find it.' (Ceinwen Sinclair).

Three nice snack bars on Indépendance: Blanche Neige (good milk-shakes, and great icecreams), Honey (very good for breakfast) and Bouffe Rapide.

For a cheap meal try the smaller restaurants (*hotely gasy*) down Ave Andrianampoinimerina. Meals usually include Chinese soup.
   Cheapest of all, and very enjoyable, is to have breakfast on Avenue de l'Indépendance. From early morning there are stalls selling bread and yoghurt. The latter seems to be safe providing you bring your own spoon and don't let them put ice in it. Fruit can be bought from numerous stalls.

Entertainment

For conventional entertainment check the Hilton Hotel for films and folk dancing (although movies are more enjoyable when shared with a Malagasy audience) or request old favourites from the pianist at the Grand Orient. But for a truly Malagasy experience, follow up the recommendation of Erik Kon of Amsterdam. 'One Sunday I got lost in the slum area of Tana and found an arena-type building where about 700 Malagasy (and four foreigners) could watch an afternoon with dances, songs and (political) declamations from various persons and groups of dancers and singers. Being there was the main attraction of my stay and I have seldom enjoyed myself so much.' The arena is in Kianja, Isotry, near the city theatre (Erik sent me a photo of the blue sign over the entrance amid suitably slummy surroundings). There are performances on Sundays, but not in August.

Transport

Trains run east to Tamatave and south to Antsirabe from the station at the end of Avenue de l'Indépendance. **Buses** (local) are always crowded and need some skill to use because of the confusing number of district names. Supposedly, however, you can buy a bus-circuit map from FTM (see below) which would help a lot. **Taxis** are plentiful and reasonable. They do not have meters so agree on the price beforehand. Taxis parked outside the large hotels are more expensive and operate on a 'fixed' rate. Bargain hard.

Taxi-brousse and taxi-be parks are on the outskirts of the city, at the appropriate road junctions: Gare du Ouest, Anosibe (Lalana Pastora Rahajason on the far side of Lac Anosy) serving the south and west; Gare du Nord, at Lalana Doktor Raphael Raboto in the north-east of the city, serving the north and the east. Taxi drivers know where these places are.

Useful addresses/information

Maps   A large selection of maps can be bought at the Institut National de Géodésie et Cartographie (its long Malagasy name is shortened to FTM), Lalana Dama-Ntsoha RJB, Ambanidia (Tel: 229-35). Hours 8.30 to 12.00, 14.00 to 18.00. They do a series of 12 maps, scale 1:500,000 covering each region of Madagascar. These are most inviting, but sadly no longer completely accurate, especially in their concept of a village, which may turn out to be one hut which fell down last decade. There are also excellent maps of Nosy Be and Ste Marie. As usual, the staff are extremely pleasant and helpful. The more popular maps can often be bought from an FTM van parked at the top of the steps leading from the Lower to the Upper Town (Place de l'Indépendance), and may also be found in bookshops (see below).

Bookshops   The best bookshop is Librairie de Madagascar, near the Hotel de France on Ave de l'Indépendance. Another, Tout pour l'Ecole, on the left side of L.Indira Gandhi has a good selection of maps and town plans. In the Upper Town the Lutheran Bookshop (Trano Printy Loterana) opposite the Solimal building sells *English-Malagasy Vocabulary* if you can't get it in the other shops.

Départment des Eaux et Forêts. Nanisana. Open 8.00 – 12.00, 14.00 – 18.00. Apply here for your *Autorisation d'Acces* to visit national parks and reserves.

Bank For the best rate and least hassle, try the bank near the Ny Havana (Roxy) cinema, half way up the steps to the Upper Town. Banking hours: 8.00 – 11.00, 14.00 – 16.30.

Supermarket. Though poorly stocked by our standards the supermarket on Ave 26 Juin nevertheless has useful picnic/travel goodies: dried fruit, honey, etc. For a better range of goodies try Prisunic, by Place de l'Indépendance near the Colbert Hotel.

Hairdresser On Indépendance on the left near the station. Excellent.

British Embassy (Ambassador Dennis Amy.) Immeuble Ny Havana, Cité des 67 Ha, Antananarivo (B.P. 167). Tel 277-49 or 273-70.

US Embassy (Ambassador Howard Walker.) 14 Lalana Rainitovo. Tel: 200-89, 209-56.

Medical Clinic (private). MM 24 X 24, Mpitsabo Mikambana, Route de l'Université, Tel: 235 55. Opened February 1990. Current rate of consultations: GP – 5,000 FMG. Specialist – 8,000 FMG. 1,000 FMG more at night. Hospitalisation: 25,000 FMG per day, excluding medication, with a 300,000 FMG deposit payable on admission.

Church services Anglican (contact tel: 262 68); Cathedral St Laurent, Ambohimanoro; 9.00 service each Sunday. Roman Catholic (tel: 278 30); three churches have services in Malagasy, and three in French. Phone for details.

THE TWO-MAN INDUSTRIAL REVOLUTION

Technology was introduced to Madagascar by two remarkable Europeans, James Cameron, a Scot, and Jean Laborde, a Frenchman.

James Cameron arrived in Madagascar in 1826 during the country's 'British' phase when the LMS had attempted to set up local craftsmen to produce goods in wood, metal, leather and cotton. Cameron was only 26 when he came to Madagascar, but was already skilled as a carpenter and weaver, with wide knowledge of other subjects which he was later to put to use in his adopted land: physics, chemistry, mathematics, architecture and astronomy. Cameron seemed able to turn his hand to almost anything mechanical. Among his achievements were the successful installation and running of Madagascar's first printing press (by studying the manual – the printer sent out with the press had died with unseemly haste), a reservoir (now Lac Anosy) and aqueduct, and the production of bricks.

Cameron's success in making soap from local materials ensured his royal favour after King Radama died and the xenophobic Queen Ranavalona came to power. But when Christian practice and teaching were forbidden in 1835 Cameron left with the other missionaries and went to work in South Africa.

He returned in 1863 when the missionaries were once more welcome in Madagascar, to oversee the building of stone churches, a hospital, and the stone exterior to the *Rova* or Queen's palace in Antananarivo.

Jean Laborde was even more of a 'renaissance man'. The son of a blacksmith, Laborde was shipwrecked off the east coast of Madagascar in 1831. Queen Ranavalona, no doubt pleased to find a less godly European, asked him to manufacture muskets and gun-powder, and he soon filled the gap left by the departure of Cameron and the other artisan-missionaries. Laborde's initiative and inventiveness were amazing: in a huge industrial complex built by forced labour, he produced munitions and arms, bricks and tiles, pottery, glass and porcelain, silk, soap, candles, cement, dyes, sugar, rum … in fact just about everything a thriving country in the nineteenth century needed. He ran a farm which experimented with suitable crops and animals, and a country estate for the Merina royalty and aristocracy to enjoy such novelties as firework displays. And he built the original Queen's palace in wood (in 1839), which was later enclosed in stone by Cameron.

So successful was Laborde in making Madagascar self-sufficient, that foreign trade was discontinued and foreigners – with the exception of Laborde – expelled. He remained in the Queen's favour until 1857 when he was expelled because of involvement in a plot to replace the Queen by her son. The 1,200 workmen who had laboured without pay in the foundries of Mantasoa, rose up and destroyed everything – tools, machinery, and buildings. The factories were never rebuilt, and Madagascar's Industrial Revolution came to an abrupt end.

He returned in 1861 and became French consul, dying in 1878. A dispute over his inheritance was one of the pretexts used by the French to justify the 1883-85 war.

Excursions from Antananarivo

Ambohimanga

Lying 21 km from Antananarivo, Ambohimanga, meaning the 'blue hill', was for a long time forbidden to Europeans. From here began the line of kings and queens who were to form Madagascar into one country, and it was here that they returned for rest and relaxation among the tree-covered slopes of this hill-top village.

Ambohimanga has seven gates, though several are all but lost among the thick vegetation. One of the most spectacular gates, through which you enter the village, has an enormous stone disc which was formerly rolled in front of the gateway each night. Above the gateway is a thatched-roof sentry post. Inside the village the centre-piece is the wooden house of the great king Andrianampoinimerina (1787-1810).

The simple one-roomed house is interesting for the insight it gives into everyday (royal) life of that era. There is a display of cooking utensils (and the stones that surrounded the cooking fire), and weapons, and the two beds (as in the Tana *rova* with the top one for the king and the lower for one of his wives). The roof is supported by a 10 metre rosewood pole.

Andrianampoinimerina's son, Radama, with British help, went a long way to achieving his father's ambition to expand his kingdom to the sea. After Radama came a number of queens and they built themselves elegant summer houses next to Andrianampoinimerina's simple royal house. Outside influence is strongly evident here, especially British, and you can see several gifts sent to the monarchs by Queen Victoria.

This is a beautiful, peaceful place. Before leaving Ambohimanga you can have a drink at a cafe/bar inside the royal palace area with quite superb views towards Antananarivo. On weekends there are sometimes displays of traditional dancing.

Ambohimanga is reached on a good road by private taxi (have him wait for you – costs about 20,000 FMG) or taxi-brousse from the Gare du Nord. There are reportedly also buses.

Lake Mantasoa

Sixty kilometres east of Antananarivo is Mantasoa where in the 19th Century Madagascar had its first beginnings of industrialisation. Indeed, historians now claim that industrial output was greater then than it ever was during the colonial period. It was thanks to Jean Laborde that a whole range of industries was started including an iron foundry which enabled Madagascar to become more or less self-sufficient in swords, guns and gunpowder, thereby increasing the power of the central government. Jean Laborde was soon highly influential at court and he built a country residence for the Queen at Mantasoa. Sadly most of the remains of the buildings have disappeared, drowned to make a reservoir. The scenery is spectacular, and camping is permitted in the pine forests.

One of the fanciest hotels in Madagascar is located here, L'Ermitage (B.P. 16, Manjakandriana; tel: 05). In 1989 they started running daily tours from Tana to Mantasoa. The price of 40,000 FMG includes transport, a welcome cocktail, a boat trip on the reservoir, lunch, and a visit to the remains of Jean Laborde's factory. If your French is good, this should be a worthwhile trip. The bus departs from the hotels Hilton, France, and Auberge Cheval Blanc.

The Chalet, run by a Swiss family (tel: 20), is recommended as alternative accommodation.

Mantasoa can be reached by taking a train to Manjakandriana and then a taxi-brousse for the last 15 km, or a taxi-brousse all the way from Tana.

Lake Itasy

On the road to Tsiroanomandidy, this lake and its surrounding area is particularly beautiful and is easily reached by taxi-brousse. The nearby village of Ampefy has a basic hotel.

Tsiroanomandidy

Lying about 200 km to the west of Tana, on a good (surfaced) road (4 hours by taxi-be), this town is worth visiting for its huge cattle market, held on Wednesdays and Thursdays. There is one fairly good hotel ('clean, food OK, and sometimes even hot water in the – only – bathroom.'). Tsiroanomandidy is linked to Maintirano and Majunga by Twin Otter, and also Morondava. See Chapter 11.

RICE

The Malagasy have an almost mystical attachment to rice. King Andrianampoinimerina declared 'Rice and I are one' and the loyalty to the Merina king was symbolised by industry in the rice paddies. Today the Betsileo are the masters of rice cultivation, but it is grown throughout the island, either in irrigated paddies or as 'hill rice' watered by the rain. Rice accounts for half of the country's agricultural produce.

The Malagasy eat rice three times a day, the annual consumption being 135 kg per person (about a pound of rice a day!). Rice marketing was nationalised in 1976, but this produced such a dramatic decline in the amount of rice reaching the open market that restrictions were lifted in 1984. However, many small farmers grow rice only for their own consumption. The government is making great efforts to increase rice production (yields are very low compared with other countries) and to make Madagascar once more sufficient in this staple food. Once an exporter of rice, their needs must now be met by imports.

ANTSIRABE

Antsirabe lies 169 km south of Antananarivo at 1,500 m. It was founded in 1872 by Norwegian missionaries attracted by the cool climate and the healing properties of the thermal springs. The name means 'the place of much salt', and the hot springs are still one of the town's main attractions.

Damien Tunnacliffe, who lived for some years in Antsirabe, describes it: 'This is also one of Madagascar's few elegant cities. A splendidly broad avenue leads from the station to the famous Hotel des Thermes, with a monolith depicting Madagascar's eighteen tribes as added interest. The town is divided into two distinct parts: to the right of the station is the former European quarter with its grid-iron streets, gardens and aura of gentle decay. Norwegians still maintain a presence in the town, both through missionaries and an aid programme. To the left of the station is the Malagasy town, though first you pass a line of banks and shops and the Catholic church.

On a promontory overlooking the Baths or *Thermes*, as the French call them, stands the Hotel des Thermes: an amazing building both in size and architectural style. It would not be out of place along the French Riviera and must be the most atmospheric colonial-style hotel after the Raffles Hotel in Singapore.

'Saturday is the best time to be in Antsirabe because that is the main market day. Ask for the 'Asabotsy' market on the far side of the lake which is close to the middle of the town. The market is like Antananarivo's *zoma* in miniature but with an even greater cross-section of activities (no handicrafts, though).

'Antsirabe is in the heart of one of the more productive regions of Madagascar. You will find a great variety of European and tropical produce on sale. It is a town which is relaxed and relaxing; there is not the 'edge' that is sometimes felt in the capital. People are genuinely friendly. There are a few beggars but not the same distressing poverty as in Antananarivo.

'In addition to agriculture, Antsirabe is one of the centres of industry (food processing, aviation), and produces much of the woven cotton goods that are sold throughout the island. Above all it is the home of the excellent Three Horses Beer.

'If you are travelling from May to September you will need a sweater or cardigan at night. It really does get quite cold. A stroll at night will be repaid by the sight of the *pousse- pousses* silently moving like fireflies, each with a lighted candle at their back. Unlike the *pousse-pousses* in Antananarivo and on the coast, those of Antsirabe are well cared-for and there is a feeling of pride about them and the men who pull them.'

Antsirabe is one of the best places to buy semi-precious stones. There are a number of little shops where stones are cut and sold; the best place is said to be a red-painted restored Colonial house on the road south of Rue de la Myre de Villers (see map). The French owner

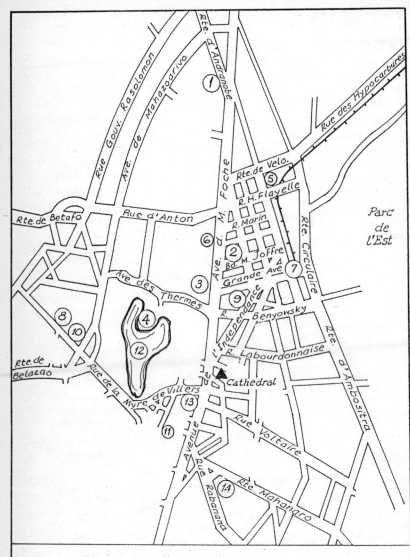

Antsirabe

① Hotel Diamant ② Hotel Trianon ③ Hotel des Thermes
④ Thermal Baths ⑤ la Halle ⑥ Cercle Mess Mixte
⑦ Railway Station ⑧ Taxi-Brousse Station ⑨ Hotel Baobab
⑩ Main Market ⑪ Shop for Precious Stones
⑫ Lake Ranomaimbo ⑬ Small Market
⑭ Taxi-Brousse Station

of the Hotel Trianon also has a shop in front room of his hotel.

Getting there

The more interesting way is by train from Antananarivo. It is a four hour journey and there are two trains a day on weekdays: 5.20 and 13.30. Weekends you have a choice of three departure times: 5.20, 11.30, and 17.15. The fare is 28 FF (first class) or 3,000 FMG (second class). There are also buses and taxi-brousses.

On arrival at Antsirabe you are met by a bevy of *pousse-pousse* drivers who will enthusiastically try to persuade you to use their services. Indeed, this is the *pousse-pousse* capital of Madagascar, and some travellers have resorted to sneaking out of the back door of the hotel to avoid their attentions. Everywhere in Antsirabe is within easy walking distance.

If you pay a visit to Lake Ranomaimbo bear in mind Angela Newport's observation: 'The lake's name was sweetly translated for me as "Water of the Unpleasant Smell" and it is known to receive the town's liquid waste. It's a beautiful sight to see the men with their nets wading in waist-high water in the early morning light, but what they catch can hardly be recommended for human consumption...'

Where to stay

David Bonderman reports on one of his best finds in Madagascar: 'Villa Nirina is owned by Mrs Zanoa Rasanjison. The villa has four very modern bedrooms with private bath and Mrs Rasanjison's home cooking, which is very good. It is just across the road from Diamant Restaurant, opposite the Clinique Ave Maria. Mrs Rasanjison speaks fluent English as well as French and German. She and her husband also rent cars with drivers.' Prices from 14,500 FMG to 18,000 FMG (for a triple room). For bookings write B.P. 245, 110 Antsirabe; tel: 485 97/486 69.

Hotel des Thermes. Tel: 487 61. Although atmospheric should not be equated with luxurious or even tasteful ('awful decor, ruined in the seventies') most people find a stay in the hotel worth the expense and it is never full. Room prices (1990): 1 to 2 persons – 200 FF, 3 persons – 250 FF and 4 persons - 300 FF. Apart from the hot baths, you can get a massage here.

Hotel Baobab. Clean and friendly, with hot water in some rooms. Room with shower 10,000 FMG, without shower 7,000 FMG.

Hotel Trianon. Tel: 488 81. This is the most popular hotel with *vazahas*, being reasonably priced, spacious, clean and comfortable, with hot water (7,500 FMG).

Also possible is the Hotel Diamant (mid price range – Chinese). Do not be tempted to stay at the Cercle Mixte, an old officers' mess, opposite the Trianon. Sheila Tunstall, a most forgiving traveller, writes: 'The room was dirty, unmade bed from the last occupants, used sanitary towels on the floor...'

Sheila found several good supermarkets with a wide range of cheese and salami for picnics. Also 'a little shop by the taxi-brousse station that sold tremendous yoghurt – the best we had!'
   A recommended eatery is La Halte, in the European (northern) part of the city.

Horses
Raniero Leto, who prefers to travel by horseback, reports that horses of reasonable quality can be hired near the Hotel des Thermes, the stables being near Parc d'Est. Their most popular excursions are to the lakes (see below). For serious riding contact Jean-Michel Rakotondra-fara, lot 23 A 38 Est de la Gare.

Excursions from Antsirabe
By Damien Tunnacliffe

Lake Andraikiba
About 5 km from Antsirabe you can see one of the several volcanic lakes. In colonial French times, Andraikiba was a popular place for water-skiing and other water sports but it is now rather run down. Like many such lakes it has its legends, the most famous one being the story of the local prince who could not make up his mind which of two women to marry and decided that the first to swim across the lake would be his wife. One of the young women, however, was pregnant with his child and drowned as she tried to swim across. Local people say that every day near dawn a beautiful young woman emerges from the water and rests on a rock, disappearing as soon as anyone approaches.

Lake Tritriva
Continuing past Lake Andraikiba on a dirt road for 12 km or so, you come to another volcanic lake, this one quite dramatic. Deep (80 m), green water is trapped in a perfect volcanic cone, fringed with trees. From the edge of the cone you have views for miles across to Antsirabe in the far distance. It is possible to get down to the water to swim (but very cold!).
   Tritriva also has its legends, especially of a young couple whose parents refused to let them marry and who threw themselves to their death in the water. They were changed into two trees whose interlaced branches grow from the rock at the edge of the lake.

Making Antaimoro paper, Ambalavao. (John R. Jones)

Sorting coffee beans, east coast . . .   *(John R. Jones)*   *. . . and vanilla in Antalaha.*

Antananarivo

Lake Anosy.

Wagon train returning from market. (John R. Jones)

Antsirabe market. (John R. Jones)

Charcoal sellers near Fort Dauphin (Taolañaro).

Sisal workers at Berenty.

Didiereaceae, spiny forest, Berenty.

This is an excellent place for ornithologists and botanists, and bats live in caves in the cliffs. A highly recommended excursion.

Betafo

About 20 km west of Antsirabe by a tarmac road that goes as far as Morondava, lies Betafo. It is a good example of a town in the highlands with red-brick churches and houses. Dotted among the houses are 'vatolahy', standing stones erected to commemorate warrior chieftains. These standing stones are inscribed and decorated.

At one end of the town is another volcanic lake, Lake Tatamarina, edged with weeping willows and with almost equally bent and silent anglers. From there it is a walk of 2½ km to the Antafofo waterfalls among beautiful views of ricefields and volcanic hills.

'Ask for the hot springs outside the town. They are not advertised at all from the main road, but can be seen at the end of a track up a little slope as two lines of grey buildings. Five of us shared a hot footbath for 100 FMG.' (Angela Newport)

Ambositra

If you go south from Antsirabe along Route Nationale 7 for 100 km you come to Betsileo country, and the small town of Ambositra in a beautiful setting surrounded by hills. Ambositra is the centre of Madagascar's wood carving industry, and even some of the houses have ornately carved wooden balconies and shutters.

The reason the wood carving industry is here is the proximity of the small remaining area of primary forest with its rare and beautiful wood and also because to the east of Ambositra live the Zafimaniry people who maintain the real traditions of Malagasy wood carving. One reader wonders if by buying wooden artefacts we aren't contributing to the further destruction of this forest. A good point – but I think the quantities used are relatively small when balanced against a much needed source of income for the village. I just wish that less junk-carving was produced.

In Ambositra there is abundant choice but little taste and even less tradition: carved elephants and other African animals, for instance, and endless warriors with spears. One carver stands out as a real artist: he signs his name "Jean" on the bottom of his pieces which are exquisite portraits of Malagasy villagers carrying out traditional activities. I don't know where he lives (having bought my carving in Diego Suarez) but someone should be able to tell you.

The best place to buy top quality carvings is at the 'Arts Zafimaniry', a co-operative run by a French Catholic mission, and housed in their monastery. This splendid complex of buildings is well worth a visit for its location and views, and is reached from the south side of town, up the hill. The address is ECAR, Boulevard Circulaire. Within the monastery the shop is not easy to find – you will have to ask one of the

A TAXI BROUSSE RIDE

By Robert Stewart

I thought my luck was in when I arrived at the taxi-brousse station in Ambositra and found a vehicle that was already half full and destined for Tana. This was 9.00. We waited three hours before the engine started and we all climbed aboard. Alas, the driver was only going for a spin around town, and half an hour later we were back where we started from. Then it was time for lunch so everyone piled into the nearest *hotely*. After lunch two of the passengers disappeared so we had to wait for them. Then two of the others decided that they didn't want to go after all so their luggage had to be offloaded from the roof. At 2.00 we started again. This time we got as far as the petrol station, but unfortunately by this time they had run out of petrol, so we had to drive across town at about 2 kph to another one.

At last we were underway. There was only about 6 inches of leg room between the rows of seats, so I had my knees jammed up against the iron bar at the back of the rows in front where sat a very sick soldier, who spent most of the journey with his head out of the window spewing lurid green bile at passers-by like something out of a horror movie. To my right sat a couple who were obviously very much in love though it was hard to see what attraction either of them had for the other. He was blind drunk and lolled around with complete lack of muscular control and she stank like a pole-cat. The rest of the passengers were delightful.

After about 20 minutes we had to stop by a roadside stall to buy mangoes. Since I was now on the sunny side of the vehicle the temperature of my shirt rose to what, had it been made of polyester, would have been melting point. Our next stop was in Antsirabe where we were surrounded by about 50 apple vendors and all and sundry went absolutely berserk. I hadn't seen so many apples since ... since we left Ambositra, which I *had* thought was the apple capital of Madagascar. We pressed on eventually, the left half of my body glowing like a Supernova again. At about 5.00 the radio was turned on so that we could listen to two men shouting at each other at a volume that would have caused bleeding eardrums in Wembley Stadium. When one passenger complained our driver managed to find a few extra decibels.

At about 6.00 we were treated to a spectacular sunset, but shortly after that it started to get decidedly brisk, and since the ailing squaddie in front of me showed no sign of having rid himself of toxic enzymes, I now had to endure an icy blast in my face. Our next stop was for grapes. We now had enough fruit on board to start a wholesale business in Covent Garden, and I was getting a bit tetchy. We got caught in a traffic jam coming into Tana so it was 8.30 when I finally disembarked. Fabulous experience; wouldn't have missed it for the world.

monks.

With all this carving around, you would expect the town's name to have some connection, but no, it means 'town of gelded cattle' because a former landowner raised admirably plump steers!

Where to stay/eat

Grande Hotel. Not very grand but there's nothing better. 13,000 FMG.

Angela Newport suggests a cheaper alternative: 'Ask at the Centre d'Hebergement du MPJS (Ministre de la Population de la Jeunesse et des Sports) which is a one storey white building with red shutters on the opposite side of the road from the Grande Hotel. There are about nine beds, some with mattresses, others with the regulation Malagasy slats – bedding not provided. Nor food.' The price quoted was 1,000 FMG (but will, no doubt, change if they realise they are on to a good thing). Another alternative is La Bonne Lave Mahavantana – if it still exists.

Zafimaniry villages

Most of the Zafimaniry villages can only be reached on foot. The starting point is 10 km south of Ambositra at the village of Ivato. From there a good road goes to the village of Antoetra, perched on the

Houses in Ambositra

mountainside at about 1,874 m. Their elaborately decorated wooden houses have geometrical and figurative carvings. Ifasina is two hours away on foot, and there are other villages in the area (see sketch map) and each has its carving speciality. This is rugged country, between 1,500 m and 1,800 m, and you must be fully equipped and prepared to camp. FTM map no 8 would be very helpful for this trip. Madagascar Airtours do a four day trek in Zafimaniry country: an excellent and safe way of seeing the more remote villages.

Interestingly, the Zafimaniry are unique in Madagascar in using the backstrap loom for weaving. This method of tensioning the warp is unknown in Africa, but common in Asia. Their traditional speciality is woven bark, where the fibres are separated after soaking in water. The resulting cloth is used for burial purposes.

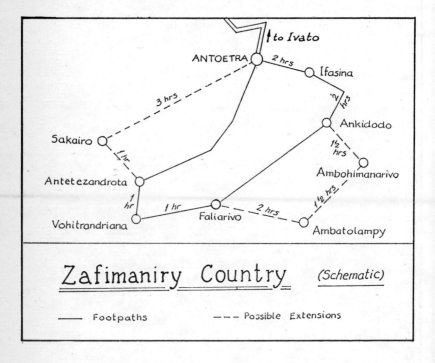

Zafimaniry Country (Schematic)

—— Footpaths   — — — Possible Extensions

Continuing south down R.N.7, the scenery becomes increasingly spectacular. Just before Ambositra the grassy hills have given way to the western limit of the rainforest, and the road climbs up steep hills where the roadside shrubs are spray-painted red from dust and mud. The steepest climb comes after about two hours, when the car labours up an endlessly curving road, through thick forests of introduced pine, and reaches the top where orange and tangerine sellers provide welcome refreshment. Then it's down through more forest, on a very poor stretch of road, to Ambohimahasoa. 7 km from here, at Ilanjana, are the remains of a Betsileo king's estate. There are also tea plantations at Sahamhasoa.

Leaving Ambohimahasoa you pass through more open country of rice–paddies and houses as you begin the approach to Fianarantsoa.

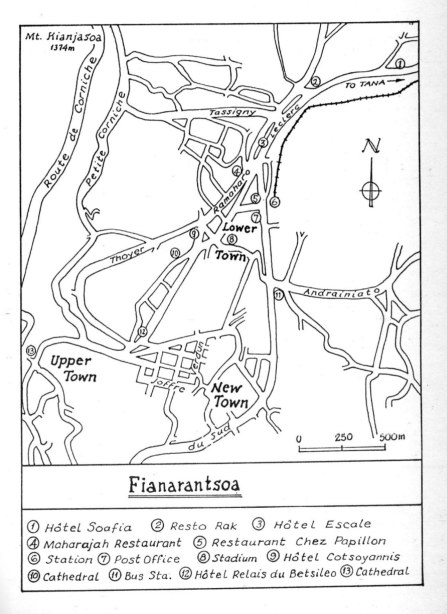

Fianarantsoa

① Hôtel Soafia ② Resto Rak ③ Hôtel Escale
④ Maharajah Restaurant ⑤ Restaurant Chez Papillon
⑥ Station ⑦ Post Office ⑧ Stadium ⑨ Hôtel Cotsoyannis
⑩ Cathedral ⑪ Bus Sta. ⑫ Hôtel Relais du Betsileo ⑬ Cathedral

FIANARANTSOA

The name means 'Place of good learning'. Fianarantsoa (Fianar for short) was founded in 1830 as the administrative capital of Betsileo. It is one of the more attractive Malagasy towns, built on a hill like a small scale Antananarivo.

In addition to access by road there are flights four days a week from Tana (485 FF).

Present-day Fianar is as notable for the number of churches, both Protestant and Catholic, as for its confusing lay-out, with the town being situated on three levels. For travellers making only a brief stop this arrangement is daunting, since the lower town, dominated by a huge concrete stadium, is decidedly dreary apart from the station itself which is a splendidly elegant piece of French colonial architecture, and quite out of keeping with the buildings in its neighbourhood.

The upper town, with its narrow winding streets and plethora of churches is worth a visit. It's quite a way – take a taxi up and walk down.

Where to stay
Category A
Hotel Soafia. (A large building hiding behind a high wall on the right-hand side of the road from Tana as you enter the town). Chinese-run and very good. 12,000 FMG to 14,000 FMG.

Hotel Moderne (above the restaurant Papillon). Near the station. Comfortable. Only a limited number of rooms.

Category B
Hotel Relais du Betsileo. In the upper town. Decayed but interesting. About 12,000 FMG.

Hotel Cotsoyannis. Friendly, modestly priced (7,800 FMG to 9,000 FMG) and with very hot water. Yummy hot chocolate for breakfast.

Category C
Hotel Escale. Cheap and grotty.

Where to eat
Chez Papillon. Some people feel its reputation as the best restaurant in Madagascar is overrated, but the majority praise the quality and wide choice of dishes unreservedly (I've had several letters full of mouth-watering details). Not cheap, but good value.

Restaurant Maharajah. At the bottom of Rue Pasteur.

Restaurant Canonnaise (near Cotsoyannis).

Resto Rak. On the northern end of town on the right hand side (if coming from Tana) after passing three petrol stations on the left.

'You can buy bread fresh from the bakery to the left of the Sofia Hotel. Just find the door in the left-hand corner of the big grey building early in the morning.' (Alison Newport)

Further information
There is a tourist office (Syndicat d'Initiative) near the station run by Stella Ravelomanantsoa. He (sic) speaks English and is very helpful.

Excursions

Wine tasting
The Isandra estate (Domaine Côtes d'Isandra) and the Famoriana estate (Domaine Côtes de Famoriana) are two of the largest and best known wine producers in Madagascar. Both vineyards are open to visitors. Isandra is 20 miles north-west of Fianarantsoa and Famoriana is a little further on beyond the small town of Isorana.

Tea estate
The Sahambavy Tea Estate is situated on one side of a very pretty valley beside Lake Sahambavy, 25 km by road from Fianar, or by rail to the Sahambavy station on the way to Manankara. Although tea-growing was encouraged in Madagascar in pre-Colonial times, this is a relatively new estate and is now managed by the British company Tate and Lyle. Over 80% of the tea produced is for export and is of high quality.

Visitors are welcome at the estate which is a beautiful place for picnics.

Ranomafana
A pleasant small town, north-east of Fianar, known for its hot springs and newly-discovered lemur species in the nearby rain forest. Accessible by taxi-brousse on a once-good, now terrible road ('Mud, glorious mud stopped us reaching Ranomafana. We turned back eventually when we reached a lorry that had done about 13 km in three days and was at that moment nestling amongst the road-side vegetation...'– Angela Newport). The road descending to the town follows the course of a spectacular river (with waterfalls). There is, of course, the hot-water swimming pool which costs a nominal fee (if it's open) or you can have a private bath. Officially open from about 7.00 and closed at midday and in the evening.

Where to stay
Hotel Thermal de Ranomafana (B.P. 13, Tel: 1 (!)). Rooms from about 9,000 FMG. A bit damp but quite adequate. Good communal washing facilities, but ironically no hot water despite the name of the

town (*Rano* – water, *mafana* – hot). Good food.

Monsieur Bobo's. Easily found through the Micky Mouse sign outside, it's friendly and inexpensive (2,500 FMG). 'He has one place to stay – a two-roomed building with a tin roof and no electricity; an earth closet is tucked away round the back of some pig-sties!' Sheila Tunstall.

Ranomafana Forest

Expected soon to be designated a reserve, this remnant of montane forest sprang to public attention with the discovery of the golden bamboo lemur in 1986.

The lack of comfortable accommodation and poor road means that Ranomafana will not be on the main tourist circuit for the foreseeable future, but anyone with a serious interest in Malagasy fauna (this is also an excellent bird-watching area) would be well advised to pay a visit.

The forest is reached by walking (uphill) back up the road towards Fianar for ... some say 6 km, some say 10 km. On the way you will pass the village of Ambotilahy where you can find a guide. Sheila Tunstall and Martin Kitzen were allocated a guide by Monsieur Bobo; he seemed quite competent initially, spotting two species of lemur (probably one was the fairly common red-bellied lemur) but trouble started when he left the main path to look for a rarer species. 'We went through denser and denser forest til there was no path at all and then headed downhill to try to cross the river. We jumped from rock to rock and then the guide wanted to to cross a wider part, fell in, and would probably have been swept away if Martin had not held a branch out for him to grab hold of. We then refused to try to cross at that place and went up and down so many almost vertical slopes – rotten branches, thorns – the forest just seemed to get thicker and thicker. And then we discovered how revolting leeches can be ... no matter how often we pulled them off more would find the broken skin and tuck in. They climbed over our shoes, through the socks and popped out of the lace holes once full and bloated.' Sheila and Martin eventually got back to the town just before dark, fairly shaken by the experience.

It all sounds horribly familiar (see page 166). The conclusion is that all guides are enthusiastic and most are knowledgeable and good lemur-spotters. They may, however, be so determined to give visitors the experience they have come for that ordinary safety procedures are forgotten. If you can find a recommended guide (see page 54) you will feel more confident.

Until Ranomafana is made a reserve it is not necessary to have a permit and there are no restrictions on visiting the forest. You would be wise to check its status while applying for other permits at the Direction des Eaux et Forêts.

The Golden Bamboo Lemur, and other Hapalemurs

The story of the golden bamboo lemur (*Hapalemur aureus*) goes back to 1972 when another similar Hapalemur, *Hapalemur simus*, thought to be extinct, was re-discovered by André Peyrieras in the south east.

In 1986, two scientists arrived to study this new lemur in the forest near Ranomafana where it had been seen by Corinne Dague, a local French school teacher and lemur devotee. Patricia Wright, from Duke University, North Carolina, did some studies on what she thought were *Hapalemur simus* followed by Bernard Meier from Germany. Both initially assumed that they were observing a different form of the lemur Peyrieras had described. It was only after Ms Wright saw two dissimilar groups sharing the same habitat but feeding on different plants, that she realised these were probably two distinct species; *Hapalemur aureus* are smaller and browner than *Hapalemur simus*, and were later found to have other differences which put them firmly in the category of a new species. The brachial scent gland is in a different location and, to clinch the matter, the golden bamboo lemur has more chromosomes.

The different English names given to the Hapalemur genus are confusing. They are called bamboo lemurs and also gentle lemurs, as well as the more straightforward hapalemur. The three species and their various names are: *H. griseus*, grey gentle lemur, grey bamboo lemur, lesser hapalemur; *H. simus* broad-nosed gentle lemur, greater bamboo lemur, greater hapalemur; *H. aureus*, golden bamboo lemur (no doubt a 'gentle' name will follow).

Ambalavao

56 km south-west of Fianarantsoa is a town of outstanding interest for its scenery, cultural history and modern handicrafts. 'Nowhere in Madagascar have I seen a town so resembling a medieval European village as here. Although the main street was not narrow, the wooden balconies with their handsomely carved railings leaned into the street, giving them that look of a fairy-tale book tilt. The roofs were tiled, and lending that final touch of authenticity, pails of water were emptied onto people passing too near the gutter.' (Tim Cross).

This is where the famous Malagasy 'Antaimoro' paper is made. This 'papyrus' paper impregnated with dried flowers is sold as wall-hangings and lampshades, and the *zoma* in Tana is full of good examples. The people in this area are Betsileo, but paper-making in the area copies the coastal Antaimoro tradition which goes back to late Moslem immigrants, who wrote prophesies or verses from the Koran on this paper. This Arabic script was the only form of writing known in Madagascar before the LMS developed a written Malagasy language nearly five hundred years later using the Roman alphabet.

Antaimoro paper is traditionally made from the bark of the *avoha* tree from the eastern forests, but sisal paste is now often used. After the bark is pounded and softened in water, dried flowers are pressed into it before it finally dries. The factory where it is made is behind the church in Ambalavao, but travellers heading south will prefer to defer their shopping until Tana.

There is a good market on Wednesdays and a cattle market on Thursdays.

Although Ambalavao is on R.N.7, southward bound travellers are advised to make it an excursion from Fianarantsoa, since vehicles heading to Ihosy and beyond will have filled up with passengers in Fianar and you will be in for a long wait.

Where to stay
Tsi Kivy Hotel. 'Good value for 3000 FMG; the lavatory was a noisome dark pit with a couple of planks across it – I crept out in the dark and found a bush.' (Eleanor Clarke).

Excursions from Ambalavao
The area around Ambalavao has arguably the finest mountain scenery in Madagascar. Coming from Fianar the landscape is a fine blend of vineyards and terraced rice-paddies (the Betsileo are acknowledged masters of rice cultivation) then after 20 km a giant rock formation seems almost to hold the road in its grasp. Its name is, appropriately, Tanan'Andriamanitra, or Hand of God.

Beyond Ambalavao, as you continue on the road south-west, granite domes of rock dominate the grassy plain. The most striking one, with twin rock towers, is called Varavarana Ny Atsimo, the 'Door to the South', which dominates the pass of the same name. Beyond is the 'Bonnet de l'Évêque' (Bishop's Hat), and a huge lump of granite shaped like an upturned boat, with its side gouged out into an amphitheatre; streams run into the lush vegetation at its foot. Then comes the flat Horombe plateau and the south.

Pic Boby
South of Ambalavao lies the Andringitra massif, crowned by Madagascar's second highest mountain, Pic Boby (2,658 m). The area constitutes Réserve Naturelle Intégrale de l'Andringitra, which has recently been given special attention by the WWF and government conservation agencies. A permit to visit must be obtained in Tana. Guides may be hired at the village of Antanifotsy, which is 50 km from Ambalavao down a very bad road. There are footpaths in the reserve, including one running 25 km from the village to Pic Boby. Be prepared for weather extremes: a record temperature of -8°C was recorded in June 1980 near the summit of Pic Boby, and there is occasionally snow.

The reserve is likely to be gradually opened up to tourism, and is rich in endemic fauna and flora. A large variety of vegetation may be seen, depending on the altitude, ranging from aloe and pachypodium in lower, rocky areas to cloud forest. A correspondingly large number of fauna species are found also, especially amphibians.

Another more accessible town for mountain excursions is Ambohi-mahamasina. No permit is needed here.

Ifandana

This historic spot in the Andringitra region (about 18 km from Ambalavao) marks the place where the Betsileo made their last stand against King Radama I. Thanks to British guns and military training Radama brought two thirds of the island and all the main centres of population under his control. Ifandana crag is a conical rock, from which the besieged Betsileo are said to have committed mass suicide rather than be subjected to Merina rule. Supposedly their bones can still be found beneath the crag, and the area is, understandably, sacred. It is *fady* even to point at the peak.

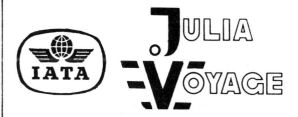

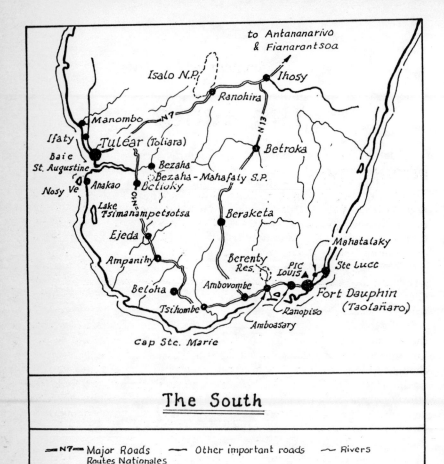

The South

--N7-- Major Roads   — Other important roads   ～ Rivers
Routes Nationales

John Mack, the British Museum's expert on ethnology in Madagascar tells the following story to illustrate the sensitivity to local conditions required of those westerners who wish to help the rural Malagasy. Some time ago the government gave the people of rice growing areas extra funds to encourage them to boost rice production. The people did the obvious (to them) thing: they spent the money on cement to improve the tombs of their ancestors. After all, it was the *razana* who were responsible for the quantity and quality of rice produced.

Chapter 8

The South

INTRODUCTION

This is the most exotic and most famous part of Madagascar, the region of 'spiny forest' where weird cactus-like trees wave their thorny fingers in the sky, where pieces of 'elephant bird' shell may still be found, and where the Mahafaly tribe erect their intriguing and often entertaining *aloalo* stelae above the graves.

This is also where Madagascar's most popular nature reserve (Berenty) is found, and arguably the country's most beautiful beach (Fort Dauphin) so no visitor is likely deliberately to omit the south from his or her itinerary.

Europeans have been coming to this area for a long time. Perhaps the earliest were a group of shipwrecked Portuguese sailors. Six hundred men were cast ashore in the south-west in 1527 and some are thought to have taken refuge in the Isalo massif in a cave now known as the *grotte des Portugais* (although a research project in the 1960s concluded that it was probably of Arab origin dating from the eleventh century). Later, when sailors were deliberately landing in Madagascar during the interest in the spice trade in the 16th and 17th centuries, St Augustine's Bay, south of the modern town of Tuléar, became a favoured place. They came for reprovisioning – Dutch and British – trading silver and beads for meat and fruit. One Englishman, Richard Boothby, was so overcome with the delights of Madagascar and the Malagasy, 'the happiest people in the world', that fired by his enthusiasm the British attempted to establish a colony at St Augustine's Bay. It was not a success. The original 140 settlers were soon whittled down to 60 through disease and murder by the local tribesmen who became less happy when they found their favourite beads were not available for trade and that these *vazahas* showed no sign of going away. The colonists left in 1646. Fifty years later St Augustine was a haven for pirates, and by 1754, when a British Admiral called at the Bay, many of the Sakalava aristocracy had English names.

The most important tribes in the south are the Mahafaly, Antanosy and Antandroy, occupying areas along the coast and into the hinterland, and the Bara in the centre. These southern Malagasy are tough, dark-skinned people, with African features, accustomed to the hardship of living in a region where rain seldom falls and finding water and grazing for their large herds of zebu is a constant challenge.

In contrast to the highland people, who go in for second burial and whose tombs are the collective homes of ancestors, those in the south commemorate the recently dead. There is more opportunity to be remembered as an individual here, and a Mahafaly man who has lived eventfully, and died rich, will have the highlights of his life perpetuated in the form of wooden carvings (*aloalo*) or colourful paintings adorning his tomb. Formerly the *aloalo* were of more spiritual significance, but just as we, in our culture, have tended to bring an element of humour and realism into religion, so have the Malagasy. As John Mack says (in *Island of Ancestors*) '*Aloalo* have become obituary announcements when formerly they were notices of rebirth'.

Antandroy tombs may be equally colourful, if less entertaining. Large and rectangular (the more important the person the bigger his tomb) and like the Mahafaly, topped with zebu skulls left over from the funeral feast. A very rich man may have over 100 skulls on his grave. They usually have 'male and female' standing stones (or in modern tombs, cement towers) at each side. Modern tombs may be brightly painted with geometric patterns on the sides. The Antanosy have upright stones, cement obelisks, or beautifully carved wooden memorials. These, however, are not over the graves themselves. This sacred and secret place will be elsewhere.

Tomb painting showing cause of death and boozy funeral procession.

Getting around

Road travel in the south is a challenging affair (just how challenging is described by Dervla Murphy in *Muddling through in Madagascar*) but roads *are* being improved, and R.N.7 to Tuléar is now paved almost its entire length! (Anyone who travelled on it before paving will appreciate the exclamation mark.) Apart from this new road, and the road between Fort Dauphin and Ambovombe ('the best in Madagascar') the tracks that link other important towns are abysmal, so most people will prefer to fly. Apart from flights to the main towns of Fort Dauphin and Tuléar I note that in 1990 Air Mad have optimistically scheduled a Piper to fly on Tuesdays to Ampanihy, Bekily, and Betioky, and also to Ihosy twice a week. If they actually manage to take off this would be a great way of getting to one of those small towns.

Ihosy

Pronounced 'Ee-oosh', this small town is the capital of the war-like Bara people, who resisted Merina rule and were never really subdued until French colonial times. Cattle rustling is a time-honoured custom in this region. Ihosy is the junction for Tuléar and Fort Dauphin; the road to the former is now quite good, to the latter is terrible. Ihosy is about five hours from Fianarantsoa by taxi-brousse, and in the midst of spectacular scenery.

The rather overpriced Zaha Motel is here, plus the Hotel Relais-Bara; 'Quite dreadful. 5,000 FMG. Toilet minus ten on a scale of 1-10. Worst meal and accommodation of the whole trip. Rooms like stables built in a row; no windows but louvred doors, so when I couldn't lock mine a fellow-traveller had to lock me in and pass the key through the louvre!' (Liz Roberts). There is also a nice little square of open-sided *Hotelys* serving quite good Malagasy food.

Isalo National Park

The combination sandstone rocks (cut by deep canyons and eroded into weird shapes), rare endemic plants, and dry weather (between June and August rain is almost unknown, but note that November is the wettest month), makes this park well worth a visit. For botanists there is *Pachypodium rosulatum* or elephant's foot – a bulbous rock-clinging plant – and a native species of aloe, *Aloe isaloensis*, and for lemur-lovers there are sifakas, brown lemurs and ring-tails. 55 bird species have been recorded here.

A permit is best obtained in advance in Tana, but is also available from the Départment des Eaux et Forêts in the adjacent town of Ranohira, 97 km south of Ihosy. The park chief, Monsieur Ferdinand Kasambo, is exceptionally knowledgeable having been in this job since 1969. Guides can be hired here to show you the park, including a three day trek to the Grotte de Portugais. It is well worth taking a guide (current price: 4,000 FMG per day) to avoid wandering aimlessly. There is a small river, for instance, that broadens into a waterfall and deep pool. You wouldn't want to miss that!

For any extensive excursion into the park, boots are a must: here even the grass cuts like a knife and the rocks play havoc with ordinary shoes. If exploring without a guide, a compass is essential.

This is one of only two National Parks in Madagascar (the others are Reserves) and seldom visited, yet tourism brings in money and – as important – helps deter poachers or plant collectors. Few who go there are disappointed. Sheila Tunstall writes: 'Four of us spent three days hiking in the park – the scenery is breathtaking, and it was one of the highlights of our trip.'

There is a basic hotel in Ranohira. 'It was full so they let us camp in the yard for 500 FMG per person. The couple in charge were delightful – charming, helpful, nothing was too much trouble and the food was excellent.'

ROBERT DRURY

The most intriguing insight into 18th century Madagascar was provided by Robert Drury, who was shipwrecked off the island in 1701 and spent over 16 years there, much of the time as a slave to the Antandroy or Sakalava chiefs.

Drury was only 15 when his boat foundered off the southern tip of Madagascar (he had been permitted by his father to go to India with trade goods). The shipwreck survivors were treated well by the local king but kept prisoners for reasons of status. After a few days they made a bid for freedom by seizing the king as a hostage and marching east. They were followed by hundreds of warriors who watched for any relaxation in their guard, they were without water for three days as they crossed the burning hot desert, and just as they came in sight of the river Mandrare (having released the hostages) they were attacked and many were speared to death.

For ten years Drury was a slave of the Antandroy royal family. He worked with cattle and eventually was appointed royal butcher, the task of slaughtering a cow for ritual purposes being supposedly that of someone of royal blood – and lighter skin. Drury was a useful substitute. He also acquired a wife.

Wars with the neighbouring Mahafaly gave him the opportunity to escape north across the desert to St Augustine Bay, some 250 miles away. Here he hoped to find a ship to England, but his luck turned and he again became a slave, this time to the Sakalava. When a ship did come in, his master refused to consider selling him to the captain, and Drury's desperate effort to get word to the ship through a message written on a leaf came to nothing when the messenger lost the leaf and substituted another less meaningful one. Two more years of relative freedom followed, and he finally got away in 1717, nearly 17 years after his shipwreck.

Ever quick to put his experience to good use, he later returned to Madagascar as a slave trader!

Endearing though lemurs are, remember they are wild animals and should be respected as such. Except for Berenty and Nosy Komba, where they are thoroughly at home with tourists, do not try to feed them or stroke them. It is illegal to sell or purchase lemurs as pets and the trade must be stamped out.

TULÉAR (TOLIARA)

Getting there

Road   Now that Route Nationale 7 has been improved, access by taxi-brousse or taxi-be is not bad (1990 price for a taxi-be: 22,000 FMG). One traveller who took the bus reported that it was tolerably comfortable, but took 22 hours to go 560 km (between Fianar and Tuléar).

After Ranohira the rugged mountains give way to grasslands with flat-topped mountains (which would be called mesas in America) topped with forest. On the last stretch you pass the forest of Zombity where there are lemurs.

Air   There are flights four days a week (885 FF), currently (1990) on Tuesdays, Wednesdays, Thursdays, and Saturdays, and also a Twin Otter service but be careful: flights are often fully booked, and in the high season the Air Mad office in Tuléar is full of desperate *vazahas* trying to get back to Tana.

Tuléar today

Tuléar's history is centred on St Augustine's Bay, described at the beginning of this chapter, although the name of the town (Toliara or Toliary) is thought to derive from an encounter with one of those early sailors who asked a local inhabitant where he might moor his boat. The Malagasy replied: *Toly eroa*, 'Mooring down there'. The town itself is relatively modern – 1895 – and designed by an uninspired French architect. His tree-planting was more successfully aesthetic, and Tuléar's shady tamarind trees, *kily*, give welcome respite from the blazing sun.

There are two good reasons to visit Tuléar: the rich marine life with excellent snorkelling and diving, and the Mahafaly tombs. The only place of interest in the town itself is the small museum of the Sakalava and Mahafaly culture on Blvd Philbert Tsiranana. The museum occupies the upper storey of the building and the exhibits are labelled in English and French. There are some Sakalava erotic tomb sculptures here.

The beaches north and south of Tuléar have fine white sand and are protected by an extensive coral reef. However, this is too far from shore to swim out to – a *pirogue* (for hire at the beach hotels) is necessary. Tuléar itself, regrettably, has no beach, just mangroves and mudflats.

Taxis in town: 500 FMG; to the airport: 2,000 FMG.

Where to stay

IN TOWN:
Category A
Hotel Plazza. B.P. 362. Tel: 427-66. In June 1989 was 20,000 FMG to

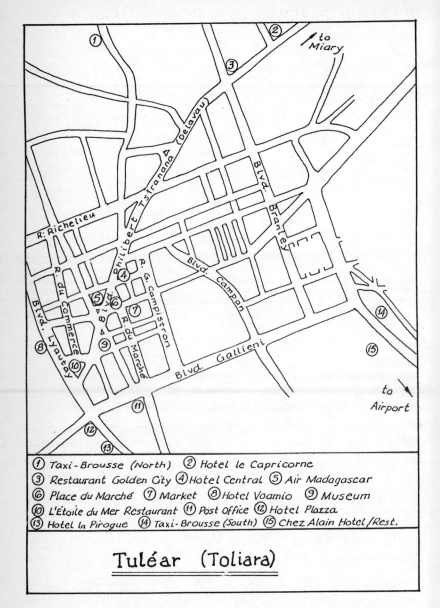

1. Taxi-Brousse (North) 2. Hotel le Capricorne
3. Restaurant Golden City 4. Hotel Central 5. Air Madagascar
6. Place du Marché 7. Market 8. Hotel Voamio 9. Museum
10. L'Étoile du Mer Restaurant 11. Post Office 12. Hotel Plazza
13. Hotel la Pirogue 14. Taxi-Brousse (South) 15. Chez Alain Hotel/Rest.

Tuléar (Toliara)

'A noisy intruder sees nothing of this splendid [dawn] pageant. The animals, warned of his approach, either take to flight ahead of him or else stop singing until he has passed. As a result he walks in a pool of silence which travels with him as he goes, and the bush, to him, seems totally deserted except for the invisible insects which persevere with their insistent shrilling no matter what goes on around them.'

David Attenborough, *Zoo Quest to Madagascar.*

35,000 but now hard currency prices. Central, facing the ocean (or – to be more accurate – the mud flats). Hot water, airconditioned. Good food. Recommended.

Hotel Capricorne. B.P. 158. Tel: 414-95. 106 FF. About 2 km from the town centre (Betania), but fewer mosquitoes and friendly (English spoken). Airconditioned. Very good food. Considered by most to be the best hotel in town (it's owned by M. De Heaulme, who owns most of Fort Dauphin).

Category B
Chez Alain. New bungalows, well run by Alain who is very helpful. 14,000 FMG semi-detached, 18,000 FMG detached. No hot water.

Category C
La Pirogue. 11,500 FMG. Pleasant bungalows near the Hotel Plazza. Good food and atmosphere.

Hotel Voamio. Similar price. Very primitive bungalows and noisy (this is one of Tuléar's main night clubs), but friendly.

Hotel Soava Dia, on the main road into town near the bus station. 4,000 FMG, clean and comfortable.

Warning: In the cool season (May to October) the nights in Tuléar are very cold. The cheaper hotels rarely supply enough blankets.

BEACH ACCOMMODATION OUT OF TOWN

Mora Mora, Ifaty (26 km north of Tuléar on a terrible road). B.P. 41. Tel: 410-71. Full board about 80 FF. Very comfortable beach bungalows, good food, and equipment for snorkelling, scuba diving or deep sea fishing (but the beach itself is unpleasant – covered with dried sea-weed). Rustic – no hot water. Recommended. Just inland from the hotel is an excellent area of spiny forest. 'What a treat of a place – first class food and a trio of highly entertaining ring-tailed lemurs who specialised in eating sugar and knocking over flower- arrangements.' (Keith Hern). But be warned: there are reports of travellers getting food-poisoning at Mora Mora. Refrigeration problems.

Safari Vezo. Run by Jean-Louis Prévot, this unpretentious set of beach bungalows by an unspoilt Vezo fishing village (Anakao) costs 28,000 FMG per person full board (36,000 FMG single occupancy). The two hour *pirogue* journey is organised by M.Prevot and costs 25,000 FMG return, leaving at 7.00 and and after lunch. Book in advance. 'The early morning trip can be very cold and windy, but Anakao is a superb experience – fresh fish, lobster, prawns, wonderful hors d'oeuvre... best food I've ever eaten, including in France!' (Liz

Roberts). The accommodation is basic and water rationed since it has to be brought in from Tuléar.

While there take a pirogue to Nosy Ve (see *Excursions*).

Safari Vezo run three other adventurous trips: river running on the Onilahy; Lac Tsimanampetsotsa (a lake renowned for its birdlife and very difficult to reach on your own); Sea safari from Tuléar to Morombe. Tours run with a minimum of four people.

Bookings should be made to Safari Vezo, B.P. 427, Tulear (tel: 413 81).

Where to eat

One of the best meals (seafood) in town is in an unpretentious wooden building on the sea front, the Etoile de Mer, between the Plazza Hotel and the Voamio. Nearby is the Club Zaza and Corail, both recommended. According to French expatriates, the best food in town is at Chez Alain, located on the road to the airport.

A little thatched kiosk at the junction of the seafront and the main boulevard serves good *pommes frites* and sandwiches.

Excursions from Tuléar

Madagascar Airtours has an office in the grounds of the Plazza Hotel and runs some very good tours. Given the problems of public transport, these are well worth considering. They include St Augustine and Ankilibe (fishing village), and Betioky.

St Augustine and Nosy Ve

Accessible by *vedette* or *pirogue* this historically important spot is also a very pleasant beach resort. St Augustine was the haunt of pirates and was mentioned by Daniel Defoe in *The King of Pirates*.

Off shore is the island of Nosy Ve. The first landing there was by a Dutchman in 1595, and it was officially taken over by the French in 1888 before their conquest of the mainland. This is a lovely little island offering fabulous snorkelling and of particular interest to ornithologists because there is a breeding colony of red-billed tropic birds.

Betioky

A very dusty 138 km (four hours each way) trip that can be made by taxi-brousse or through Madagascar Airtours which gives you a chance to see the Mahafaly tombs for which the area is famous.

The surrounding landscape is dry scrub and gentle hills. The first tombs that you come to, after about an hour, are painted with scenes from the life of the deceased, and his often sticky end, shot or run over by a truck. On one of these the cost of building the tomb is boldly painted on the side (200,000 FMG). I was told that these are Bara, not Mahafaly. Most of the huts beside the road have tall sacks of charcoal for sale: a source of income for the impoverished people, but seriously depleting the already sparse forests. In this arid area water must sometimes be trucked in from Tuléar.

After the simple rectangular tombs come classical (but unpainted) *aloalos* or stelae, topped with zebus, wrestlers, and a taxi-brousse. The most magnificent tomb is on the edge of a village off the road to the left. Well worth scrambling down to. The deceased was evidently an extremely wealthy man, there are numerous brightly painted *aloalos* on his tomb, showing all sorts of things: soldiers, cattle, houses, cars, horse and rider, aeroplane... That man had really *lived*! And died: the list of animals slaughtered for his funeral, and proudly noted on the side of the tomb, comes to 116.

There is nothing much at Betioky except cheerful people and a little *Hotely*. Tours take you there mainly because there is a craft centre which the guides like to call a museum. It isn't, it's a souvenir shop, and the quality is not particularly good. There is a basic hotel near the petrol station – inexpensive, full of character, with good food. Ask to be taken to the tomb of judge Zama Joseph, about an hour's walk from there.

An alternative to spending the night in Betioky, is to take the road to Bezaha, on the great river Onilahy. The Taheza hotel is very basic – 'It has a four poster bed – well, an iron frame. It was so hot in the room we didn't fall asleep, we passed out. The loo is a hole in the ground. If you open a window a swarm of mosquitoes dance in looking for yummy foreigners. A hotel for the tough. Very good food though, and a great bar adjoining. Everyone very friendly, and it's very cheap.' (Harry Sutherland-Hawes.)

Bezaha-Mahafaly Special Reserve

A visit to this reserve is highly recommended by David Bonderman. 'The reserve is located on the south side of the Onilahy, only a few kilometres as the crow flies from Bezaha, but not accessible from that town. Instead it is 30 km from Betioky along a motorable track. The reserve is owned by the University of Tana and run by the WWF. There are several rooms where visitors can stay; bedding provided but bring your own food. This was one of our best experiences with lemurs in the entire country. The reserve has a lot of ringtails and sifakas, and some of the best spiny forest we saw. It makes an ideal two day trip from Tuléar, the drive taking about five hours. By going about 25 km beyond Betioky you could see some of the more interesting tombs before returning to Tuléar.' For a permit apply to the Départment des Eaux et Forêts in Tana, or to the School of Agronomy at the University of Antananarivo.

The road to Fort Dauphin

The 1989 price for a taxi-brousse to Fort Dauphin was 15,000 FMG. 'We set off at 1am and drove for 18 hours, stopping at Beloha for the night. The driver was great – put us in the front so we got good views and a comfier seat. He took us to the (basic) hotel in Beloha – 3,000 FMG including breakfast, and found us a hotel in Fort Dauphin.' (Sheila Tunstall). In 1990 a taxi-be was quoted at 32,000 FMG.

David Bonderman hired a car and driver in Tuléar and sent this report: 'We drove between Tuléar and Fort Dauphin via Betioky, Ampanihy, Beloha, and Ambovombe. We had a fabulous time, the vegetation and the tombs were worth the trip... There were tombs all along the road between Betioky and Ambovombe, but the highlights are in four spots: a stretch of about 15 km starting at kilometre 70 before Ejeda; the last 20 km coming into Ejeda; the first 20 km after Ampanihy; and the first 15 km after Beloha. The drive from Tuléar to Fort Dauphin in a hired car takes about 20 hours, allowing time to see tombs and so forth.'

Accommodation en route is very basic. At Ejeda the Lutheran Mission is sometimes able to put up travellers, as are the Pères Blancs in Beloha.

Ampanihy

The name means 'the place of bats', but it's more famous as the place of mohair weaving. The industry collapsed, however, and Ampanihy is once more just a town on the road south. Accommodation seems to be limited to what you can find in private houses.

After Ampanihy you enter Antandroy country and will understand why they are called 'People of the thorns'. Continuing on R.N. 10 you reach Beloha then Tsihombe. The road improves and at Ambovombe reaches glorious perfection (for Madagascar) in its home run to Fort Dauphin.

Ambovombe

The junction for R.N.10 and R.N.13, which runs to Ihosy is, if anything, in even worse condition than R.N.10, but taxi-brousses run there. There are several hotels: the Relais de Androy and the Hotel des Voyageurs, both on the main street, and another across the road from the taxi-brousse station.

Cap Ste Marie

If you are in a four wheel drive vehicle you should consider taking a sidetrip west to the southernmost point of Madagascar. Cap Ste Marie (Tanjona Vohimena) is a wonderfully spectacular region, with high sandstone cliffs and dwarf plants resembling a rock garden.

Never get on a taxi-brousse without something to keep you warm; a day trip may well turn into a night trip.

FORT DAUPHIN (TAOLAÑARO)

History

The remains of two forts can still be seen in or near this town on the extreme south-east tip of Madagascar: Fort Flacourt, built in 1643, and the oldest building in the country was erected by shipwrecked Portuguese sailors in 1504. This ill-fated group of 80 reluctant colonists stayed about fifteen years before falling foul of the local tribes. The survivors of the massacre fled to the surrounding countryside where disease and hostile natives finished them off.

1642 saw a French expedition, organised by the Société Française de l'Orient and led by Sieur Pronis with instructions to 'found colonies and commerce in Madagascar and to take possession of it in the name of His Most Christian Majesty'. An early settlement at the Bay of Sainte Luce was soon abandoned in favour of a healthier peninsula to the south, and a fort was built and named after the Dauphin (later Louis XIV) in 1643. At first the Antanosy were quite keen on the commerce part of the deal but were less enthusiastic about losing their land. The heavily defended fort only survived by use of force and with many casualties from both sides. The French finally abandoned the place in 1674, but their 30 year occupation formed one of the foundations of the later claim to the island as a French colony. During this period the first published work on Madagascar was written by Pronis's successor, Etienne de Flacourt. His *Histoire de la Grande Isle de Madagascar* brought the island's amazing flora and fauna to the attention of European naturalists, and is still used as a valuable historical source book.

Getting there

The overland route is reportedly best done with a company called Sonatra, which operate from the taxi-brousse station on the far side of Lake Anosy in Tana. They go via Ihosy, Betroka and Ambovombe. You should book your seat as far in advance as possible.

For the wimps, there are flights to Fort Dauphin on Tuesdays, Thursdays, Fridays and Sundays (1990 schedule), 885 FF. Sit on the right for the best views of Fort Dauphin's mountains and bays. Flights are usually heavily booked. The airport is chaotic. It's tiny and looks as though it has recently been bombed (it hasn't) and there's always an exceptionally long wait for luggage.

Fort Dauphin today

This is the most beautifully located of all towns in Madagascar. Built on a small peninsula, the town is bordered on three sides by beaches and breakers and backed by high green mountains which dwindle into spiny forest to the west. More geared to tourism than any other Malagasy mainland town, Fort Dauphin offers a variety of exceptionally interesting excursions (Berenty, the spiny forest, the Portuguese fort, the bay of Sainte Luce) and one of the country's most beautiful beaches, Libanona. If you visit only one place in Madagascar, make it this.

Warning Fort Dauphin is buffeted by almost continuous strong winds in September and much of October.

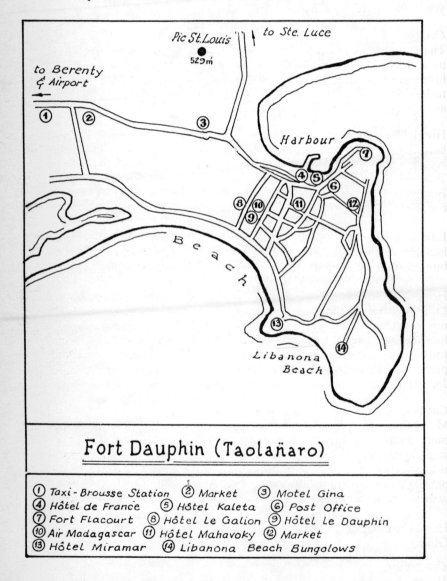

Fort Dauphin (Taolañaro)

① Taxi-Brousse Station ② Market ③ Motel Gina
④ Hôtel de France ⑤ Hôtel Kaleta ⑥ Post Office
⑦ Fort Flacourt ⑧ Hôtel Le Galion ⑨ Hôtel Le Dauphin
⑩ Air Madagascar ⑪ Hôtel Mahavoky ⑫ Market
⑬ Hôtel Miramar ⑭ Libanona Beach Bungalows

Empty film cannisters are useful salt containers for de-leeching or dehydration therapy.

Where to stay

Most of Fort Dauphin belongs to M. Jean de Heaulme, the owner of Berenty reserve, who has done so much for conservation and scientific study of wildlife in Madagascar. His hotels are the Dauphin, the Galion, and the Miramar. You are expected to stay in one of these if you want to visit Berenty, but it is not compulsory.

Category A

The Dauphin and Galion. The Dauphin is the main hotel and Galion its annexe. Meals (excellent) are taken in the Dauphin which has a lovely garden with a crocodile pool. Prices range from 125 FF (single) to 160 FF (double). The manager, Saymoi, is very friendly and helpful and speaks some English.

Hotel Miramar. The most beautifully situated hotel and best restaurant in Fort Dauphin. On a promontory overlooking Libanona beach, which is excellent for swimming, sunbathing and tide-pooling. There is a limited number of rooms costing 30,000 FMG double. Bookings must be made through the Hotel Dauphin (B.P. 54, Taolañaro. Tel: 210-48). Excellent restaurant (oysters, lobster).

Libanona Beach (B.P. 70, Fort Dauphin; tel: 213 78; telex 22430.) Its location vies with the Miramar as the best in Fort Dauphin, and new bungalows have made it excellent value. 20,000 FMG – 30,000 FMG

Hotel Kaleta (tel: 212 87/213 97). Under the same management as Libanona Beach (both are government-owned), so the same B.P. number and telex. Prices are also the same. A brand new 32 room hotel in the centre of town offering a good alternative for those looking for comfort and lemurs but unable to afford the De Heaulme/Berenty prices. See *Excursions*. Run by a husband and wife team, Armand and Janette Rivert.

Category B

Motel Gina. Six pleasant thatched bungalows, with a new one being built, located on the outskirts of town. Good restaurant. They run some interesting-sounding tours, including one to Lokaro, with a boat ride starting at Lake Lanirano, just north of Fort Dauphin, then passing through various waterways. The trip culminates in a 1½ hour walk to the final destination, a beach resort.

Hotel Casino. A little further out of town and similar in quality to the Gina.

Category C

Hotel Mahavoky, town centre. 8,500 FMG. Occupies an old missionary school which gives added interest, and is recommended by everyone for its helpful, English-speaking manager. Good restaurant.

Where to eat

Apart from the restaurants attached to the above hotels, there are the Panorama (Malagasy, with quite a good disco) and the Chez Jacqueline (Chinese). Gina's, part of the hotel of the same name, is said by some to serve the best food in town. All these restaurants are on the road to the airport.

'About 100 metres from the main market and almost directly opposite the large Kaleta supermarket there are three little *hotelys*. The middle one is run by a lovely lady who speaks good French and serves the best steak we've tasted anywhere; seafood pizza with great chunks of fresh lobster and prawns swimming in sauce, and excellent crab, prawns, etc – and all for 1,500 FMG a portion!' (Sheila Tunstall).

Excursions

Around town

Fort Dauphin offers a choice of beach and mountain, and a particularly lively, interesting market (the locals are used to seeing *vazahas* shopping for bananas for the Berenty lemurs, so are more outgoing than in many areas).

The beach is **Libanona**, with excellent swimming (I've never checked the shark situation, though) and superb tidepools. Admirers of the weird and wonderful can spend many hours poking around at low tide. The pools to the right of the beach seem the best.

Pic Louis, the mountain that dominates the town, is quite an easy climb up a good path and offers excellent views. The trail starts opposite SIFOR, the sisal factory 2 to 3 km along the road to Lanirano. Allow a half day to get up there and back – or better still take a picnic. (If you're unsure about doing it on your own, the Libanona Beach Hotel/Kaleta do excursions there.)

Another arm of the De Heaulme empire is the **Botanical Gardens** situated about 16 km out of town towards St Luce.

Further afield

Apart from Berenty, which is described later, there are numerous places to visit in this beautiful area of Madagascar. If you haven't a car you will probably need to join an organised excursion.

Portuguese Fort (Île aux Portuguais)

The tour to the old fort, built in 1504, involves a *pirogue* ride up the river Vinanibe, about 6 km from Fort Dauphin, and then a short walk to the sturdy-looking stone fortress (the walls are one metre thick) set in zebu-grazed parkland. Arranged through the Hotel Dauphin: 95,000 FMG.

Baie Sainte Luce

About 65 km north-east of Fort Dauphin is the beautiful and historically interesting St Luce Bay where the French colonists of 1638 first landed. I haven't been there, but met a couple who raved about the beach, the lobster, and the swimming in a natural pool. You can go there on a tour (150,000 FMG from Hotel Dauphin) or, if you have a tent, make your own way as best you can.

Rainforest

If you have your own transport there is a wonderful area of true rainforest a 1½ hour drive up the coastal road north of Fort Dauphin on the road to Ranomafana Sud (Manangotry). Intrepid backpackers could get there by taking a taxi-brousse to Ehazoambo (Ezoambo) then walking 1 to 2 hours.

Berenty reserve

I've never known a visitor – traveller or package tourist – who hasn't loved Berenty (well, there was one...). The combination of semi-tame lemurs, the tranquillity of the forest trails (which are *swept* daily!), and the superb food makes this *the* Madagascar memory for most people. The danger is that Berenty is already becoming overcrowded, with reports of up to 50 visitors descending on the place at a time. Fortunately there is only a limited amount of accommodation, so if you can arrange to spend a night or two you can still have the reserve to yourself in the magic hours of dawn and dusk.

Visits to the reserve must be organised through the Hotel Dauphin. 1989 prices were: 780 FF per person (1 – 3 people), a little less for a larger group, plus 33,000 FMG (equivalent in hard currency) – double – per night (25,000 FMG single) in simple but clean accommodation (no hot water and if you have a mosquito net, bring it).

The reserve lies some 80 km to the west of Fort Dauphin, amid a vast sisal plantation, and one of the most exciting aspects of a visit to Berenty is the drive there. For the first half of the journey the skyline is composed of rugged green mountains often backed by menacing grey clouds or obscured by rain. Groves of travellers palms (*ravenala*) dot the landscape and near Ranopiso is a small reserve protecting the very rare three-cornered palm, *Neodypsis decary*. To see an example close to, wait until you arrive in Berenty where there is one near the entrance gate. Your driver will show you a grove of pitcher plants – *Nepenthes Madagascariensis* – whose nearest relatives are in Asia. The yellow 'flowers' (actually modified leaves) lure insects into their sticky depths where they are digested, probably for their nitrogen content.

Shortly after Ranopiso there is a dramatic change in the scenery: within a few kilometres the hills flatten and disappear, the clouds clear, and the bizarre fingers of Didierea appear on the skyline, interspersed with the bulky trunks of baobabs. You are entering the spiny forest, and have made the transition from eastern climatic zone to southern. There are four genera of Didiereacea, but non-botanists are most interested in two: *Alluaudia* and *Didierea* and some broad ground rules will help you tell the two apart. In Alluaudia the spines and leaves are arranged in spirals, in Didierea they are random. One of the most common Alluaudia is the finger-like *Alluaudia ascendens*; *Alluaudia procera* has a tall, woody trunk with a clump of flowers at the tip of each branch; *Didiera trolli* or Octopus Tree, has 'tentacles' that cover the ground, making walking among them impossible. Another conspicuous family is the Euphorbiaceae: *Euphorbia stenoclada* is leafless and flat-topped; *Euphorbia oncoclada* has branches that look like strings of green sausages. Look out also for the 'money tree', *Xerosicyos danguyi* with coin shaped leaves.

Though often mistakenly called cacti, and bearing many similarities, a close inspection will show that these plants are like nothing else you've ever seen. They are taller, too, than any cactus – fifteen metres high or more. Shorter, but equally spiny plants provide ground cover. The strange thing about the spiny forest is that the lack of large native browsing animals makes one wonder what the Didierea are protecting themselves from? (Alison Jolly speculates that this protection evolved when giant lemurs could have posed a danger by fracturing the precious water-storing stems.)

Soon after the beginning of the spiny desert you will be taken to see an Antanosy 'tomb' (actually the dead are buried elsewhere), with some beautiful carved wooden figures. There are zebu, 'the tomb of Ramaria' (she has a bible and cross), someone losing a leg – or worse – to a crocodile, and the most famous piece – an exquisitely carved boatload of people. This has been described as portraying the soul voyage of the dead, but in fact – more prosaically – is a memorial to a group who died in a canoe accident. These were done by the famous Antanosy carver Fasira who worked on a series of commemorative sculptures shortly after the war.

In the area are other memorials, but without carvings. These cenotaphs commemorate those buried in a communal tomb or where the body could not be recovered, and look like clusters of missiles lurking in the spiny forest.

Amboasary is the last town before the bridge across the river Mandrare and the turnoff to Berenty. The rutted red road takes you past acres of sisal, beautiful in the evening light, to the entrance of the reserve.

Berenty is famous for its population of ring-tailed lemurs and sifakas. Henri de Heaulme and his son Jean have made this the best protected and studied 100 hectares of forest in Madagascar. Although in the arid south, its location along the river Mandrare and the introduced shady tamarind trees ensure a well watered habitat (gallery forest) for the large variety of animals that live there. The forest itself is threatened by the rampant spread of the cactus-like 'rubber vine', *Cissus quadrangularis*. Scientists are studying ways to check their growth.

The following species of lemur are sure to be seen: brown lemur, ring-tailed lemur and sifaka. The lemurs here are well-used to people and the ringtails, becoming cockier each year, will jump on your shoulders to eat proffered bananas. They have an air of swaggering arrogance, are as at home on the ground as in trees, and are highly photogenic with their black and white markings and waving striped tails. These fluffy tails play an important part in communication and act as benign weapons against neighbouring troops which might have designs on their territory. Ring-tailed lemurs indulge in 'stink fights' when they scent their tails with the musk secreted from wrist and anal glands and wave them in the neighbours' faces; that is usually enough to make a potential intruder retreat. There are approximately 160 ring-tail lemurs in Berenty, and the population has stayed remarkably stable considering that only about a quarter of the babies survive to adulthood. The females, which are dominant over the males, are receptive to mating for only a week or so each year, in April/May, so there is plenty of competition amongst the males for this once a year treat. The young are born in September and at first cling to their mother's belly, later climbing onto her back and riding jockey-style.

Attractive though the ring-tails are, no lemur can compete with the sifaka for soft-toy cuddliness with their creamy white fur, brown cap, and black faces. Sifaka belong to the same sub-family of lemur as the indri (seen in Périnet). Unlike the ring-tails, they rarely come down to the ground, but when they do the length of their legs in comparison to their short arms necessitates a comical form of locomotion: they stand upright and jump with their feet together like competitors in a sack race. The best places to see them do this is on the trail to the left at the river, and across the road near the aeroplane hangar near the restaurant/museum. Sifaka troop boundaries do not change, so your guide will know where to find the animals. The young are born in July. Sifaka make a speciality of sunbathing – spreading their arms to the morning rays from the top of their trees. They feed primarily on leaves so are not interested in the tourist-proffered bananas that so excite the ring-tails and brown lemurs.

The brown lemurs of Berenty were introduced from Analabe, near Morondava, and are now well established and almost as tame as the ring-tails.

There are a few other lemurs which, being nocturnal, arc harder to see: the mouse lemur, and lepilemur which may be seen peering out of its hollow tree nest during the day.

Apart from the lemurs, another striking mammal is easily seen in the reserve – fruit bats or flying foxes. Thousands of them live in noisy groups on 'bat trees' in one part of the forest; with their wingspan of over a metre they are an impressive sight. (In 1989 their area was closed off to tourists to protect the animals from constant disturbance. At the time of writing you can only see them from a distance.)

Bird watching is rewarding in Berenty, with 56 species recorded. You are likely to see several families unique to Madagascar, including the hooked-billed vanga, and two handsome species of couas – the crested coua and the giant coua with its dramatic blue face-markings. The latter likes to nest in the tops of acacia trees. The cuckoo-like coucal is common, as are grey-headed love-birds and the beautiful paradise flycatcher with its long tail feathers (a subspecies of the genus that occurs in East Africa). Look out for its nest which is built 3 to 4 feet from the ground. It's also worth watching tree holes for the several species that may be nesting there: kestrel, vasa parrot, love bird and the broad-billed roller. If you visit from mid–October to May you will see a variety of migrant birds from south east Africa: broad-billed roller, dwarf cuckoo and lots of waders (sanderlings, greenshank, sandpiper, white-throated plover).

The joy of Berenty is the selection of broad forest trails that allow safe wandering on your own, including nocturnal jaunts (remember, many creatures are only active at night and are easy to spot with a torch – see page 00); also moths' and spiders' eyes shine red, and all sorts of other arthropods and reptiles can be easily seen. By getting up at dawn you can do your best bird-watching, see the sifakas opening their arms to the sun, and enjoy the coolness of the forest before going in to breakfast. Just writing this brings back such strong memories of last October that I feel that two days in Berenty is hardly enough – make it three if you possibly can!

Excursions from Berenty include an area (within the reserve) of spiny forest, and a visit to the sisal factory, which sounds boring but is, in fact, very interesting and enjoyable. Also, don't forget to take a look at the museum attached to the dining room; small, but very good.

COMMONLY SEEN SPECIES
* = endemic

BIRDS
Little egret (black form) (*Egretta garzetta dimorpha*)
Night heron (*Nycticorax nycticorax*)
Purple heron (*Ardea purpurea Madagascariensis*)
White-faced whistling duck (*Dendrocygna viduata*)
Madagascar turtle dove* (*Streptopelia picturata*)
Helmeted guinea-fowl (*Numida mitrata*)
Yellow-billed kite (*Milvus migrans*)
Madagascar kestrel* (*Falco newtoni*)
Madagascar harrier hawk* (*Polyboroides radiatus*)
Madagascar buzzard* (*Buteo brachypterus*)
Madagascar Scops owl* (*Otus rutilus*)
Lesser Vasa parrot* (*Coracopsis nigra*)
Greater Vasa parrot (*Coracopsis vasa*)
Madagascar coucal (* – but also breeds on Aldabra) (*Centropus toulou*)

Giant coua* (*Coua gigas*)
Crested coua* (*Coua cristata*)
Hooked-billed vanga* (*Vanga curvirostrus*)
Madagascar crested drongo* (*Dicrurus forficatus*)
Madagascar Magpie robin* (*Copsychus albospecularis*)
Madagascar paradise flycatcher* (*Terpsiphone mutata*)
Souimanga sunbird* (*Nectarinia souimanga*)
Madagascar bulbul* (*Hypsipetes madagascariensis*)
Broad-billed roller (*Eurystomus glaucurus*)
Madagascar cuckoo shrike* (*Coracina cinerea*)
Grey-headed love bird* (*Agapornis cana*)
Madagascar white eye* (*Zosterops maderaspatana*)
Pied crow (*Corvus albus*)

MAMMALS
Ring-tailed lemur (*Lemur catta*)
Brown lemur (*Lemur fulvus rufus*)
White sifaka (*Propithecus verreauxi verreauxi*)
Lepilemur (*Lepilemur microdon*)
Mouse lemur (*Microcebus murinus*)
Flying fox (*Pteropus rufus*)

Lemur reserve of Amboasary-Sud

The management of the Kaleta and Libanona hotels have gone into competition with Berenty by starting their own lemur reserve, just south of the Berenty turnoff. This is considerably cheaper than its rival, and those who have been there speak very highly of it. For the specialist naturalist it cannot compare to Berenty because it is degraded forest (ie not in its natural state) and has been browsed by domestic animals, so you are unlikely to see the rarer small creatures. That said, however, the average Berenty visitor is only interested in lemurs, which can be seen here in abundance, so a visit to Amboasary can be equally rewarding.

The reserve is run by Monsieur Rolande, who for many years worked in Berenty and makes guests feel really special; it is geared to independent travellers rather than groups. Camping is usually allowed in the reserve (provided you have your own equipment) for no extra charge on the basic excursion rate of 25,000 FMG.

Liz Roberts took the excursion: 'Included in the day trip was the zebu market at Ambovombe held on Mondays – cost 35,000 FMG plus a picnic at the reserve for a further 4,000 FMG. In the reserve were lots of ringtails, brown lemurs and the wonderful sifaka. The visit also includes a ride in a zebu cart. On the return trip we were taken to the sisal factory which was fascinating.'

The usual Berenty extras along the road to Ambovombe – tombs and pitcher plants – are also visited.

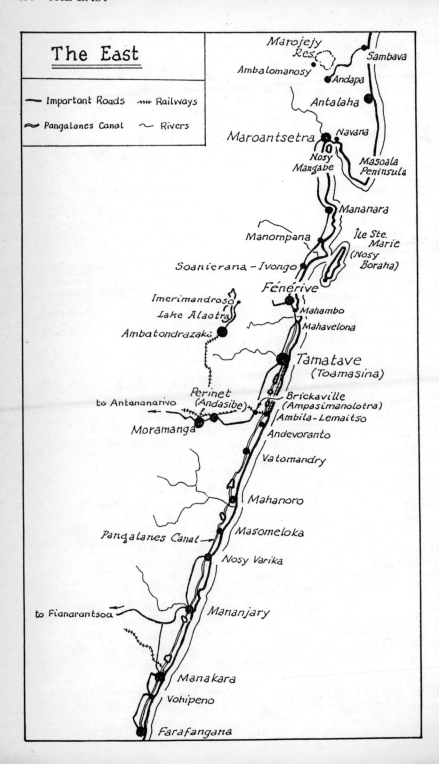

The East

— Important Roads ⋀⋀ Railways
≈ Pangalanes Canal ～ Rivers

Marojejy Res.
Ambalomanosy
Sambava
Andapa
Antalaha
Maroantsetra
Navana
Nosy Mangabe
Masoala Peninsula
Mananara
Manompana
Île Ste. Marie (Nosy Boraha)
Soanierana - Ivongo
Fénérive
Imerimandroso
Lake Alaotra
Mahambo
Ambatondrazaka
Mahavelona
Tamatave (Toamasina)
Perinet (Andasibe)
to Antananarivo
Brickaville (Ampasimanolotra)
Ambila-Lemaitso
Moramanga
Andevoranto
Vatomandry
Mahanoro
Masomeloka
Pangalanes Canal
Nosy Varika
to Fianarantsoa
Mananjary
Manakara
Vohipeno
Farafangana

Chapter 9

The East

INTRODUCTION

Punished by its weather (rain, cyclones), the east coast is notoriously challenging to travellers. In July 1816 James Hastie wrote in his diary: 'If this is the good season for travelling this country, I assert it is impossible to proceed in the bad'. This statement still holds true. There is no point in visiting this region during the months of heaviest rainfall (December, January, February). The driest months are September, October and November, with March, April and May being fairly safe, apart from the possibility of cyclones. From June to August you take your chance – and you may well be rewarded by a fine spell.

The east coast has another problem: sharks (see Box, page 177). So despite beautiful beaches swimming is only possible in areas protected by coral reefs.

Despite this, there is plenty to draw the adventurous traveller. Much of Madagascar's unique flora and fauna is concentrated in the eastern rainforests and any serious naturalist will pay this area a visit. So should others for the rugged mountain scenery with rivers tumbling down to the Indian Ocean, the balmy (and sometimes barmy) tropical atmosphere, friendly people, abundant fruit and seafood, and the supremely unspoilt island of Sainte Marie (Nosy Boraha).

The chief products of the east are coffee, vanilla, bananas, coconuts, and cloves.

This region has an interesting history dominated by European pirates and slave traders. While powerful kingdoms were being forged in other parts of the country, the east coast remained divided among numerous small clans. It was not until the eighteenth century that one ruler, Ratsimilaho, unified the region. The half-caste son of Thomas White, an English pirate, and briefly educated in Britain, Ratsimilaho responded to the attempt by Chief Ramanano to take over all the east coast ports and his successful revolt was furthered by his judiciously marrying an important princess; by his death in 1754 he ruled an area stretching from the Masoala peninsula to Mananjary.

The result of this liaison of various tribes was the Betsimisaraka, now the second largest ethnic group in Madagascar. Some (in the area of Maroantsetra) practice second burial, although with less ritual than the Merina and Betsileo. The Betsimisaraka use *ombiasy* (native healers) for foretelling the future as well for diagnosing illnesses and prescribing cures which may involve rituals as well as the use of appropriate herbs.

Getting around

Although the map shows roads of some sort running almost the full length of the east coast, this is deceptive. Rain and cyclones regularly destroy roads and bridges so it is impossible to know in advance whether a selected route will be usable, even in the 'dry' season. The rain-saturated forests drain into the Indian Ocean in numerous rivers, many of which can only be crossed by ferry. And there is not enough traffic to ensure a regular service. For those with limited time, therefore, the only practical way to get to the less accessible towns is by Air Madagascar: pretty good, but inevitably problems arise with such a hard-pressed service.

For the truly adventurous it *is* possible to work your way down (or up) the coast, as will be seen by the quotes from Helena Drysdale who managed to go from Diego Suarez to Mananjary without taking a plane.

TAMATAVE (TOAMASINA)

History

As in all the east coast ports, Tamatave began as a pirate community. In the late 18th century its harbour attracted the French, who were already a presence in Île Sainte Marie, and Napoleon I sent his agent Sylvain Roux to establish a trading post there. In 1811, Sir Robert Farquhar, governor of the newly British island of Mauritius, sent a small naval squadron to take the port of Tamatave. This was not simply an extension of the usual British/French antagonism, but an effort to stamp out slavery at its source, Madagascar being the main supplier to the Indian Ocean. The slave trade had been abolished by the British Parliament in 1807. The attack was successful, Sylvain Roux was exiled, and a small British garrison remained. During subsequent years trade between Mauritius and Madagascar built Tamatave into a major port. In 1845, after a royal edict subjecting European traders to the harsh Malagasy laws, French and British warships bombarded Tamatave, but a landing was repelled leaving 20 dead. During the 1883-85 war the French occupied Tamatave but Malagasy troops successfully defended the fort of Farafaty just outside the town.

In 1927 a catastrophic cyclone hit Tamatave flooding the town to a depth of three metres. With the sea came large ships that had been lying in the harbour and ended up in the centre of town.

Theories on the origin of the name Toamasina vary, but one is that King Radama I tasted the sea-water here and remarked 'Toa masina' – It's salty.

BY TRAIN TO THE EAST COAST

The train from Antananarivo to Tamatave is considered to be one of the great railway journeys of the world. Between 1901 and 1913 thousands of Chinese coolies laboured to complete the line, and, as with its counterpart in East Africa, many lives were lost in the process. For 375 km the railway runs through tunnels, over viaducts, and on the edge of cliffs overlooking tumbling rivers.

After a dawn start from Tana, the train goes south, circling the city before heading east through typical scenery of the *Hauts Plateaux* – paddy fields, villages, and rocky outcrops (if you sit on the right you'll have the best views). Then comes an area of forest before the train climbs up to the Angavo massif, gateway to the eastern rainforest. Here it reaches its highest point, just before Anjiro, where the railway makes a complete loop, running under itself, before starting the descent. The scenery gradually changes, from the transition zone of bamboo, to evergreen rainforest (moist montane forest). Look out for the large river Mangoro which you cross soon after Ambohibary. Moramanga is reached in four hours, and Périnet (Andasibe) in another half hour. Here the train takes a lunch break (20 to 30 mins), to allow the first class passengers to dine at the Hotel Buffet de la Gare (see page 172). After Périnet the railway leaves the road (R.N.2) which it has hugged since Tana, and strikes out on its own following the river Sahatandra (Vohitra). Sit on the left for this leg of the journey; the views are spectacular. This is the stretch with tunnels and bridges every kilometre or so – an impressive feat of engineering. Passing through the remnants of virgin rainforest, you don't need an experienced eye to see the ravages of slash-and-burn agriculture.

Shortly before dusk the train stops at Vohibinany (Brickaville – but it seems to be called Ampasimanolotra on maps), then passes through groves of traveller's palms before heading north to its destination. The map shows the tracks running right along the edge of the sea, up the narrow ribbon of land isolated by the Pangalanes lakes and canal. Sadly the view is obscured first by dense brush and then by darkness, and the arrival in Tamatave, after a journey of twelve hours, comes as a relief.

There are two other eastern railways, one a branch from Moramanga to Lac Alaotra (see page 173), and the other from Fianarantsoa to Manakara (page 175). Opinions vary as to whether the latter is even better than or not as good as the Tana to Tamatave route. It is certainly shorter.

Getting there

In 1985 the long-awaited new road from Tana to Tamatave was completed, halving the time to go by car to the coast. Chinese work crews spent nearly ten years on the project, with further felling of the depleted eastern rainforest. Four years later the weather and heavy vehicles bringing goods up from the main port have taken their toll, and the road is no better – and sometimes worse – than other 'good' Malagasy roads.

The train to Tamatave: third class compartment.

Taxi-brousses leave Tana throughout the day, and the journey takes from six to eight hours. It's best just to go along to the taxi-brousse departure point in the east of the city.

There are daily flights between Tana and Tamatave (350 FF), and regular ones to Île Sainte Marie. Air service between Tamatave and Diego Suarez, however, is only once a week (Sundays), although there are flights every day except Tuesday and Sunday (1990 schedule) to Maroantsetra, Antalaha and Mananara. This year there are no flights from Tana to Sambava. If you need to wait at Tamatave airport, visit the very pleasant bar upstairs.

Most visitors take the train. The railway from Tana to Tamatave via Périnet (Andasibe) is justly famous (see Box). The train leaves Tana at 6.00 and is due to arrive at Tamatave at 18.30. There is one first class carriage with 54 seats which can (should) be booked in advance (65 FF). Second class is always very crowded (but no worse, as one reader points out, than British Rail's commuter trains) and fun, some of the discomforts being counterbalanced by the delightful Malagasy and their offspring who will be your cheek-by-jowl co-passengers. Price 7,500 FMG.

The train back from Tamatave to Tana leaves even earlier: 5.30 am.

Tamatave today

Tamatave has an agreeable look of shabby elegance, with some fine palm-lined boulevards and once-fine colonial houses. As befits the country's main port, it is always full of foreigners. Sailors speaking a variety of languages hang around the bars and tea shops, and the hotels are often full to bursting since tourists from Tana also spend their holidays here. Consequently there is a good variety of bars, snackbars and restaurants, but hotels may be full.

Tamatave is a pleasant place to stay for a day or two (although as usual there are no specific 'tourist sights'). The market *Bazar be* is colourful and interesting, and a good place to buy vanilla, cloves, black pepper, etc. The footsore should take a *pousse-pousse* (but beware of overcharging— one traveller was quoted 15,000 FMG from the station to the town centre! locals would pay 500 FMG).

Where to stay
Category A
Neptune, 35 Boulevard Ratsimilaho (on the seafront). Tel: 322 26. The poshest hotel in town. 26,000 FMG (but now payable in hard currency). Very pleasant but impersonal. Full meal, 5,500 FMG.

Noor Hotel, 150 FF (airconditioned), 100 FF (with fan).

Hotel Joffre, Boulevard Joffre. Tel: 323 90. 150 FF to 180 FF.

Le Flamboyants, Av. de la Libération. 323 50. Air–conditioned room

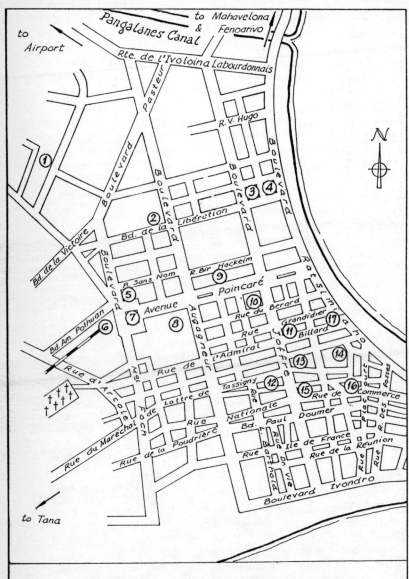

Tamatave (Toamasina) -centre

① Taxi-Brousse ② Hotel Flomboyants ③ Hotel Plage ④ Hotel Neptune
⑤ Hotel l'Escale ⑥ Railway Station ⑦ Town Hall
⑧ Air Madagascar ⑨ Post Office ⑩ Bank ⑪ Salon de Thé 'Saify'
⑫ Hotel-Restaurant Etoile-Rouge ⑬ Adam & Eve Snack Bar
⑭ S.C.A.C. ⑮ Hotel Joffre ⑯ Hotel Beau Rivage ⑰ Auximad

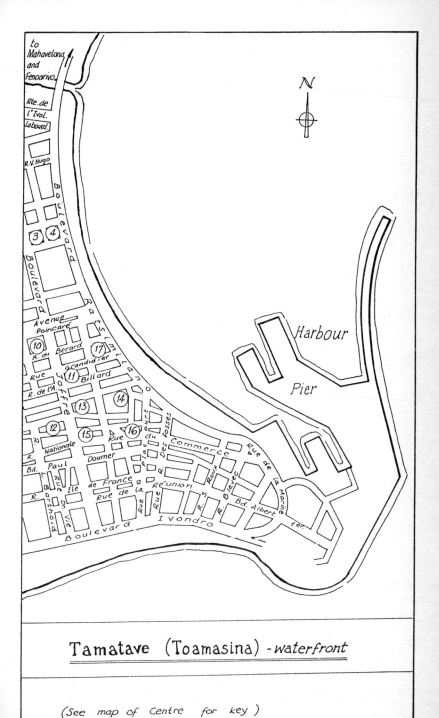

Tamatave (Toamasina) - waterfront

(See map of Centre for key)

with WC and shower: 150 FF, same but no WC: 100 FF.

Hotel Miramar. Tel: 328 70. Refurbished in 1989, the hotel offers 22 rooms, all with hot showers. Chalet (double bed) 20,000 FMG, studio and bungalow (2 single beds) 27,000 FMG, family bungalow (2 double beds) 33,000 FMG. Currently payable in FMG but the English-speaking manager, Mr Young Didier, warns me that if the hotel is upgraded to 3 star it will become hard currency only. The Miramar lies a couple of kilometres north of Tamatave, on the beach road, and can arrange airport transfers. There is a large swimming pool, tennis and basketball, also bicycles for rent, information, maps: 'I can organise circuits along the east coast for people who want to discover the country with their hearts and guts even if they have to sweat for it.'

Category B
Hotel Etoile-Rouge, 13 Rue de Lattre de Tassigny. 18,000 FMG for a room with twin beds, 15,000 FMG for one bed. Highly recommended – very friendly and comfortable (but no mosquito nets). Only 6 rooms so often full. Excellent restaurant.

Category C
Hotel Plage, Boulevard de la Libération (round the corner from the Neptune). About 10,000 FMG. Very noisy at times (night club downstairs) and possibly doubles as a brothel, but quite clean and comfortable.

Hotel Beau Rivage (better known by the name of its restaurant, La Paillotte). Rue de Commerce (near the Adam and Eve Snack Bar). 12 rooms. Good value at 12,000 FMG-14,000 FMG.

Hotel Niavo. Near the station (Blvd Ponthiau) so convenient for the 5.30 train to Tana. About 7,500 FMG. Other very basic hotels on the same street. Hotel L'Escale is another simple hotel near the station.

Where to eat
The Hotels Joffre and Flamboyants have the best restaurants, with the Neptune almost as good (especially its all-you-can-eat buffet for Sunday lunch). Other restaurants are on or around Boulevard Joffre.

Restaurant Fortuna. Highly recommended Chinese restaurant near the Joffre Hotel (11 Rue de la Batterie). Open lunchtime and 18.00 to 21.30. 'We had a good meal there, although neither of us had the courage to attempt the *Poulet des Oreilles de Chat*' (Robert Stewart).

Queens Club (round the corner from the Hotel Plage). Recommended.

Tahiti Kely. On the road to the airport. Said to have the best seafood in town.

Salon de Thé Saify (near Hotel Joffre). Excellent selection of cakes and snacks.

Adam & Eve snack bar. Near Hotel Joffre. 'Best cuppa in Madagascar'.

Warning Beware of thieves in Tamatave. Even robbery with violence has been reported here.

Excursions from Tamatave

Jardin de Ivoloina
This was once a grand and enormous Botanical Garden, created in 1898 but allowed to deteriorate. It is now being rehabilitated by conservation groups and lies 11 kilometres north of town: taxi drivers are reluctant to go all the way because of the atrocious road. Good botany and bird watching, and some captive and semi-tame brown lemurs.

The road north
The road north is mostly in good condition – although a recent cyclone washed away part of it – and a taxi or bus ride at least as far as Mahavelona is recommended (1990 taxi-be price: 1250 FMG). This can be done in a day, but for those with more time there are some excellent beach bungalows for eating and relaxation.

It is an interesting drive (and for a day trip worth going by taxi so the driver can point out things of interest). You will pass cinnamon trees, palms, bananas, tropical fruit trees such as lychee, breadfruit, mangoes, and perhaps the vine that produces pepper and clove bushes. About 30 km from Tamatave, on the left, you will see some open-sided sheds with corrugated iron roofs. These are Betsimisaraka grave sites: not, as sometimes stated, 'canoe burials' but the exposed part of wooden coffins containing several bodies (which are buried underground). In this area the Betsimisaraka do not practice second burial.

Mahavelona (Foulpointe)
The town itself is unremarkable, but nearby is an interesting old circular fortress with mighty walls made from an iron-hard mixture of sand, shells and eggs. There are some old British cannons marked GR. This fortress was built in the early nineteenth century by the Merina governor of the town, Rafaralahy, shortly after the Merina conquest of the east coast. There is a splendid contemporary picture of Rafaralahy in all his finery in John Mack's book *Madagascar, Islands of the Ancestors*.

Before reaching the town you will pass the uninspiringly named Motel Hotel – a cluster of beach bungalows with a good restaurant and safe swimming. An alternative is Au Gentil Pêcheur, another set of bungalows, recently refurbished, a few hundred metres south of the Motel Hotel. Excellent food (meals about 6,000 FMG), showers and mosquito nets, and a good beach.

Mahambo
A beach resort with safe swimming and two groups of chalets, Le Récif and Le Gîte. Both have good food and are recommended.

Continuing north to Soanierana-Ivongo and Manompana

Beyond Mahambo is **Fénérive**, formerly capital of the Betsimisaraka empire (basic hotels) and continuing north on a very poor road you finally reach Soanierana-Ivongo and Manompana – possible departure point for Ste Marie. 'We taxi– broussed it up to Soanierana-Ivongo (4 a.m. start) which is the end of the road as far as they are concerned. It being Sunday we were told we would have to wait until Monday for a lorry to take us further. There was talk of a night crossing to Ste Marie by pirogue for 25,000 FMG, but having subsequently been in one I suspect this would have resulted in certain death. Midway through the

afternoon we were rescued by a mad German called Dieter, in a battered old Land Rover, who has just bought a hotel in Mananara. The road to Manompana (pronounced Manompe) is a bit rough, and largely submerged at this time of year [February]. We didn't have any seats and Dieter was in a hurry so it was a spine–jolting experience involving hanging onto the roll bars for dear life. The last bridge before Manompana now resembles a rather dilapidated roller-coaster. Several of the sections have collapsed, and one in particular slopes sideways alarmingly. It was slippery with rain and no-one in their right mind would have attempted it, but luckily for us Dieter was not in his. We walked across – he took it at speed in one of the most courageous pieces of driving I have ever witnessed.' (Robert Stewart). Had I not received Robert's letter shortly before going to press, I would have firmly said this route was impossible in the rainy season. Indeed, I say just that in other parts of the book, which all goes to show...

There is a friendly hotel in Manompana, often taken over by *vazahas* trying to get to Ste Marie. For a description of the boat trip see page 180.

NORTH OF TAMATAVE (TOWNS ACCESSIBLE BY AIR)

Mananara

Mananara, 185 km north of Soanierana-Ivongo, at the entrance to the Bay of Antongil, is a well-guarded secret; the risks of getting there (or rather leaving by overbooked Twin Otter) precludes it from short stay itineraries.

Monique Rodriguez, who organises adventurous trips through Liounis, writes: 'This is the only place in Madagascar where one can be pretty much assured of seeing the aye-aye in the wild, on Aye-Aye Island (otherwise known as Roger's Island). This is part of the U.N. Biosphere Conservation Project in the Mananara area.

The only choice of accommodation is Chez Roger in simple bungalows. Two of my groups last year survived and rated Mananara as the highlight of their trip. No running water, of course, but plenty of clean water in buckets brought to your bungalow. Good and plentiful Chinese and Malagasy food. Full board Chez Roger is 10,000 FMG, transfers and excursion to Aye-Aye Island is 11,000 FMG per person. Reservations not necessary for individuals if they speak some French – just show up and say you read about Mananara in Hilary's book. For groups, advance and careful planning is a must.'

There will soon be a second accommodation option when Dieter opens his hotel. If his management has the same panache as his driving it should be a winner!

Maroantsetra

The rainiest place in Madagascar (you'd know that without reading the record books) but the Mecca of naturalists and wildlife enthusiasts because of the nearby island reserve of Nosy Mangabé which has been set aside to protect the aye-aye and other lemurs.

As so often happens in Madagascar, I spent rather longer than planned in Maroantsetra, so got to know the town quite well. I liked it. There is a modest air of prosperity (relatively speaking) a small but bustling market selling a wonderful variety of fish, including little hammerhead sharks and vanilla laid out to dry in the sun. However, that visit was in 1986. Helena Drysdale went in 1989 and reports: 'Lots of beggars and a feeling of hopelessness. Flights out booked two months ahead, and no roads.' (So how to leave? See *Excursions*).

The airport is 8 km from town. There may or may not be a taxi, but it is a pleasant walk.

There is sometimes a boat service from Maroantsetra to Île Sainte Marie and Tamatave. Enquire at the Motel Coco Beach or the shipping office in the main street. You may also be lucky enough to find a cargo boat going south to where you can pick up a vehicle to Manompana (the departure point for Ste Marie).

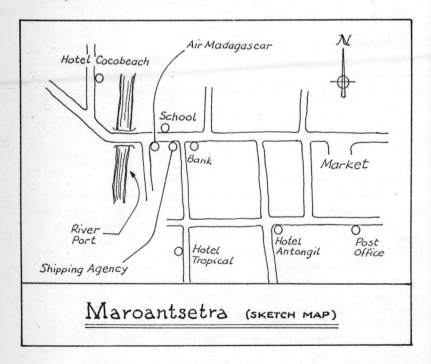

Maroantsetra (SKETCH MAP)

Where to stay/eat

Motel Coco Beach (B.P. 1, Maroantsetra. Tel: 18) on the outskirts of town. This is a typical series of beach bungalows, with cold-water showers, and only one loo. However, when Fidel, the manager, is there he is very helpful and can advise on boats (if they are not *en panne*).

Antongil. Centre of town. Under the same management as Coco Beach, and recently refurbished.

Le Tropical. Three bungalows, 7,000 FMG. Excellent food. Very helpful manageress, Mme Eveline Therese, whose brother in law Alain Costo, has a small boat and will take you to Nosy Mangabe for 35,000 FMG.

Excursions

Nosy Mangabe

To visit the island you must have a permit from the Eaux et Forêts people in Tana. There is usually a naturalist doing field studies on the island. He/she would probably be happy to answer questions providing you don't interrupt the work. A simple shelter may be available, but those wishing to spend the night should bring a tent (the Dept Eaux et Forêts could advise you). Aye-ayes are secretive and nocturnal but are becoming somewhat habituated so more often seen these days. Even without aye-aye there is a wealth of other creatures: ruffed lemurs (two species), brown lemurs, bright red frogs, and reptiles such as the marvellous leaf-tailed lizard *Uroplatus fimbriatus*, chameleons, and snakes.

Nosy Mangabe is also an extraordinarily beautiful island, with sandy coves (no swimming, alas, because of sharks) and a hill (a very hard, slippery climb) topped by a lighthouse with lovely views.

Other excursions

A very worthwhile tour is a pirogue trip up the **Andranofotsy** river to the village of the same name. The vegetation and riverlife viewed on the way is fascinating, and the unspoilt (so far) village, with its inquisitive inhabitants, is peaceful and endearing.

Bob Gillam and Helena Drysdale both recommend visiting **Navana**. Follow the coast east along a beach backed by thickets, through waterways clogged with flowering water-hyacinth and past plenty of forest. You need to cross a lot of water on a pirogue, a regular local service (4,000 FMG). It takes an hour through little canals and costs very little. There is a hotel in Navana and you can also get there by boat from Maroantsetra.

HELP! ... see page 227

The Masoala Peninsula

The peninsula, which is road-free, is one of the largest and most diverse area of virgin rainforest in Madagascar, and probably harbours the greatest number of unclassified species. No wonder the WWF would like to see it receive protected status in the form of a National Park.

It is possible to walk across the peninsula between Maroantsetra and Antalaha. It's a distance of 152 km, takes five days and involves much walking along river beds or ankle deep mud in the pouring rain or baking heat – around 35°C. Added to this, the path is mostly by rice fields so doesn't cross large areas of virgin forest. The trek can be arranged through Madagascar Airtours, who describe it evocatively in their brochure as going through 'dense underwoods bearing orchids, villages, rivers and streams ... the contact with the forest inhabitants takes smoothly back to the well-spring of life'. Helena Drysdale and her husband Richard did it from Antalaha: 'We had two excellent guides. You were right about the mud and paddy fields but it was a tremendous adventure and wonderful staying in the villages. My feet still have not fully recovered (after five months). We did about 25 km each day; a tent would not have been much use since there were not many flat places to pitch it.'

Antalaha

Quite a pretty town dominated by the vanilla industry. The European-run Hotel du Centre (6,000 FMG)is comfortable. Meals 4,000 FMG. More upmarket is the Ocean Hotel (15,000 FMG to 20,000 FMG, with meals costing 10,000 FMG).

The road to Sambava is fairly good, with a regular taxi-brousse service.

Sambava

A straggling town in the centre of the vanilla and coconut growing region. It is also an important area for cloves and coffee production, and a base for exploring the eastern rain forest.

The airport is 1.5 km to the south of the town. The market is at the north end.

Where to stay/eat

Category A

Hotel Carrefour. (1988 prices) 16,000 FMG, 24,000 FMG and 28,000 FMG (air conditioned). Restaurant. Poor value.

Category B

Orchidea Beach (B.P.86. Tel: 128) Very pleasant new bungalows overlooking the ocean. 10,000 FMG. Very good value and recommended. Run by an Italian, M. Filosi, and his family.

Calypso Hotel. 11 rooms: 4 at 6,500 FMG, 3 at 7,500 FMG, and 3 at 10,000 FMG (1988). Clean. Recommended.

Category C
Hotel Pacifique. 3 rooms at about 7,500 FMG. Bungalows at around 15,000 FMG.

Dragon d'Or. 6 rooms at about 6,000 FMG. Central. Basic. Good restaurant. Nearby is Chez Sam, a good Chinese restaurant.

Excursions
A travel agency, Sambava-Voyages (B.P. 28a. Tel: 110) not far from the Air Madagascar office at the south end of the town, will organise excursions by *pirogue* on the nearby river Bemarivo to an island rich in birdlife, Nosiharina, or to the Réserve Naturelle Intégrale of **Marojejy**. This is one of the WWF's priority reserves because the rugged hillsides of the Massif of Marojejy are covered with vegetation which varies according to altitude, producing great diversity. The accompanying fauna is equally varied. 17 amphibians and 22 species of reptile have been recorded here. The 23 species of mammal include the very rare sub-species of diademed sifaka, *Propithecus diadema candidus*.

There are no tourist trails so if you want to see the reserve (and not as I saw it (see next page) you had better let Sambava Voyages help you. Give them plenty of advance warning and preferably get your own permit in Antananarivo. The trip to Marojejy takes at least three days. A tent is needed plus provisions. It is worth knowing that the rainfall on the eastern slopes is thought to reach 3,000mm a year!

Sambava Voyages have now increased their operations to include a variety of river and hiking trips which sound ideal for those wishing to get off the beaten track but not quite ready to go it alone.

The Manageress of Sambava-Voyages is Mme Seramila. She speaks a little English.

Boats also go up the Bemarivo to the village of Amboahangibe to transport coffee. You may be fortunate enough to get a lift, or arrange your own pirogue.

The relative prosperity of the area is shown by the rather good road to **Andapa**. When I went there twelve years ago I was enchanted by the villages en route: Manantenina and Andranomifototra. I remember tracks leading to the villages, and masses of butterflies. And friendly people. I also remember my attempt to walk west from Antanimbaribe. However, I still believe this area has a lot to offer explorers; or at least I still find the 1:500,000 scale Antalaha map (no 4) as tantalising as ever, so it's a good thing I'm writing this in England!

A CAUTIONARY TALE

I first came to Madagascar in 1976 with an insatiable appetite for seeing wildlife. In those days you could fly direct from East Africa to Majunga, so George and I started our clockwise exploration of the island without going to Tana. No Tana meant no official permits for visiting nature reserves. No problem in Montagne d'Ambre – we got our permits in Diego – but *beaucoup de problèmes* in our next choice, Marojejy, which attracted us because our map showed a footpath running right across the reserve: just right for a two day backpacking trip.

As we made our way to the trail head we tried hard to get a permit. We spent three days walking to sundry villages on the edge of the reserve, meeting some delightful Malagasy and equally appealing chameleons and butterflies, but failing to find a representative from *Eaux et Forêts* willing to give us the necessary permission. When an *Eaux et Forêts* man appeared on the scene – while we were being told of the comparative merits of cat and lemur meat by our otherwise charming hosts in Antanimbaribe – we were amazed. And when he asked for our passports and started to write out a permit, (laboriously copying all our passport details such as 'Name and address of bear') we were thrilled. When we gathered that he also intended to accompany us into the reserve we were less happy, normally preferring to follow our own route at our own pace. However, local information was that the path was not easy to follow, so it seemed sensible to have expert guidance.

Our Man (we never learned to pronounce his name) was not really equipped for backpacking; he had plastic sandals, a brief case containing three hats, two clean shirts, and about 5 lbs of official papers. He carried no food or bedding so I had to add a blanket to my already laden pack, and George crammed in some extra biscuits. We were also carrying a fair bit of unnecessary weight – our packs (the old-fashioned external-frame variety) weighed around 35lb, and I was further hindered by a movie camera with which to make a David Attenborough style record of the wildlife.

Unencumbered, Our Man took a bold route up the side of the mountain, through vanilla groves, while we sweated in the rear. I'd forgotten how exhausting it is climbing steeply in very hot, very humid weather. When we caught up with him he was gazing possessively at a distinctive stone. 'This marks the edge of the reserve', he told us. And added that it was the furthest he'd been. He'd never actually tried to walk 'our path'. We felt a twinge of doubt. Another twinge came when we met our first fallen tree; we'd known about the recent cyclone – indeed we'd caught the edge of it in what had seemed the very appropriately named Hell-ville – but we'd forgotten the effect cyclones can have on trees. This shows the effect Madagascar can have on one's grey cells since we'd looked down in amazement at the spilled-matches effect as the plane flew over the forest on its approach to Sambava.

By the time we'd crawled under, or teetered over, our fifth or sixth fallen giant, I was in a thoroughly bad mood. With sweat running down my face, ants dropping down my neck, and my hateful pack and even more hateful movie camera throwing me off balance, it didn't seem that I was having much fun.

We camped by the river, pitching our tent across the path, this being the only flat space available, and cooked a rather sumptuous meal. We deserved a treat, and our map showed that tomorrow would be downhill all the way. We should reach our destination in the early evening. No need to save any

Bemarivo river, Sambava.

The beach at Cocoteraie, Île Sainte Marie (Nosy Boraha). (Sarah Moon)

Montagne de Français, Diego Suarez (Antseranana).

Petite Cascade, Montagne d'Ambre National Park.

Crater lakes on the way to Mont Passot, Nosy Be

Cirque Rouge, near Majunga.

Baobabs near Morondava. (John R. Jones)

food, apart from our emergency nuts and raisins. Our Man, miserable for lack of rice, nevertheless had a hearty appetite for freeze-dried food.

After breakfast and self-reminders that we should spend more time looking for wildlife we set off. The path evidently crossed the river so we obediently did likewise, and equally obediently followed our man as he decided to follow the river when the path disappeared. This was fine for him in his plastic sandals, but dodgy when we wished to keep our hiking boots dry. We boulder-hopped athletically until we came to a high, vine-draped cliff. There was no way round the base, we had to climb up the slippery, steep sides and let ourselves down, Tarzan-style, on the lianas.

'*Ou est le sentier?*' we asked Our Chap. We asked him the same question in increasing desperation for the next two days. I expect he was asking himself where the path was; áfter all, he probably wasn't very happy either at being lost in the eastern rain forest without cigarettes or rice and with two stroppy *vazahas* who never should have been there in the first place. However, I bet he wasn't as unhappy as I was. Certainly he wasn't stumbling along sobbing quietly. I'd given up being brave when the first fire-ants landed down my neck. Up until then I'd been quite stoical, taking a detached scientific interest in the leeches that decorated our legs and hands (what do they eat when there aren't juicy tourists stumbling past their bushes?) and even allowing something approaching joy at the sight of a rare *Brookesia* chameleon.

The terrain we were struggling through deserves some description. In fact there *is* a description in the *Flora* section. I note with interest that we were floundering through moist montane forest where there is 'more undergrowth [than lowland forest] ... and abundant epiphytes, ferns and mosses, and large lianas and bamboo. As the altitude increases, so the height of the canopy decreases,... permitting the growth of epiphytes and shrubby, herbaceous undergrowth with an abundance of moss.' Yes, I remember it well. The large lianas had a habit of snagging our pack frames, bringing us to an abrupt halt, and the bamboo had tiny cactus-like hairs that became imbedded in our hands if we grabbed bamboo for support. The shrubby, herbaceous undergrowth with an abundance of moss formed a safe-looking carpet over treacherous drops into hidden streams, and rotting logs that broke when we stepped on them. And they are certainly right about the density of this rain forest being greater than in other parts of the world. Without a panga to cut our way through the obstructing vegetation, we had to sidle, push and thrust our way through.

People ask if being lost in the jungle of Madagascar wasn't frightening. No, it wasn't frightening. When you're as miserable as I was, there isn't the leisure to be frightened as well. Apart from the hostile plants, almost all of which seemed to sting, slice, prick or trip, and the sweat running into our cuts and scratches, there was the effort of climbing near-vertical hillsides to cut off loops of the river, then easing ourselves down again, clinging onto whatever booby-trapped plant happened to be handy. At least we became blasé about crossing white water on moss-slicked tree trunks (a mild death-wish does wonders for your balance) and stopped caring about whether we got our boots wet. Since we were sometimes wading through waist-deep water it hardly seemed to matter. We had to follow the river, since the only certainty was that eventually we would come to a village.

After twelve hours of unmitigated effort we stopped for the night. Supper was broth, nuts and raisins. We passed the map wordlessly between us, and gave up guessing our location. With the knowledge of what was to come, breakfast (a cup of tea) was even less cheerful, and with nothing to eat we felt exhausted by ten. Then Our Man gave us a surge of hope and energy when he pointed to something in the soft sand at the edge of the river. A human footprint! If you've ever thought how splendid it must be to set foot where no white man has trod – forget it. It's greatly over-rated. But a footprint in the sand? We were unequivocably excited. No matter that we saw no other, and that our progress was as slow and painful as before, we had seen the light at the end of the tunnel. At noon (no lunch) we saw another, even more cheering sign of human life: an abandoned hut on the hillside. It took four hours to reach it, and much to our disappointment there was no clear trail nearby, but at least there was a flat area for our tent, and sugar cane and tobacco, much to Our Man's delight. He hastily picked some and dried it by the fire before smoking it. He also found leaves for *bredes* and gave a great shriek of excitement at his tastiest find: inch-long weevils with long snouts. We helped him collect the revolting creatures in a plastic bag.

Our fourth day in the jungle started in extreme gloom. We expected a village to lie just below the rim of the hill beyond the hut, but on reaching the top we saw ... miles and miles of forest. There was also the twinkling silver of a corrugated iron roof, but the sight of the distance between us and it and the hilly nature of the intervening jungle sapped our energy before we started. We were both getting very, very tired. The jungle was the densest, steepest, nastiest yet, with more fallen trees and more thorny branches than any before. Every step had to be carefully judged, every forward progression forced through the dense vegetation. Six hours later when we found a path we had no energy left for elation or even relief. We just walked numbly on, and it was only when a voice greeted us from behind that we could take in that we really had made it. We sat down and let Our Man and the woman jabber away. 'She knows my family', he told us excitedly 'My wife's wondering where I am!'.

The woman led us to her neat thatched hut made from woven bamboo, and we sank thankfully onto the clean floor mats. Our Man had regained all his old aplomb and described our adventures at length, with illustrative gestures. The family regarded us with gratifying respect and sympathy, tut-tutting in horror at our festering cuts and leech bites. We let the condolences wash over us until roused by a marvellous sound – the clinking of cutlery. Mats were spread on the floor and an enormous bowl of rice was carried in, followed by two different kinds of greens. We ate huge quantities, but Our Man filled his plate again and again. We were feeling almost human when he said jovially: 'You remember that little house we slept near last night? They say it's only half an hour over that hill.' We didn't laugh.

As we followed the path to Ambatobe we felt physically and mentally renewed and for the first time realised how we must appear to others. Our shirts had been wringing wet with sweat for four days; we were smelly, grubby and scabby, and we badly needed a bath. When we came to a stream we told Our Man to go on ahead.

The river formed a deep pool with a natural rock seat. It was hard to tear ourselves away but eventually, with clean bodies and fresh clothes, we approached the village. All the inhabitants were lined up on both sides of the path to greet us. 'Salama, salama!' we called, shaking the outstretched hands, sometimes twice as people raced round to have another turn.

Reverently we were guided to the biggest hut and two chairs were drawn up. In the dim light we could see our man already comfortably enthroned and surrounded by an admiring audience. The villagers crowded in and gazed at us in awe. Our story was told again and again, and when every detail had been lovingly described and all questions answered, supper arrived. A veritable banquet, with chicken stew, many varieties of greens, and the inevitable mound of rice. A plateful of small brown objects was added. Good heavens, we'd completely forgotten the weevils! Here they were, nicely roasted, and it seemed ungrateful not to try them. They had an agreeable nutty flavour. Forgetting my former disgust, I ate my share.

After supper Our Man changed his shirt, produced an official hat from his briefcase, and started reading to the villagers from one of his many papers. They listened respectfully, nodding at intervals. Eventually the audience trickled away and we could climb into our sleeping bags and sink into blissful sleep.

Next day two stalwart youths were enlisted to carry our packs and we practically floated down the wide trail to the road. The view was magnificent, birds sang, butterflies danced and a rustle in the trees made us look up: a troop of lemurs gazed mockingly down at us. We arrived at the road in just under two hours. The distance covered in that time was rather more than we'd gone in the three previous days.

WEST OF TAMATAVE
Périnet (Andasibe)

A visit to Madagascar's most accessible Special Reserve, Périnet-Analamazoatra, is a must for anyone interested in the flora and fauna of the eastern rainforest (moist montane forest at this altitude: 930 – 1049 m). Périnet protects the largest of the lemur family, the indri *Indri indri.* Standing about three feet high, with barely visible tails, black and white markings and surprised teddy-bear faces, the indri looks more like a gone-wrong panda than a lemur. The long back legs are immensely powerful, and an indri can propel itself backwards thirty feet, execute a turn in mid-air, and land face-forward to gaze down benevolently at its observers. And you will be an observer: most people see indris in Périnet, and if they don't see them they hear them. For it is their voice that makes this lemur extra special: whilst other lemurs grunt or swear, the indri sings. It is an eerie, wailing sound somewhere between the song of a whale and a police-siren, and it carries for up to two miles as troops call to each other across the forest. The indris are fairly punctual with their song: if you are in the reserve between one to two hours after daybreak and shortly before dusk you should hear them. There's no point in looking for indri at other times; they spend much of the day dozing in the tops of trees.

In Malagasy the indri is called *Babakoto.* There are various legends connected with the indri, and explaining the esteem with which the local people hold them (it is *fady* to kill an indri). One that links the indri with the origin of man (thus supporting modern evolutionary thought) is described by Alison Richard on page 49, and another popular legend tells of a man who climbed a forest tree to gather wild honey, and was severely stung by the bees. Losing his hold, he fell, but was caught by a huge indri which carried him on its back to safety.

There are nine species of lemur altogether in Périnet, (including the recent discovery of aye-aye) although you would be very unlikely to see them all. Your most likely encounter will be with a troop of grey bamboo lemurs (*Hapelemur griseus*) which are diurnal and sometimes feed on the bamboo near the warden's house. It is well worth going on a nocturnal lemur hunt (the guides are experts at this) to look for mouse lemurs, and the greater dwarf lemur (*Cheirogaleus major*) which hibernates during the cold season.

Lemurs are only a few of the creatures to be found in Périnet. There are tenrecs, beautiful and varied insects and spiders, and lots of reptiles. One of Madagascar's biggest chameleons lives here: *Chameleon parsonii*, which is bright green, about two feet long and has twin horns at the end of its snout. Local boys often collect chameleons for tourists to photograph. They expect a small tip. With Malagasy help you may also find a *Uroplatus* or leaf tailed lizard. Boas are quite common and more easily seen.

This is a good place for bird watching. Near the warden's house there are flowering trees of a species much favoured by the Madagascar green sunbird (*Cinnyris notatus*) which has an iridescent green head and throat, and sucks nectar like the New World hummingbirds. There are also plenty of the cuckoo-like blue couas, blue pigeons, paradise flycatchers, two species of falcon (Newton falcon and Madagascar falcon), two species of black vasa parrot, and many others.

Botanists will not be disappointed. In French colonial days an orchid garden was started by the lily pond to the right of the road to the reserve, and a variety of species flourishes here although most flower in the warm wet season. For a detailed description of the flora found in moist montane forests such as Périnet, see page 30.

Leeches can be an unpleasant aspect of Périnet if you've pushed through vegetation and it's been raining recently. Tuck your trousers into your socks and carry salt; this usually dislodges the creatures before they get dug in. A lighted cigarette or petrol does the same trick. Malagasy leeches are very small – not African Queen proportions – but the anti-coagulant they inject when they bite means you bleed dramatically.

To visit the Reserve you need a permit from Eaux et Forêts in Tana, and a guide (although the latter is not compulsory). The star guide, the warden's son Bedo, was tragically murdered in 1989 (see page 93). His brother, Maurice, and his sister are very competent and experts at finding indri and nocturnal lemurs. Other village kids also offer their services.

There is an urgent need to standardise the tipping of guides in Périnet and bring it more in line with other reserves. No one can blame young people for 'milking' affluent-seeming tourists when they get the opportunity, but visitors in 1988/90 reported being asked for exorbitant sums for guide service: 36,000 FMG was one invoice! (At the time the minimum monthly wage in Madagascar was 38,000 FMG.) See page 54 for the WWF recommended daily salary for a guide, and agree the price before you set out.

Sleeping and eating

There is only one place to stay in Périnet: the Hotel Buffet de la Gare, which at first sight is mistaken for the station itself. It is one of those places you either love or hate (although it can't be *too* bad – Prince Philip has stayed here). The hotel is old (1938), and in desperate need of some financial investment. Water supplies are erratic, the beds saggy and uncomfortable (don't expect to share a double bed and get much sleep) and interesting creatures sometimes pop out of cracks in the ceiling. The hotel is run by Monsieur Joseph with an old world charm and courtesy that more expensive hotels would do well to emulate. Joseph's attention to his guests was exemplified when someone asked for a hot bath. Fifteen minutes later I watched a team of men running up and down the stairs carrying buckets of steaming water.

The dining room is truly elegant – fresh flowers on the tables and a marvellous rosewood bar. The food is good too.

There are eight rooms costing 12,500 FMG to 15,500 FMG, and seven new chalet-bungalows (plumbing still a bit dodgy) for 21,850 FMG. Joseph has recently bought some land a hundred metres or so up the road towards the reserve. At present you can camp here (2,500 FMG) in idyllic surroundings – there is a lake and nearby forest to investigate, but there are plans to build a further 12 chalets as well as a small snack bar. Joseph wants to continue to make a campsite available, however, and also has tents for hire.

If you don't want to eat in the Buffet, there are huts serving food in the village across the river, and a place behind the hotel which does basic but tasty rice dishes when a train arrives.

Moramanga

This formerly sleepy town gained a new lease of life with the completion of the Chinese road (there is a memorial here to the Chinese workers). There is rather a good place to stay, the Grand Hotel, which has *hot* water and is successfully wooing some visitors (especially groups) who would normally stay at Périnet. Without your own transport, however, you cannot get to the reserve in time to hear the indri call in the morning. Another hotel, the Emerald, is said to be equally good and also has hot water and private showers. The restaurant Au Coq d'Or is recommended.

Marovoay

This is the first stop on the railway line north towards Lake Alaotra, and the name means 'Many Crocodiles'. Appropriately, a commercial crocodile farm has been started here and tourists will be able to visit from mid-1990. There are over a thousand *Crocodylus niloticus*, some over two and a half metres in length, living in semi-wild conditions. The best season to visit is January, when the eggs are hatching, and at feeding time at other times of the year. To arrange a visit write to: Reptel Madagascar, 50 Ave Grandidier, BP 563, Isoraka, Antananarivo. Tel: 348 86. Fax: 206 48.

Lake Alaotra

This is the largest lake in Madagascar and has been designated a Site of Special Biological Interest by the WWF because of its endemic waterfowl. 74 bird species have been recorded, and two are of particular interest since they probably breed only on Lac Alaotra: Delacour's grebe or Alaotra grebe (*Tachybaptus rufolavatus*) and Madagascar pochard, (*Aythya innotata*).

A spur of the railway runs from Moramanga to Lac Alaotra and the village of Imerimandroso. This is the start of the so-called Smugglers Path to the Indian Ocean – a five-day walk. Like the similar path across the Masoala peninsula this sounds both unpleasant and difficult. It is described in the German guide *Madagaskar* (published by DuMont, Cologne) but the Germans I met who had attempted it had all turned back. However, perhaps I just didn't meet the successful ones, so if you're enthusiastic, well equipped, and adventurous by all means give it a try. It goes to Antsikafoka, just south of Fénérive and has a romantic history: before the road and railway this was the normal route for smuggled goods from Réunion and Mauritius to be brought to the highlands. Now there is talk of making a road along this route – it may even be underway.

If you only go as far as Ambatondrazaka, there is a Chinese-run hotel with just adequate food. The Salon du Lac opposite is a good patisserie. The road goes right round the lake but there is no public transport much of the year.

SOUTH OF TAMATAVE
Pangalanes

This series of lakes was linked by artificial canals in French Colonial times for commercial use, a quiet inland water being preferable to an often stormy sea. Over the years the canals became choked with vegetation and no longer passable, but attempts are now being made to rehabilitate the canals and re-establish the unbroken waterway which stretched from Tamatave to Vangaindrano.

It is possible to travel stretches of the canal yourself on barges carrying cargoes of bananas, coffee, etc. This is particularly attractive for fishing enthusiasts since there are many deep-sea fish in the the lakes. There are no sharks, so swimming is safe. Bird watching is also rewarding and crocodiles may be seen, especially at night with the use of a torch.

Some companies run escorted trips to the Pangalanes: Turisma, 15 Ave de l'Indépendance, Antananarivo (B.P. 3997). Tel: 289-11/287-57. Telex 22366 Somatram) and Caravanserai, B.P. 627, Antananarivo. Tel: 302-79. Turisma has a three and five day itinerary, the latter allowing a two and a half day stay at the village of Ankanin'ny Nofy, 61 km south of Tamatave.

There is also a hotel near Ambila Lemaitso, Les Everglades, on Lac Rasoabe (Tel: 442-97 in Tana for further information and bookings). It is reportedly a rather sad, gloomy place, but perhaps it just needs more visitors. Excursions can be arranged from the hotel.

Both Ankanin'ny Nofy and Ambila Lemaitso are on the Tana – Tamatave railway.

Andevoranto, south of Ambila Lemaitso, is said to be a cheerful, friendly small town. There may not be accommodation however (but camping would be no problem).

Continuing south

You can travel down the coast as far as Mahanoro (occasional transport) and can sometimes find a *pirogue* to take you to Nosy Varika and Mananjary, which is linked by road to Fianarantsoa. This is adventurous stuff, and not for those with limited time. Helena Drysdale writes: 'We travelled from Tamatave to Mananjary over 2 weeks. Generally people assured us it was impossible, that there were no roads, that all the bridges were down in the cyclone, and the ferries were *en panne* (that familiar phrase). But with luck and ingenuity it was possible. One taxi-brousse per week from Tamatave to Mahanoro (2 days), otherwise river boats available at Tamatave's river port for hitching (we went on boats travelling south to a graphite mine in Vatomandry – a very uncomfortable three days).

'In **Vatomandry** we stayed in the Hotel Fotsy (7,000 FMG); thatched bungalows, full of rats, but good food and friendly. Nice town but nothing much to see.

'From there to **Mahanoro**, one day by taxi-brousse, two by boat. Hotel Pangalanes, 7,000 FMG. Boat from Mahanoro to **Masomelika** one day; very simple hotel (2,000 FMG) but friendly people (I asked for the toilet and was pointed to a bucket. This was the shower – the toilet was in the bushes). From Masomelika to **Nosy Varika** took half a day hitchhiking. There's a relatively expensive Chinese hotel here (rooms 4,000 FMG, but a pot of tea cost almost as much). Then on to Mananjary, one night by boat.'

Mananjary

A centre for coffee, vanilla, and pepper. Accessible by good road and taxi-brousse, this town is famous for its circumcision ceremony which takes place every seven years: most recently in October, 1986 (see overleaf).

Hotels: Jardin de la Mer (Ambinany) and Solimotel (Bd Maritime). The latter has come up in the world; excellent food.

Helena warns against camping here: 'The tent was slashed with a knife while we slept; we chased the man off and retreated to the verandah of the Solimotel, but he came back and succeeded in taking a camera and several other things while we slept.'

'In this area you can see a stone sculpture called "The White Elephant". Since there are no elephants in Madagascar, some historians think that people from India or Africa made this elephant just after their arrival 1000 years ago. You need a guide and three days to go to this sculpture.' (Jytte Arnfred Larson).

Fianarantsoa to Manakara by train.

Not as popular as the Tana-Tamatave train, this is nevertheless a spectacular railway trip, especially the early part. The train leaves every day at 7.00 and takes six hours to reach Manakara. There are also taxi-brousses.

Manakara

There are two hotels: Sidi Hotel (15,000 FMG) and Hotel Manakara (6,000 FMG), reported to be dirty with poor food. From Manakara you can continue south by taxi-brousse to two towns described here by Jytte Arnfred Larson of Denmark.

Vohipeno

'About 30 km south of Manakara. No hotels, only a very small Malagasy *hotely* with one room (only for adventurers). This area is inhabited by the Antaimoro tribe who came from Arabia about 600 years ago, bringing the first script to Madagascar. Originally Moslems, most of them have now been converted to Christianity. From Vohipeno you can walk about 5 km to Ivato, where you can visit the old Antaimoro kings' tombs. But first you must go to the office of the *président du Fokontany* to get permission. The substitute for the *président* who gave me the permit was a passionate lover of Malagasy history and told me stories about the kings and queens for one hour, although I was anxious to start the excursion. The path to Ivato goes through several small villages – very unspoilt. All over I met very friendly people. In Ivato I met a man who spoke some French and was willing to guide me to the present king. There was a big gathering for a funeral so many local village chiefs were in the king's house. I was invited to enter and after greeting ceremonies, we sat down to negotiate a price for permission to take photos. I was asked to pay 3,000 FMG – but was only allowed to take photos of the tomb from the outside.'

The Antaimoro people also demonstrate their Islamic history through their clothing (turban and fez, as well as Arab-style robes). They are the inheritors of the 'great writings' *sorabe*, written in Malagasy but in Arabic script. *Sorabe* continue to be written, still in Arabic, still on 'Antaimoro paper'. The scribes who practise this art are known as *katibo* and the writing and their knowledge of it gives them a special power. The writing itself ranges from accounts of historical events to astrology, and the books are considered sacred.

Farafangana

Accessible by taxi-brousse from Manakara. Nice fishermen's cottages. Restaurant Le Lac. There's one reasonable hotel near the sea, about 17,000 FMG, and a good Malagasy *hotely* near some *bungalows administratifs*.

Warning   To vary the route back to the *Hauts Plateaux* there is a temptation to take the very rough – but marvellously scenic – road from Farafangana to Ihosy. The advice is don't: this road is notorious for bandits.

SAMBATRA IN MANANJARY

By Sally Crook

Sambatra means 'blessed' or 'happy' in Malagasy, and it is the word used for the circumcision ceremonies which are performed in much of Madagascar. The Antambahoaka, probably the smallest tribe in Madagascar, live around Mananjary on the east coast, and young boys and their families from the surrounding villages congregate every seven years for a communal circumcision ceremony there. They become 'blessed', though the actual deed of removal of the penis foreskin is now performed at a different time, usually in the hygienic conditions of a hospital.

In October 1986, the week-long celebrations commenced at a leisurely pace and culminated (after a Thursday of inactivity, due to the *fady* nature of this day) on a Friday. Women collected reeds and wove mats in preparation for the big day, and later men carved and painted wooden birds, three of which were fixed on the roof of each *trano be* (literally 'big house'), facing east. This in itself caused much excitement and some unwished for precipitous descents from the sloped, thatched roofs, while the men continued to beat their oval wooden or hide shields with sticks wielded like swords. Similar activity, drumming and chanting continued below, and the women chanted as they stepped from side to side in their dance. A boy standing astride a barrel on a wheeled cart, brandishing shield and stick gave the most fiery display, encouraging the crowds around.

The fathers of boys to be circumcised wore long colourful robes, gathered at the neck. The *trano be* in which the people drink and talk for days, should not be entered by foreign females, and even the Malagasy women must wear their hair in the traditional style – the many plaits on each side of the centre parting being drawn to a cluster at each side of the neck.

In the afternoon of the Wednesday, women shuffled around the *trano be* in an anti-clockwise direction, chanting and holding aloft the white braided and tasselled red ceremonial caps of their young sons. At the front and back of the procession, the rolled mats woven especially for the occasion were held aloft. After several circuits of the house, the crowds proceeded to the beach where, apparently spontaneously, the women's cries were periodically renewed.

The excitement spilt over into a kind of fighting between men with green pointed sticks cut from the mid ribs of palm fronds, and soon the fathers of the circumcision candidates were being routed and chased back into town as the green sticks were hurled at their retreating backs. The apparent terror with which men fled from these harmless weapons indicates a far greater symbolic significance than their physical power.

As Thursday became Friday at midnight, sacred water was collected from the wide River Mananjary where it enters the sea. In the morning gloom nine zebu were sacrificed – one for each clan – by the cutting of the jugular vein after prayers. Some escapees caused excitement before the animals could be bound and lain on their sides with a piece of wood between the teeth. At the first sight of blood, little boys rushed forward to collect it in buckets or in bamboo pipes, just as their 'cousins' in Toraja, Sulawesi, do to this day.

Dancing, music and the women's chant of 'Eeee-ay' changed to processions and a chorus of 'Aaa-ooh' as crowds converged once again on the beach. The young boys, in red and white smocks and wearing their tasselled caps, were carried on their fathers' shoulders. The mind-dulling chant continued as the separate clans were herded along like sheep by men with sticks, following the man with the sacred water held in a small pot on his head, protected by a movable 'hedge' of four poles carried by other robed men.

That night, the boys, bearing white marks on their faces to indicate their clan, were carried on the shoulders of adults around the *trano be*. Each was passed through the west door of the house, and, wearing a string around the waist, was sat upon the severed head of a fine male zebu for a while in the presence of the clan leader, adorned with colourful striped cloth and a fez. The virility of the animal was thus conferred on the boy, and, as he was passed through the east door he had become a man.

These tiny men were almost dropping with exhaustion as they were paraded once again near the house, whose outside northern end had been cordoned off and guarded from trespass throughout the ceremonial days. The joy of their mothers was vocal and infectious as if they were relieved to have their sons now accepted as adults.

JAWS

Sharks are a real danger to swimmers in unprotected bays on the east coast, where an average of 12 people a year die this way. Shark associated deaths seem particularly high in Tamatave — everyone has a gruesome story. Often the victims were in quite shallow water and one tourist died of his injuries after an attack when he was wading.

So, however inviting the water, only swim in areas protected by a coral reef or artificial shark barrier. Ask local advice – the French for shark is *requin* and in Malagasy *Antsantsa*.

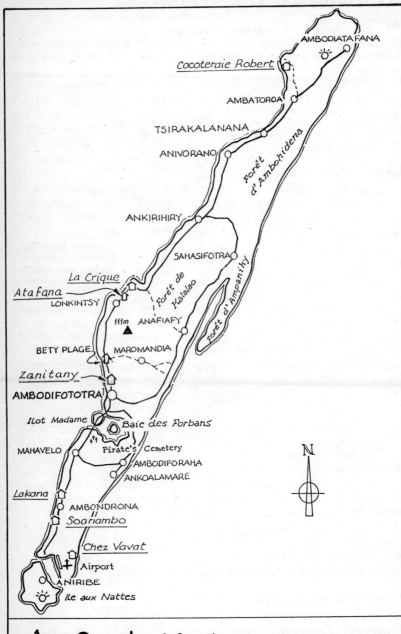

Île Sainte Marie (Nosy Boraha)

——— road
– – – footpath
⌂ hotel/bungalows
☼ lighthouse

0 |–|–|–|–|–| 5 km

ÎLE SAINTE MARIE (NOSY BORAHA)

History

The origin of the Malagasy name is obscure. It either means Island of Abraham or Island of Ibrahim, with probable reference to an early semetic culture.

It was re-named Île Sainte Marie by European sailors, and became the major hideout of pirates in the Indian Ocean. From the 1680s to around 1720 these European pirates dominated the seas around Africa. There was a Welshman – David Williams, Englishmen – Thomas White, John Every, William Kidd, and an American – Thomas Tew, among a Madagascar pirate population which in its heyday numbered nearly one thousand.

Later a Frenchman, Jean-Onésime Filet ('La Bigorne') was ship-wrecked on Ste Marie while escaping the wrath of a jealous husband in Réunion. La Bigorne turned his amorous attentions, with remarkable success, to Princess Bety, the daughter of King Ratsimilaho. On their marriage the happy couple received Nosy Boraha as a gift from the king, and the island was in turn presented to the mother country by La Bigorne (or rather, put under the protection of France by Princess Bety). Thus France gained its first piece of Madagascar in 1750.

Île Sainte Marie today

A cliché of a tropical island with endless deserted beaches overhung by coconut palms, bays protected from sharks by coral reefs, hills covered with luxuriant vegetation, and an absence of unsightly tourist develop-ment and of vehicles: there are five on the island. The serpent in this Garden of Eden is the weather: as in all the eastern region cyclones strike regularly and you can expect several days of rain and wind all year round, but interspersed with calm sunny weather. The best months for a visit seem to be June and mid-August to November.

The only real town in Ste Marie is Ambodifototra. Other small villages are comprised of bamboo and palm huts.

Ste Marie attracts a more rugged breed of visitor than its island rival, Nosy Be. This is partly because of the weather, partly because there is more choice of low-cost accommodation and an absence of tourist hoo-ha, and partly because it can seem almost impossible to get there, and quite impossible to leave. Travellers have demonstrated the heights of initiative in finding transport off the island when planes are habitually booked solid for months in advance.

Getting there and back

By boat   A very crowded and uncomfortable passenger boat leaves Tamatave once a week, usually on a Tuesday at 6.00. The shipping line is SCAC, a couple of blocks behind AUXIMAD, along the seafront, which used to operate these boats. Price about 10,000 FMG for an often rough ten hour crossing, leaving at 6.00 am. It returns on Fridays, leaving at midnight.

It is also possible to take a boat from Manompana, on the mainland 25 km away (see page 161). Manompana is not always accessible – it depends on the state of bridges and ferries crossing the several rivers up the east coast – and once there you must try your luck over boats. If a group of *vazahas* has collected at the one very basic (but friendly) hotel you could charter a pirogue from the Chinese owners (15,000 FMG) – an exciting, not to say dangerous, trip in these shark infested seas. The journey will take three to six hours. The *Vedette Alize* seems a bit safer and runs to Ste Marie on Tuesdays and Fridays (returning Mondays and Thursdays). It costs 10,000 FMG, and takes 4 hours (it generally leaves at 3.00 or 4.00, and it is often raining).

'The ferry is a small, barely seaworthy launch, skippered by a chap who could well be descended from pirates. He is toffee-coloured, with a hook nose and blue eyes, but appears to have inherited none of his ancestors' swashbuckling courage. Indeed, he appears absolutely terrified of going to sea at all, and refuses flatly to do so unless it resembles a mill pond...' (Robert Stewart).

A further boat alternative is to stay at the Miramar in Tamatave and make use of Monsieur Didier's offer of a sailing boat (50,000 FMG) from Foulpointe to the beach hotel of Betty Plage.

By plane   Air Madagascar currently (1990) flies to Ste Marie from Tana or Tamatave every day except Tuesdays, costing 486 FF from Tana and 200 FF from Tamatave. All flights are heavily booked, especially in July and August, and you should make your reservations well in advance. As soon as you arrive, reconfirm your return flights. However adamant the Air-Mad people are that the flight is full, it is worth going stand-by. I have got on twice this way, and other travellers report the same success. It's a nerve-racking business, though.

There are no taxis on the island, but one truck serves as hotel transport. Some hotels have their own vehicles and meet the incoming planes. Check with the 'courtesy vehicles' if there is room at their hotel before climbing aboard.

Where to stay
There are no large hotels on Ste Marie, only palm-thatched bunga-lows. Most are some way from the airport and charge about 10,000 FMG for transfers.

Category A
Soanambo (B.P. 20, tel: 40). 3 km from airport; 10 km from Ambodi-fototra. The most luxurious and expensive at 150 FF single, 195 FF double. Breakfast 29 FF, other meals 75 FF. Very comfortable with many facilities – ping pong, volley ball, swimming pool, hot water, bicycles, 'pedalos' (pedal boats) for hire, plus sailing, wind-surfing and deep sea diving at the nearby Centre Nautique. Main meal 15,000 FMG. Good food.

La Cocoteraie Robert. In the extreme north of the island, described by one who knows as 'the most beautiful beach in the world', and has recently added 40 more bungalows. Access by land difficult, but a boat goes there from Soanambo (it's run by the same French family). Similar price to Soanambo.

Category B
La Crique. (B.P. 1). Deservedly the most popular of all hotels, in the prettiest location, a kilometre north of Lonkintsy, with a wonderful ambience and good food (Meal 7,000 FMG). Room prices (1990): bungalows 11,500 FMG (single), 14,000 FMG (double), 17,500 FMG (triple); also family bungalows, 2 rooms with 2 beds in each, 18,000 FMG. Often full, so try to book ahead.

Lakana. Six simple but very comfortable bamboo and palm bungalows, 5 km from the airport, and including four perched along the jetty. Bed, breakfast and one meal per day cost 20,000 FMG or 95 FF. Lunch/dinner 30 FF. 10 speed bicycles for hire (7,500 FMG – full day). Some English spoken. Near the Centre Nautique.

Betty Plage. 3 km north of Ambodifototra. Owned by Mr Young Didier, who runs the Miramar in Tamatave. For bookings and details enquire at the Miramar.

Atafana. A new Malagasy-run hotel about 4 km south of La Crique, in a very pretty bay. Room 7,000 FMG, meal 5,000 FMG.

Category C
Chez Vavate. 6 rooms/bungalows, about 9,000 FMG. On first appearance an unprepossessing collection of local huts built on a ridge overlooking the airstrip. Don't be taken in by first impressions, the food here must be some of the best in Madagascar (and the *punch coco* ensures that you spend your evenings in a convivial haze) and the relaxed family atmosphere makes this a very popular place with young travellers. The only catch is you must walk 1½ km from the airport. There is no road, and the 'courtesy vehicle' from the airport is a man with a wheelbarrow! If you miss him take the wide grassy track which runs parallel to the airstrip then veers to the left up a steep hill, but be warned – if Chez Vavate is full you will have missed the vehicles going to the other places. Camping is usually permitted here.

Lafalafa. This restaurant in Ambodifototra also has a few rooms for about 5000 FMG.

Zanitany. 1 km north of Ambodifototra. French run, clean bungalows with shower 15,000 FMG to 18,000 FMG; the main building is an old colonial house with lovely decor and a sitting/dining room on the water's edge. Excellent food. Friendly. Universally praised.

Warning
There is talk of 'developing' Île Ste Marie as a major tourist resort.

Excursions around Ste Marie
From Chez Vavate, Soanambo or Lakana

Île Aux Nattes
A population of some 300 live on this island off the south of Ste Marie so transport by *pirogue* is easy and frequent. Cost 500 FMG approx. *Pirogues* leave from the southernmost tip of Ste Marie (the path there is an extension of the airport runway) and will land you near the little village of Aniribe. From here it is a short walk to the lighthouse (a villager will show you the path) which can be visited both for the view and for the fascination of seeing a 1914 model of a petrol-powered lighthouse still in operation – when there is petrol. Walk back along the very beautiful beach.

Île Aux Nattes was the home of 'Napoleon', a larger than life chief who used to enjoy entertaining *vazahas*. He died in 1986 but his family continue to cook *Poulet au coco* (chicken in coconut milk) if you order it a day in advance. There is a sort of 'restaurant' where this scrumptious dish has become a tradition. It's a lovely, and still unspoiled place. It is possible to stay in local huts – make enquiries.

Two walks from the south
1. Two hours. Take the ridge path leading from Chez Vavate for about 2 km to an intersection. The path to the right takes you down to the beach, and that to the left crosses the narrow tail of the island and brings you out on the coastal road a couple of kilometres from the airport.

2. Six to seven hours. At low tide it is possible to walk up the almost deserted east coast (great swimming) of Ste Marie to the village of Ankoalamare and to the motorable track which crosses the island, winding round the rim of steep cultivated valleys and past small settlements. (You can also pick up one of the transverse paths). Return by the coastal road.

Bike rides
Bikes can be hired from many of the hotels, from Ambodifototra (the shop is opposite the bank – 4000 FMG per day), and from the little village near the airport. This way you can see quite a lot of the island (but don't reckon on covering much ground – the roads are very rough

and the bikes often very bad). The main town, Ambodifototra, shows signs of past elegance, and two restaurants (Lafalafa recommended for good food and fruit juice) make it a suitable place to stop for lunch.

If you are staying at Ambodifototra you will have time to explore the north of the island, which is more dramatic scenically than the south. There is quite a good stretch of tarred road between the town and La Crique.

Mopeds are also available in Ambodifototra for 50,000 FMG per day.

Pirates' Cemetery

This can only be visited at low tide since there are several tidal creeks to be crossed. Just before the bay bridge to the town is a track leading off to the left. Children will guide you (whether you want them to or not) to the pirates' cemetery, 20 minutes away. This is quite an impressive place, with grave stones dating from the 1830s, one with a classic skull and cross bones carved on it.

Harry Sutherland-Hawes writes 'Check out the local graveyards on the island, especially the one north of Ambodifototra. Keep an eye out on the right hand side of the road and you will suddenly see a stone coffin or two through the leaves. If you wander in, it will surely give you a fright: hundreds of coffins, all laid next to each other, some with carvings next to them. One of the locals who took me there was going to open a couple up to show me, but I declined his kind offer!

'These graveyards are all over the place, always next to the villages, but the one by the main town is the most impressive.'

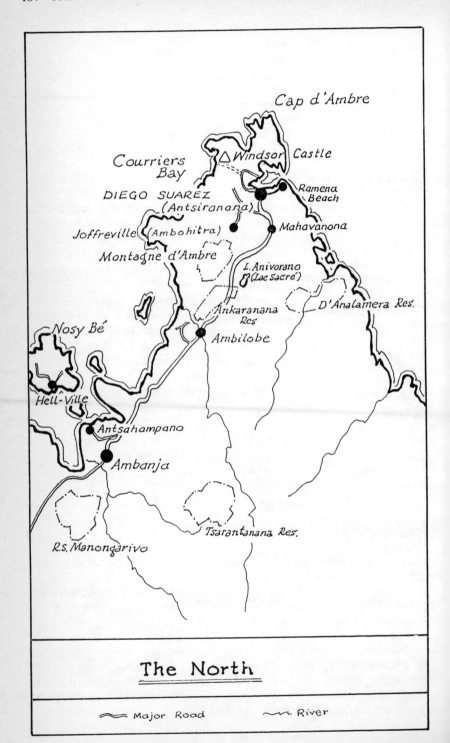

Cap d'Ambre

Courriers
Bay

△ Windsor Castle

DIEGO SUAREZ
(Antsiranana)

Ramena
Beach

Joffreville (Ambohitra)

Mahavanona

Montagne d'Ambre

L. Anivorano
(Lac Sacré)

Ankaranana
Res.

D'Analamera Res.

Nosy Bé

Ambilobe

Hell-Ville

Antsahampano

Ambanja

R.S. Manongarivo

Tsarantanana Res.

The North

〜 Major Road   〜 River

Chapter 10

The North

INTRODUCTION

The northern part of Madagascar is the domain of the Antakarana people. Cut off by rugged mountains, the Antakarana were left to their own devices until the mid-1700s when they were conquered by the Sakalava; they in turn submitted to the Merina king Radama I, aided by his military adviser James Hastie, in 1823.

The north is characterised by its variety. With the Tsaratanana massif (which includes Madagascar's highest peak, 2,880 m) bringing more rain to the Nosy Be area than is normal on the west coast, and the pocket of dry climate around Diego Suarez – seven months of dry weather; ninety percent of the 900 mm of rain falling between December and April – the weather can change dramatically within short distances. With changes of weather go changes of vegetation and its accompanying fauna, making this region particularly interesting for botanists and other naturalists, as well as straight forward holiday makers.

Getting around

The area retains its isolation and there are few good roads. Although you *can* get just about everywhere by taxi--brousse in the dry season most people prefer to fly.

DIEGO SUAREZ (ANTSIRANANA)

History

Forgivingly named after a Portuguese captain, Diego Suarez, who arrived in 1543 and proceeded to murder and rape the inhabitants or sell them into slavery, this large town has had an eventful history. (There is no truth, however, to the often claimed story that the Republic of Libertalia was founded here by pirates in the seventeenth century.)

The Malagasy name simply means 'port' and its strategic importance as a deep water harbour has long been recognised. The French installed a military base in 1885, and Britain captured and occupied the town in 1942 (Madagascar was then under the control of the Vichy

Government) to prevent any Japanese designs on the island as an Indian Ocean base.

Getting there and back

The best way is by air; the only reasonable road is from Nosy Be via Antsahampano (a popular route with travellers wanting a short taste of the thrills of taxi-broussing). This trip is described under *Nosy Be*. There is also a rough overland route to Vohemar, Sambava and Antalaha (see *Overland to Sambava*). There are two *gare routières* in Diego, on the Route de l'Ankarana (south) and the Route de la Pyrotechnie (west).

Flights go from Tana (returning the same day) via Majunga on Mondays, direct on Tuesdays, Wednesdays and Thursdays, via Sambava on Saturdays, via Tamatave on Sundays, and a Twin Otter wanders up the east coast on Fridays; (1990 schedule). 955 FF. There are also flights from Nosy Be, Majunga, and Vohemar.

Diego today

Traditionally rated second in beauty after Rio de Janeiro (presumably by people who had never seen Brazil) the harbour is encircled by hills, with a conical 'sugar loaf' plonked in one of the bays to the east of the town. From the air or the top of Montagne de Français, Diego's superb position can be appreciated but the city itself is in the usual state of decay, though with a particular charm. The port's isolation behind its mountain barrier and its long association with non-Malagasy races has given it an unusually cosmopolitan population and lots of colour: there are Arabs, Creoles (descendants of Europeans), Indians, Chinese, and Comorans.

It's a town you either love or hate: 'I love Diego! It is friendly, airy, with well-supplied shops, attractive architecture...' (J.Wilson); 'I have never heard a good word said for the port city. It is safe to say that Diego ... is the worst place in Madagascar. And why limit it? It is one of the worst places in the world.' (From *The Great Red Island* (1965) by Arthur Stratton).

The name Joffre seems to be everywhere in and around Diego. General Joseph Joffre was the military commander of the town in 1897 and later became Maréchal-de-France. In 1911 he took over the supreme command of the French armies, and was the victor of the battle of the Marne in 1914.

Diego is a pleasant town for wandering; take a look at the amazing, decaying building to the east of Clémenceau Square on Rue Richelieu. This was formerly a French Naval hotel, and has reportedly been bought by an American hotel group, to be restored to its original glory. Eventually.

There are several souvenir shops in Diego, but mostly selling rather tacky items (we boycotted those selling stuffed turtles or tortoises).

The best is Bijouterie Chez Babou, at 10 Rue de Colbert. They sell marvellous woodcarvings by 'Jean' of Ambositra.

Diego taxis are plentiful and cheap. They cost a set amount for any destination in the town centre (350 FMG daytime, 700 FMG at night), and usually operate on a shared system, so flag one down even if there's someone in it. To and from the airport costs 3,000 FMG.

The rainy season in Diego is from Christmas to March. There can be cyclones during that time (there was once a devastating one in Diego in April).

Guide   If you need a guide in or around Diego or to Montagne d'Ambre, 'Bob' has been recommended by Robert Stewart and Benjamin Freed, both of whom contributed to this chapter. Bob speaks good English and is very knowledgeable about the flora and fauna. He can often be found at the Hotel Rascasse.

Where to stay

Category A
Hotel de la Poste (Near Clémenceau Square, overlooking the bay. Postal address B.P. 121. Tel: 214-53). Officially the best in town, but so run-down in 1989 that it can only improve. At its best there's air conditioning, a wonderful view (from the Annexe) and a good restaurant. 19,000 FMG to 20,000 FMG double. Occasional hot water, shower, WC, etc. in all rooms.

Category B
Hotel Paradis du Nord. Rue Villaret Joyeuse, across from the market; taxi drivers know it. In 1989 this was the best value in town since everything worked – air-conditioning, hot water... The rooms themselves are cell-like (13,800 FMG) except for No 1 which is marvellously spacious and overlooks the colourful market (21,000 FMG). There is a pleasant balcony dining room, laundry service, and a secure garage if you are driving (you can rent cars from here). The noise from the Saturday night disco could be disturbing but doesn't seem to penetrate the rooms.

Hotel Valiha, 41 Rue Colbert (B.P. 270. Tel: 215-31). Going through a bad patch, but was once the best value in town. Helpful staff. 10,000 FMG to 15,000 FMG. The more expensive rooms have air-conditioning and hot water – if they're working. There's a 'villa' in the Annexe for 40,000 FMG – worth checking out.

Hotel Fian-tsilaka, 13 Bvd Etienne (tel: 223-48). Room prices range from 9,000 FMG to 20,000 FMG for a studio room with hot water. Good restaurant.

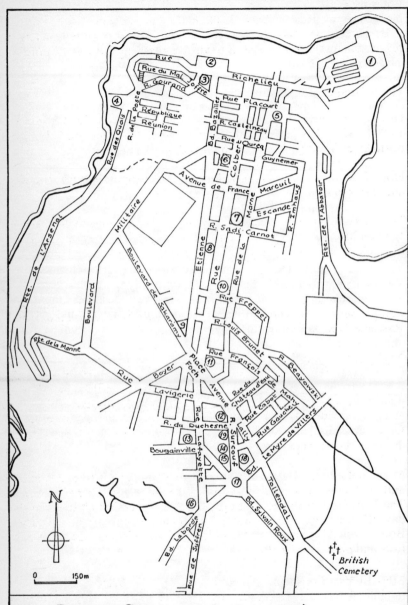

Diego Suarez (Antsiranana)

① Hospital ② Clemenceau Square ③ Hotel de la Poste
④ Place de l'Amiral Ronarch ⑤ Place Gallieni ⑥ Market ⑦ Hotel Valiha
⑧ Hotel Fian-tsilaka ⑨ Post Office ⑩ Nouvel Hotel
⑪ Bar/Restaurant Libertania ⑫ Restaurant l'Extreme Orient
⑬ Hotel Maymoune ⑭ Hotel Rascasse ⑮ Hotel Orchidée ⑯ Market
⑰ Place de l'Amiral Courbet ⑱ Air Mad./Mad. Air Tours ⑲ La Vanille Rest.

Category C
Nouvel Hotel, Rue Colbert. 7,500 FMG. Good value.
Ben Freed, who has been in the Diego area for a year, reckons their restaurant is one of the best in town. He recommends *filet de poisson au poivre verte crème*.

Hotel Orchidée, Rue Surcouf (opposite Air Mad).

Hotel la Rascasse, Rue Surcouf, near the Orchidée. 12,000 FMG to 15,000 FMG (1988). Air-conditioned and newly decorated, but reportedly unfriendly. Not recommended.

Hotel Fiadanana. 9 Rue Amiral Pierre. The cheapest in town, friendly and disreputable. About 7,500 FMG.

Tourist Hotel (renamed the Maymoune) 7 Rue Bougainville. About 10,000 FMG. Good value; rooms have fan, bidet, shower and sink. Balcony with view onto street.

Where to eat
The best food in town (described as 'superb' by two readers) is at the newly opened La Vanille restaurant, up the road from the Hotel Rascasse, and run by two Malagasy brothers.

Yachy (pronounced Yah-*shee*) about 100 metres north of La Vanille (next to the Alliance Française) is recommended by Ben Freed: 'This is a *beautiful* place, with lovely murals and chopsticks by all the place-settings. The cuisine is mixed Chinese/European, there are generous portions and the staff is probably the most courteous in Diego. Try the *Mine Rosé* and the *Poisson à l'Abricot*.' Reservations are required at weekends.

Many of the hotels serve good meals, the Nouvel, Fian-tsilaka, Valiha, and De la Poste being the best, and there are plenty of small eateries. The Hortensia, near the post office, does fast food at all times of the day. If your hotel does not serve breakfast, go to the Amicale Boulangerie, between the Orchidee and the cinema. Excellent hot rolls and *pain au chocolat*.

FINALLY... 'For shame you did not mention Ninaglace! It's good, it's reliable, it has tasty icecream, yoghurt and fruit juice. Try a *Ninaourt aux fruits*, or a khimo sandwich. The place for a good breakfast or a good nosh.' (Ben Freed).

Photocopy the maps and vocab in this book so you can easily carry them with you.

Excursions

NEAR TOWN

The British Cemetery

On the outskirts of town on the road that leads to the airport, the British cemetery is on a side road opposite the main Malagasy cemetery and is well-signposted. Here is a sad insight into Anglo-Malagasy history: rows of graves of the British troops killed in the battle for Diego in 1942, and the larger numbers, mainly East African and Indian soldiers serving in the British army, who died from disease during the occupation of the port. Maintained by the Commonwealth War Graves Commission, this is a peaceful and moving place.

Ramena Beach

20 km from the town centre. Get there by taxi-brousse or private taxi for around 8,000 FMG. On Sundays there is a bus. It's a beautiful drive around the curve of the bay, with some fine baobabs en route. Lovely white sand and good swimming – but at present no restaurant (although in the nearby fishing village there is sometimes a store open that sells drinks). However, the brothers who run La Vanille are thinking of branching out there – weekends only.

If you ask around you may be able to rent a fisherman's bungalow.

Other beaches

Ben Freed has two suggestions: 'The prettiest beach is Baie des Dunes. You need to get a permit from the military base in town (not a difficult task). There are no tourists or snack bars, there are palm trees, sand and swimming. Get a taxi to Ramena and make a right turn up to the guard house. After that it's about 1.5 km of track.

'Baie des Sakalavas. I haven't been to this one, but a military permit and four-wheel-drive are needed. My friends tell me it is more beautiful than the Dunes, and is part of Cap Oranges.'

Montagne des Français (French Mountain)

The mountain gets its name from the memorial to the French and Malagasy killed during the allied invasion in 1942. Another sad reminder of a war about which the locals can have had little understanding. There are several crosses but the main one was laboriously carried up in 1956 to emulate Jesus's journey to Calvary.

It is a hot but rewarding climb up to this high point with splendid views and some nearby caves. Take a taxi 8 km along the coast road towards Ramena beach, to the start of the old road up the mountain. You'll find it opposite a sign saying 'Ben Galow' on the left side of the road. The track winds upwards, with obvious short cuts; the big cross is reached in about an hour. It's best to go very early in the morning (good bird-watching) or in the evening. The mountain supports unusual vegetation: baobabs, aloes, and until recently pachypodium, but these have evidently all been dug up.

FURTHER AFIELD

Towards Cap d'Ambre

To reach the northerly tip of Madagascar you need a four-wheel-drive vehicle or motor-bike and nerves of steel, but there are places of great interest nearer to Diego. Phil Chapman, who was part of the Ankarana expedition, told me of a meeting with a German who was a U boat commander during the war; as they travelled close to the high cliffs of the western cape they sighted 'British smoke' billowing from a cave. Cautious investigation revealed that the 'smoke' was thousands upon thousands of bats.

The area is still fascinating for naturalists, particularly botanists, and those interested in the wartime history of Madagascar. A half day drive takes you to beautiful Courriers Bay passing the fantastic rock known as **Windsor Castle**. This monolith (visible from Diego) is steep-sided and flat-topped, so made a perfect look-out point during times of war. The views from there are superb. It was fortified by the French, occupied by the Vichy forces, and liberated by the British. A ruined staircase still runs to the top. Phil tells me this is a great place to see *tsingy*, that fretted limestone karst that features in some of the most dramatic photos of Madagascar. There is also an endemic species of pachypodium, *Pachypodium windsorii* – the best place to find it is to the left of the staircase. It goes without saying that the flora should *not* be collected.

Courriers Bay, half an hour beyond Windsor Castle, is a very pleasant beach.

There is said to be a first class restaurant in the area, run by a retired couple from Réunion, but I have no further details.

The trip to Courriers Bay is really only suitable for a four-wheel-drive vehicle, but intrepid taxi drivers have reached it in their Renault 4s. It takes about two hours. Take the road that runs west towards Ampasindava, where you turn right (north) along a rocky road, then left towards Windsor Castle. The road continuing north is the very rough one to the Cape.

In the same general area is Montagne des Miel, the southernmost mountain of the peninsula. 'Its main selling feature is the flora, in particular the baobabs and pachypodium. There are baobabs right beside the road, but what is more impressive is to look through binocs at all those beautiful baobabs placed delicately along the mountainside. If you have a guide, climb to the top.' (Ben Freed).

Lac Sacré

The sacred lake (Lac Anivorano) is about 75 km south of Diego. It attracts visitors more for its legends than the reality of a not particularly scenic lake and the possibility of seeing a crocodile. The story is that once upon a time Anivorano was situated amid semi-desert and a thirsty traveller arrived at the village and asked for a drink. When his request was refused he warned the villagers that they would soon have more water than they could cope with. No sooner had he left than the earth opened, water gushed out, and the mean-minded villagers and their houses were inundated. The crocodiles which now inhabit the lake are considered to be ancestors (and to wear jewellery belonging to their previous selves. So they say).

On the two occasions I have been there I have seen no crocs (and there are reported to be only three left now), but other travellers have been luckier. The crocodiles are sometimes fed by the villagers – some people say on Fridays and Saturdays – and you may do best to book a tour with Madagascar Airtours in Diego; they should know when croc feeding day is.

Personally I feel that Anivorano is not worth a special trip but is an interesting stop if you are coming by road from the south.

Parc National Montagne d'Ambre

A splendid example of upland moist forest, this national park ranges in altitude from 850 m to 1,474 m and has its own micro-climate with rainfall equal to the eastern region (the rainy season here is from December to May but it can rain any time of the year).

There are tall trees, orchids, unusual birds, an assortment of reptiles and insects, and two diurnal lemur species – Sanfords lemur (*Lemur fulvus sanfordi*) and crowned lemurs (*Lemur coronatus*). Both are endangered, and this is the most easily accessible place to see them. Sanfords lemur is brown, the males having splendid white/beige ear-tufts and side-whiskers surrounding black faces, whilst the females are whiskerless with a grey face. Crowned lemurs get their names from the triangle of black between the ears of the male; the rest of the animal is reddish brown, with white belly and face. Female crowned lemurs have a little red tiara across the forehead, grey backs and tails, and the same white belly and face as the male. Young are born from September to November. Ben Freed, who is studying these lemurs and provided the above description, adds: 'A useful way of locating them is to listen. The calls, particularly of the crowned lemur, are quite distinct and loud. It is a short, piercing *Waee*. Sanford's lemur often gives a raspy call that lasts for several seconds.'

Unlike the reserves, Montagne d'Ambre was set up for visitors to enjoy (as well as being an area of great scientific interest). It is one of the places targeted by the WWF's Northern Reserves Project (the others are Ankarana, Analamerana – protecting the black sifaka – and Forêt d'Ambre) so tourist facilities will be improved, and eventually there will be accommodation.

The park has, in theory, 30 km of paths, but many of these were destroyed by the cyclone that struck northern Madagascar in 1984; 10 km of paths would now be more accurate: they lead to the Petit Lac, the Jardin Botanique, and two waterfalls, Grande Cascade and Petite Cascade. There is also a Sentier Touristique.

The waterfalls provide the two focal points. If time is short and you want to watch wildlife rather than walk far, go to the Petite Cascade (along the track beyond the old warden's house). Here you'll find an idyllic fern-fringed grotto with waterfalls splashing into a pool and feeding a stream which is visited by malachite kingfishers and other water-loving birds. The area between the building and the waterfall is also the best place to see lemurs. Be quiet, take your time, and please don't leave litter in this marvellous spot. The more energetic can take the marked track (on the right as you walk up from the park entrance) to the Grande Cascade. Excellent bird watching here, some lovely tree ferns, and finally a steep descent to the foot of the waterfall (only do it when dry – it's slippery and dangerous when wet). On your way back you'll pass a path on the right (left as you go towards the waterfall) marked 'Jardin Botanique'; don't be misled into thinking this will lead you to the rose-garden. It's a tough up-and-down walk that eventually joins the main track to the old building. Rewarding, but not if you're tired, and watch out for leeches.

'I guess my main bit of advice for tourists is not to expect too much – this is *not* Berenty or Nosy Komba. For me the beauty of the place is not that you have lemurs eating out of your hands, nor that you are guaranteed to see lemurs (you are not); the beauty lies in appreciating what fate allows you to see, hear, and feel. In that respect the Malagasy have one hell of a park here.' (Ben Freed).

You need a permit to visit Montagne d'Ambre (available from the Direction des Eaux et Forêts in Diego or in Tana, costing the usual 20,000 FMG). Although the park can be done in one day with Madagascar Airtours, it is really much too nice a place to hurry through. It's best to spend the night in nearby Joffreville (Ambohitra), or better still, camp in the park (but check at the Eaux et Forêts office in Diego that this is permitted). There is an area for tents near the old visitor centre that now serves as a shelter for scientists.

Taxi-brousses run to Joffreville (but you may not find one to take you home in the evening). In the 'town' (no great metropolis) you will find the mouldering Hotel Joffre.

From Joffreville it is 7 km to the park entrance. Some taxi- drivers will take you to the barrier or to the village of Rousettes (near le Petite Cascade).

Note   The temperature in the park is, on average, 10°F cooler than in Diego, and likely to be wet and muddy. There may also be leeches. Do not wear shorts and sandals. Bring rain gear, insect repellent, and a sweater, however hot you are at sea-level.

Ankarana

About 75 km south of Diego Suarez is a small limestone massif, Ankarana. An 'island' of *tsingy* (limestone karst pinnacles) and forest, the massif is penetrated by numerous caves and canyons. Some of the largest caves have collapsed, forming isolated pockets of river-fed forest with their own perfectly protected flora and fauna. The caves and their rivers also are home to crocodiles, some reportedly six metres long.

After a preliminary look in 1981, The Crocodile Caves of Ankarana Expedition, led by Dr Jane Wilson, spent several months in 1986 exploring and studying the area, and their findings excited considerable scientific interest, a TV film and a book by Jane Wilson (see *Bibliography*).

Ankarana is a Special Reserve but hitherto has received poor protection. Thankfully, it has now been included in the WWF's project and the ecotourism will be encouraged. Ask Madagascar Airtours in Tana for information.

At the time of writing, it is only accessible to intrepid explorers. Before venturing into the reserve you should be aware that this region is of great significance to the Antakarana people (the clan kings are interred in one of the caves, and *famadihana* takes place from time to time – a huge festival for the local people). The Ankarana Expedition members asked permission of the current king before entering the area. Until controlled tourism is established there, it would be as well for others to show the same cultural sensitivity.

The village of Matsaborimanga is opposite the largest piece of forest with high lemur populations (crowned lemur, Sanfords lemur, sportive lemurs, diademed sifaka and aye-aye have all been seen here) and the villagers know the forest well. For caving, you should approach from the village of Andrafiabe. The locals will show you the entrance of the largest cave, Grotte d'Andrafiabe, but will not accompany you inside. With 11 km of passages, caving experience and reliable caving lights are essential. There is a total of 80 km of cave passages in the massif.

Other explorations

The areas adjacent to Montagne d'Ambre present excellent opportunities for adventurers. A local guide is recommended to ensure that you don't infringe any *fady* as well as for way-finding. Plan your route with the FTM Antsiranana map (no 2). Another enticing area is Ambanja (see *Nosy Be*).

Tim Cross sent me a splendidly evocative description of his explorations (which eventually brought him on foot to Diego) some of which are quoted here.

In the lychee capital of Madagascar, Antsalaka, I was put up by the local teacher and his wife. Their five children sung the national anthem for me. They lit a fire to dry my boots, and I learned some Malagasy from the Franco-Malgache schoolbooks in the schoolroom. I had announced my intention to traverse the Montagne d'Ambre rainforest the next day. The villagers were astonished at this undertaking. It was a long, long way, they gestured. They insisted I take a guide... But where would I find a guide willing to leave his village over Christmas? As it happened one presented himself to me, and for £2.50 agreed to guide me for three days over the mountains...

I had left the bitumen highway three days ago and was now trekking over the mountainous rainforests of the north. A tropical forest full of butterflies winking by the verges, lemurs singing and snorting in the branches, and exotic orchids blooming out of dense vegetation was what I had envisaged. But I was so preoccupied with keeping my balance on the treacherous, muddy and sloping zebu track that the only form of wildlife I could spot was the insidious leech. Yet once on the top ridge of the Montagne d'Ambre rainforest, we were rewarded with one of the few vantage points on the island from which to savour the split panorama of the Mozambique Channel to the west and the Indian Ocean to the east both at the same time...

We ultimately reached our destination (Bobakilandy). It was getting dark, and the first thing to do on arrival was to be introduced to the president of the community. I had become used to this procedure of being sat down and expected to explain one's origins and the purpose of the journey (hiking for pleasure does not impress)... The chief dealt out tots of rum on what appeared to be an ad hoc basis. The basis obviously precluded *vazahas*, but the hospitality *did* extend to his offer of a temporarily disused kitchen hut as a bedroom, which I gladly accepted. Despite prominent holes in the woodwork and the corrugated iron, it offered a welcome degree of privacy. For a village-faring *vazaha* the momentary seclusion is a rare privilege; whenever the door of the hut was ajar, a group of wide-eyed young village boys would crowd about me expecting to be entertained. Even the most staunch advocate of the Swiss Army Knife will admit there is a limit to its entertainment value, and ultimately it was my stabs at the Malagasy language that induced more fits of giggles amongst the assembled company. I was offered little beetles and made to pronounce their various names and even a string of mushrooms adorned by a threaded *valala* (locust). But the entertainment was reciprocated. The Malagasy eat unsalted rice three times a day. It soon became known that the *vazaha* preferred fruit and sweet things. The boys then rushed away to collect mangoes and the phenomenally sticky jack fruit... Madagascar may be best known for its lemur population, but for me it is undoubtedly the human population which exerts the greater fascination and which makes this island worth visiting, if you are prepared to leave the bitumen highway.

Overland from Diego to Sambava

'Three days of extreme pain. The road from Ambilobe to Vohemar is almost non-existent. We broke down in our *camion* several times. **Vohemar** is a pleasant town with nothing much to see, like most Malagasy towns. Solimotel excellent, with delicious food and spotless bungalows overlooking the sea.

'The bridge has collapsed just outside Vohemar. You must wade across the river and then hope for something the other side. Six hours in a *camion* to Sambava on a fairly good road.' (Helena Drysdale).

Nosy - Be

① Andilana Beach Hotel   ② Airport
③ Hotel Les Cocotiers   ④ Hotel Palm Beach
⑤ Residence d'Ambatoloaka   ⑥ Mont Passot (329m)
⑦ Oceanographic Institute

NOSY BE
History
Nosy Be's charms were recognised as long ago as 1649 when the British colonel Robert Hunt wrote 'I do believe, by God's blessing, that not any part of the World is more advantageous for a Plantation, being every way as well for pleasure as well as profit, in my estimation.' Hunt was attempting to set up an English colony on the island, at that time known as Assada, but failed because of hostile natives and disease.

Future immigrants, both accidental and intentional, contributed to Nosy Be's racial variety. Shipwrecked Indians built a magnificent settlement several centuries ago in the south east of the island, where the ruins can still be seen. The crew of a Russian ship that arrived during the Russo-Japanese war of 1904-5 with orders to attack any passing Japanese and were then forgotten are buried in the Hell-Ville cemetery. Other arrivals were Arabs, Comorans, and – more recently – Europeans flocking to Madagascar's foremost holiday resort.

When King Radama I was completing his wars of conquest, the Boina kings took refuge in Nosy Be. First they sought protection from the Sultan of Zanzibar, and he obliged by sending a warship in 1838, then two years later they requested help from Commander Passot, who landed his ship at Nosy Be. The Frenchman was only too happy to oblige, and asked Admiral de Hell, the governor of Bourbon Island (now La Réunion), to place Nosy Be under the protection of France. The island was formerly annexed in 1841.

Getting there
By boat from Majunga   Two days and two nights of acute discomfort. 15,000 FMG.

By road and ferry   From Diego take a taxi-be or taxi-brousse (always *very* crowded) or a Mercedes truck (smoother) to Ambanja on the mainland opposite Nosy Be. The journey takes about six hours. The road is quite good as far as Anivorano, then terrible to Ambilobe (but you pass through some of Ankarana), then quite good to Ambanja, which has several hotels (Croix de Sud, Hawaii, Patricia and others) and is a good place to spend a few days with plenty of natural history explorations to be taken.

From Ambanja take a taxi the following morning about 18 km to Antsahampano, the departure point for the ferry. There are two ferries a day; the sailing times depend on the tide, and the trip takes two hours. You have the alternative of going by small steam boat (*vedette*). Being smaller, they are less tied to the tides, and also call first at Nosy Komba.

If you've got time and are tough you can also go by road from Tana. Tim Cross describes his trip:

The *gare routière* is a bustling conjunction of clapped out trucks, vans and cars, all pretending to be serviceable and offering to transport the impecunious to various corners of the island. I slowly began to get the gist of taxi-brousse travel: for about £10 you could travel 400 miles in a canvas-covered utility van which was expected to accommodate sacks of manioc, charcoal, rice, baskets of fruit, three hens, two turkeys and a tortoise, and – oh, by the way – twenty human beings of various sizes and odours. I opted to perch at the back of the the van... Comfort is abandoned along with Optimism and Superstition. I had no idea how long it would take me to reach my destination of Ambanja. Nor did anyone else. After having been stopped twice by police and having experienced our first flat tyre (the first out of seven, that is) within the first hour I understood why... By midnight we were gradually descending from the highlands into the plains, where we had our third flat tyre. We were all tired by then, and welcomed the opportunity to clamber out of the van, rest and gaze up at the sky. And what a sky! I suddenly realised why other people sing of stars with such fervour and delight. Never have I seen such a star-studded sky. From one horizon to the other, there was the Southern Cross, and traversing the heavens in a scattering of luminous powder on the dark velvet blanket of the sky was the Milky Way.

The second night of taxi-brousse travel was a sore one and only mitigated by the fact that one of the road stations that night sold beer. It seemed endless, and the roads deeply rutted. My aim was to reach the Nosy Be ferry at eleven the next morning but our progress was painfully slow, for we had our seventh and final breakdown at 9 o'clock, only 10 km away. We had run out of all our spare tyres and the patches for inner tubes, and these had looked like a patchwork quilt even before we started. So we waited and waited until a vehicle would drive past and give someone a lift to fetch a new inner tube... It was mid afternoon when I arrived at Antsahampano and the *vedette* for Nosy Be...

By air   There are regular flights from Tana, Majunga and Diego to Nosy Be (885 FF from Tana) and a Twin Otter from Ambanja and other nearby towns. Flights are heavily booked at weekends and during the peak holiday season.

Nosy Be today

This is very much a holiday island, and deserves its popularity if you can face all the tourists after the emptiness of the rest of Madagascar. Blessed with an almost perfect climate (sunshine with brief showers), fertile and prosperous, with sugar, pepper, and vanilla grown for export, and the heady scent of *ylang-ylang* blossoms giving it the tourist-brochure name of 'Perfumed Isle', this is the place to come for a rest – providing you can afford it. Nosy Be is now *very* expensive.

Most of the easily accessible beaches on Nosy Be have been taken over by hotels, but adventurous visitors can find completely unspoilt places. The FTM map of Nosy Be (scale 1:80,000) which is readily available in Tana is very detailed and marks beaches.

Nosy Be even has some good roads (money from sugar and tourism has helped here). Transport around the island is by taxi-be or private taxi (of which there are plenty). Taxis are much more expensive than on the mainland.

Surprisingly, no-one so far has thought of opening up a bike-hire shop. It's such an obvious need that I would expect it to happen soon. Meanwhile bicycles and mopeds are occasionally available from the bigger hotels, and make getting around much easier and more fun. And of course you can get around on foot. With the help of the map and a tent, a backpacking trip of a few days would be a great way to escape.

Lazier visitors can now hire a car from Loca Voay, run by the dynamic English-speaking former manager of the Orchidée hotel in Diego. 'Self-drive cars can be hired for about $45 including insurance, and were well worth it, giving us the chance to see in three days what would otherwise have taken a week. The roads are good and the traffic light so there is no need to have any fear of driving there.' (David Bonderman).

Where to stay
There are several beach hotels, none of which is cheap:

Andilana Beach Hotel (ex Holiday Inn). Tel: 611 76. 117 characterless rooms with air conditioning. Swimming pool, tennis, etc. 427 FF single (high season). Dinner 82 FF. Nicest location, worst architecture. Good food and everything the package tourist could desire. Madagascar Airtours has its office here.

Les Cocotiers. Tel: 612 84. Once excellent, with lovely beach bungalows and good food but recent reports are that you'd better be Italian or an independent (wealthy) traveller to be sure of a booking here. About 250 FF full board.

Hotel Palm Beach. Accommodation ranges from rooms to beach bungalows and 'bungalow apartments'. Casino. Swimming pool. Beach not as nice as Cocotiers. From 213 FF to 243 double, per person, half board, high season.

Résidence Ambatoloaka. Tel: 61-368. Popular, but expensive at 238 FF per head (double, per person, half board, high season). Dinner 62 FF. This is one of the best swimming beaches.

A bit further down the beach is the Hotel de la Plage, with corrugated iron huts for 5,000 FMG, and masses of good food. Private houses in the village will also put up visitors for around 10,000 FMG.

Also in the area is the highly acclaimed restaurant Chez Angeline which does a superb set meal of sea food for 10,000 FMG. Universally recommended. If you want a cheaper meal there is a restaurant at the other end of the village that is apparently called Tonga Soa Horr Horr (since the first two words mean 'welcome' perhaps it is just the Horr Horr). Lobster, coconut icecream, and wonderful fruit juices.

Hell-Ville (Andoany)

The name comes from Admiral de Hell rather than an evocation of the state of the town. Hell-Ville is quite a smart little place, its main street lined with boutiques and tourist shops. There is a market selling fresh fruit and vegetables (which may also be purchased from roadside stalls), and an interesting cemetery neatly arranged according to nationality.

You can stay in Hell-Ville, but of course the hotels are nowhere near as nice as the ones on the beach, and are all overpriced:

Hotel de la Mer, Boulevard du Docteur Manceau. Tel: 61-353. The only middle-range hotel in town. Rooms vary from very nice with a view of the sea, to squalid (an alternative name is Hotel de la Merde). There's a superb view from the restaurant.

The remaining hotels in town are fairly awful. You have a choice of Hotel 'Trans 7 stop' at the far side of town (away from the harbour, 6 rooms), the Hotel Venus (4 rooms) and the Saloon Hotel.

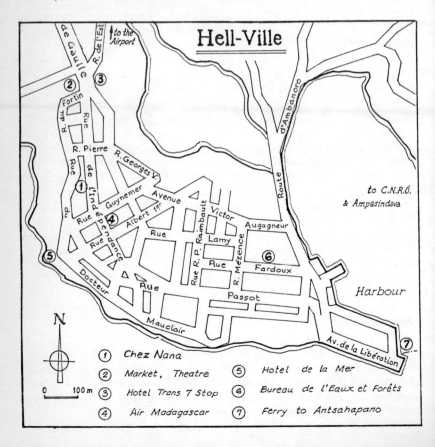

① Chez Nana
② Market, Theatre
③ Hotel Trans 7 Stop
④ Air Madagascar
⑤ Hotel de la Mer
⑥ Bureau de l'Eaux et Forêts
⑦ Ferry to Antsahapano

Although the best restaurants are at the beach hotels and Chez Angeline, there are one or two good places on the main street of Hell-Ville and one that reader David Bonderman considers the best food he ate in Madagascar: 'Chez Nana is at the far end of the main street in Hell-Ville. There are six or eight tables and Nana is a tremendous cook... Dinner with wine was about 10,000 FMG per person.'

Another possibility is the Restaurant Express, a popular meeting place for travellers. To eat really well, order your meal a day in advance. Chez Looky, opposite the cinema on Bvd General de Gaulle, is more modest.

If you are taking the ferry back to Antsahampano, check the board outside the ferry office (A.M.Hassanaly et fils) a few doors up from Air Madagascar.

Excursions

Mont Passot

The highest point of the island (315 m), affording marvellous views of a series of deep-blue crater lakes. These are said to contain crocodiles (though I have never seen one in half a dozen visits) and to be sacred as the home of the spirits of the Sakalava and Antakarana princes. It is *fady* to fish there, or to smoke, wear trousers or any garment put on over the feet, or a hat, while on the lakes' shores. It is, in any case, difficult to get down to the water since the crater sides are very steep.

The best road to Mont Passot runs from near the Andilana Beach Hotel, but the more adventurous can try walking (10 km) up the track from Djamandjary, the island's second biggest town. (Note: much has been made in some tourist literature of the 'unusual houses' at Djamandjary. You are led to believe that these are some quaint ethnic curiosity. The ugly cement igloos were, in fact, part of a foreign aid project following devastation from a cyclone. They offer no wind resistance, so do not blow down easily.) Most people come to Mont Passot to see the sunset so you may be fortunate enough to get a lift down, but you risk walking back in the dark. In any case, in the clear air of Nosy Be the sunset is generally less than spectacular, so if you are on foot make a day excursion of it and take a picnic.

Ampasindava

From Hell-Ville a road runs from the north end of the quay, hugging the north-east shoreline to the village of Ampasindava, 7 km away, where it abruptly ends – at a beautiful sandy beach, ideal for picnics and swimming or for camping (not on the beach which is almost covered at high tide, but nearby, after asking permission). There is fresh water, large shady rocks, and nothing else.

The walk there, (or taxi, if you prefer) is varied and interesting. Just outside Hell-Ville you pass some mangrove swamps. Stop and look at the mud-skippers – fish that are as at home outside the water as in it! The bulbous cheeks hold water which is washed over the gills allowing it to breathe. The mud-skippers pectoral fins are formed into a sucker for clinging onto the stems of mangroves.

After 5 km of winding tree-lined road (where I found three chameleons) you arrive at the Centre National de Recherches Océanographique on the right. This beautifully located Research Institute has a small museum. There is a good collection of shells and coral, although perhaps really only of interest to marine biologists since most of the fishy specimens are in bottles and the famous Coelacanth is now at the museum in Tsimbazaza in Tana.

A few kilometres further on you come to the remains of an early Indian settlement and graveyard. The buildings are completely in ruins, the 30 cm thick sand and coral wall in the grip of strangler figs, and flame trees thrust up through the once fine architecture. The story of the builders having been shipwrecked Indian sailors is only hearsay: one wonders if sailors would be such competent architects. It is a mysterious and beautiful place, providing a refreshing symbol (for Madagascar) of the power of nature over the work of man.

Finally, before you get to Ampasindava, you will pass the edge of the reserve of Lokobe. (To visit this you should have a permit – sometimes available from Eaux et Forêts in Hell-Ville.) A path runs up the steep hillside, and you have a good chance of seeing black lemurs (*Lemur macaco*) and other creatures. Even without going into the forest you may have exciting encounters – I saw two large snakes beside the road.

Traditional village and sacred lemurs

Another way to visit Lokobe is with Jean-Robert who works for Madagascar Airtours, speaks English, and charges 40,000 FMG to visit his village. Dick Byrne has sent the following description which I endorse, having also done the trip and greatly enjoyed it. The letters I have received since the last edition of this book have been unanimous in their praise.

First a bus takes you to the village of Ambatozavavy, amongst mangroves in a shallow bay. Then you start to *earn* your pleasure: paddling elegant outrigger dugouts along the coast! It's great fun, and actually if you get tired you don't have to paddle, it's just quicker. This gets you to Ampasipohy, Jean-Robert's home, a small traditional village. He explains the *fady*, the local crops, the produce villagers get from the forest, and so on. They grow ylang-ylang (which is used for perfume-making) and vanilla. He's also a dab-hand at finding the local species of lepilemur (*Lepilemur dorsalis*), which unlike other lepilemurs spends the day in thick bushes not in holes; they have tiny ears, a rusty coat and very big, round heads and huge eyes.

We saw it. We also saw a hefty boa constrictor, thanks to the villagers who all keep a close watch for wildlife to show visitors when Jean-Robert runs a tour (he'll award their diligence from the profits, so it's a great way to channel money to village level without profiteering middlemen, *and* helps boas to stay away from handbags). Back to the canoes, but on the way back you'll stop at an ancient royal burial ground, so sacred that you have to walk barefoot, and search for black lemurs. They're not fed as on Nosy Komba, so are more shy, but good views are nearly guaranteed all the same. A great day out, and lunch is well-cooked traditional Malagasy food, eaten under the palms at the top of the beach.

Jean-Robert will take any number of people from two up, but too many would tend to reduce the enjoyment. He can be contacted through your hotel.

Nosy Komba (Nosy Ambariovato)

A 'must' for most visitors to Nosy Be, but less popular with budget travellers who dislike the air of commercialism that has inevitably spread to this island paradise. Certainly Nosy Komba has changed since we first hitched a lift there with a missionary in 1976, to find nothing but sand, sea, shells, and lemurs. We didn't even see the village! But those days have passed and I would recommend that you go as a Tourist and pay the villagers for taking their photos, buy vanilla, clay animals and hand-carved model outrigger canoes, eat magnificently, feed the lemurs and be photographed with them all over you, and swim and snorkel, and your 'but I'm a traveller not a tourist' scruples be damned!

Tours to Nosy Komba are arranged through the various hotels (though this can be difficult in the off-season). 1990 prices are 29,000 FMG to 35,000 FMG, with an extra 10,000 FMG for a picnic (lavish). A solo traveller would need to join a group. Determinedly independent travellers can usually find a pirogue for about 5,000 FMG (late afternoon is the best time) and can stay on the island. All accommodation is simple, from the delightfully relaxing Hotel Lemuriens (German-Malagasy run, on the main beach, 7,000 FMG, eat with the family) to the Hotel Madio with its ebullient pet vasa parrot (huts 3,500 FMG). If these are both full you will probably be able to stay in a private house.

Nosy Komba's main attraction is undoubtedly the black lemurs (actually, only the males are black, the females are chestnut brown with white eartufts). To visit them you must pay a small entrance fee. These lemurs have always been fearless, being held sacred by the villagers so unmolested, but with the advent of tourists bearing bananas they have become very assertive. Lemurs always seem to possess beautiful manners and even assertive lemurs don't snatch and bite; they just reach out their black-gloved hands for the treat, and ten or so hands – while the owners are sitting on your shoulders and sliding off your head over your eyes – means you are divested of your bananas pretty quickly. So cameras at the ready!

Black lemurs mate in April and give birth to one baby in September.
When you are done with the lemurs and shopping for souvenirs in
the village, the swimming is excellent. The best snorkelling is around
the rocky promontory which juts into the sea. The water is not as clear
as Nosy Tanikely, but there is usually plenty to see. Beware of
sunburn!

Nosy Tanikely

To me this is as close to paradise as you can get. At the time of writing
Nosy Tanikely is a tiny island inhabited only by the lighthouse keeper
and his family (who offers rooms to anyone bringing their own food
and bedding), unspoiled by any of the trappings of tourism. It is
unrealistic to hope that this state of affairs can last, but I do... The
island is a marine reserve and it is for the snorkelling that most people
visit it. And the snorkelling is stupendous. In crystal clear water you
can see an amazing variety of marine life – coral, starfish, anemones,
every colour and shape of fish, turtles, lobsters... It is totally mind
boggling. The underwater world is always astonishing; perhaps because we see less of it on television than other natural wonders, or
perhaps that there is just so *much* there, so much variety, so much
colour, so much weirdness. The Mad Airtours brochure has got it right
when it says 'If you are eager for unreal surprises and pleasant
emotions, make up your mind now and discover our new world ...'

With this new world beneath your gaze there is a real danger of
forgetting the passing of time and becoming seriously sunburnt. Even
the most carefully applied sunblock tends to miss some areas, so wear
a tee-shirt and shorts.

Don't think you have finished with Nosy Tanikely when you come
out of the water; at low tide it is possible to walk right round the island.
During your circumambulation you will see (if you go anticlockwise): a
broad beach of white sand covered in shells and bleached pieces of
coral, a couple of trees full of flying foxes (*Pteropus rufus*), and
graceful white tropic birds (*Phaethon lepturus lepturus*) flying in and
out of their nests in the high cliffs. At your feet will be rock pools and
some scrambling, but nothing too challenging.

Then there is the climb up to the top of the island for the view and
perhaps a tour (tip expected) of the antique and beautifully maintained
lighthouse.

Most hotels arrange trips to Nosy Tanikely. The cost is the same as
Nosy Komba (and you should definitely include the picnic).

Further away are two more islands, seldom visited, and reportedly
even lovelier: Nosy Mitsio (60 km north-west – an uninhabited
archipelago) and Nosy Iranja (60 km south-west – a turtle nesting
reserve). Both islands are reached in four hours by fast boat. The cost
(in 1990) is 110,000 FMG for two days and a night (camping) on Nosy
Iranja, and 120,000 FMG for Nosy Mitsio.

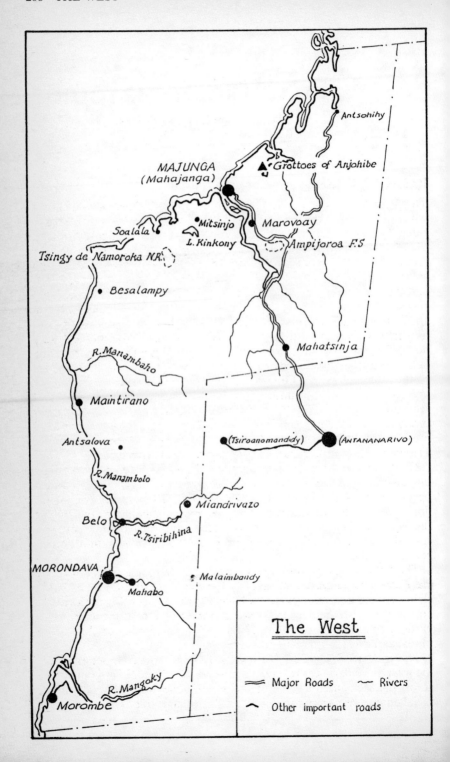

MAJUNGA
(Mahajanga)

Antsohihy

Grottoes of Anjohibe

Mitsinjo

Marovoay

Soalala

L. Kinkony

Ampijoroa F.S

Tsingy de Namoroka N.R.

Besalampy

R. Manambaho

Mahatsinja

Maintirano

Antsalova

(Tsiroanomandidy)

(ANTANANARIVO)

R. Manambolo

Miandrivazo

Belo

R. Tsiribihina

MORONDAVA

Malaimbandy

Mahabo

R. Mangoky

Morombe

The West

═══ Major Roads   ⌒ Rivers

⌒ Other important roads

207

Chapter 11

The West

INTRODUCTION

The west of Madagascar is the home of the Sakalava people. For a while in Malagasy history this was the largest and most powerful tribe, ruled by their own kings and queens. The Sakalava originate from the Menabe, the first kingdom in Madagascar, which began in the sixteenth century in the south east of the country and spread to the south west. The kingdom became progressively stronger and by the end of the century, under the rulership of King Andriamandresy, had reached the Sakalava river. Thus the Menabe became the Sakalava. In 1610 a new king, Andriandahifotsy, became the first Malagasy ruler to use firearms, acquired from traders working the Mozambique Channel. With this new battle weapon conquest became easier, and the Sakalava pushed northward until they occupied the whole western part of the island, from the Onilahy river to the Manambolo river. The unification of the tribe under one king did not last, however, and Andriandahifotsy's three sons divided up the kingdom and started their own expansion. The Boina, a new kingdom in the north (around present day Majunga), was the most successful, and under its king, Tsitavana, the northern part of Madagascar was conquered.

By the end of the eighteenth century, the Sakalava empire was huge but divided into the Menabe in the south-west and the Boina which occupied all of the north. The two rulers fell out, unity was abandoned, and in the nineteenth century the area came under the rule of the Merina. The Sakalava did not take kindly to domination and sporadic guerrilla warfare continued in the Menabe area until French colonial times.

The Sakalava kingdom bore the brunt of the first serious efforts by the French to colonise the island. For some years France had laid claims (based on treaties made with local princes) on parts of the north and north west, and in 1883 two north west fortresses were bombarded, followed by Majunga. This was the beginning of the end of Madagascar as an independent kingdom.

The modern Sakalava have relatively dark skins. Understandably the west of Madagascar received a number of African immigrants from across the Mozambique Channel. Their influence shows not only in the racial characteristics of the people of this region, but in their language and customs. There are a number of Bantu words in their dialect, and their belief in *tromba* (possession by spirits) and *dady* (royal relics cult) are of African origin.

The Sakalava do not practise second burial. The quality of their funerary art (in one small area) rivals that of the Mahafaly: birds and naked figures are a feature of Sakalava tombs, the latter frequently in erotic positions. Concepts of sexuality and rebirth are implied here. The female figures are often disproportionately large, perhaps recognising the importance of women in the Sakalava culture.

Sakalava royalty does not require an elaborate tomb, since kings are considered to continue their spiritual existence through a medium, who have the power to heal, and in royal relics. These relics are ritually washed in September every ten years.

The west offers a dry climate, deciduous vegetation, endless sandy beaches with little danger from sharks – although the sea can be very rough – and fewer other visitors than most parts of the country. Adventurous travellers will have no trouble finding their own deserted beach and some spectacular landscapes. And sun.

Opposite major rivers, the seawater along the west coast is a brick red colour: 'like swimming in soup', as one traveller puts it. This is the laterite washed into the rivers from the eroded hillsides of the highlands and discharged into the sea; Madagascar's bleeding wounds.

Getting around

Going from town to town in the west is even harder than in the east: in much of the area the roads simply aren't there (apart from the Tana to Majunga road, and the new, very good, road to Morondava) so unless you find a pirogue, flying is necessary. However, a Twin Otter serves the smaller towns of Soalala, Tambohorano, Maintirano, Belo, and Morondava. The Twin Otter sometimes stops at other small western towns from Majunga – Morafenobe and Ambatomainty.

MAJUNGA (MAHAJANGA)
History

Majunga has always been a cosmopolitan city. Ideally located for trade with east Africa, Arabia and western Asia, it has been a major commercial port since the eighteenth century, when the Boina capital was moved here from Marovoay. Majunga was founded in 1745. One ruler of the Boina was Queen Ravahiny, a very able monarch who maintained the unity of the Boina which was threatened by rebellions in both the north and south. It was Majunga which provided her with her imported riches and caught the admiration of visiting foreigners. Madagascar was at that time a major supplier of slaves to Arab traders and in return received jewels and rich fabrics. Indian merchants were active then, as today, with a variety of exotic goods. Some of these traders from the east stayed on, the Indians remaining a separate community and running small businesses. More Indians arrived during colonial times.

In the 1883-85 war Majunga was occupied by the French. In 1895 it served as the base for the military expedition to Antananarivo which established a French Protectorate. Shortly thereafter the French set about enlarging Majunga and reclaiming swamp-land from the Bombetoka river delta. Much of today's extensive town is on reclaimed land.

Getting there and back
Majunga is 560 kilometres from Tana by fairly good road or by plane.

Road I took the Air Route Service minibus which was remarkably comfortable, and runs daily (about 14,000 FMG). It leaves mid afternoon from Behoririka (the area beyond and to the right of the station) on Ar Rainizanabololona near Giraud Vinet (the glass factory – most taxi drivers know it). Seats can be booked in advance.

There are also regular taxi-brousses which leave at 9.00, giving you more time to see the scenery, take about 13 hours and cost around 13,000 FMG.

It's a lovely trip (at least until it gets dark) taking you through typical *Hauts Plateaux* landscape of craggy, grassy hills, rice paddies, and characteristic Merina houses with steep eaves supported by thin brick or wood pillars.

The taxi-brousse station in Majunga is on Ave Philbert Tsiranana. Most leave around 7.00.

Plane There is a twice weekly service (Tuesdays and Thursdays in 1990) from Tana to Majunga (which goes on to Nosy Be so is likely to be crowded) 550 FF; flights on other days by Twin Otter.

A taxi from the airport into town should be 3,000 FMG. A bus also passes the airport every half hour or so.

Boat to Nosy Be If you're determined to go to Nosy Be the uncomfortable (but undoubtedly adventurous) way, there are occasional cargo boats from Majunga. The shipping office is at Armement Tawakal, near the Sampan d'Or restaurant. Boats take 48 hours and cost around 15,000 FMG.

Majunga today
A hot but breezy town with a large Indian population and enough interesting excursions, high quality beach bungalows and sun to make a visit of a few days well worthwhile. Besides, you can eat one of the best meals in Madagascar here (Chez Chabaud)!

The town has two 'centres', the town hall (Hotel de Ville) and statue of Tsiranana (the commercial centre), and the baobab tree on the seafront boulevard (some offices, including Air Madagascar are near here). It is quite a long walk between the two – take a pousse-pousse, of which there are many. There are also some smart new buses, and taxis which operate on a fixed tariff of 500 FMG.

A wide boulevard follows the sea along the west part of town, terminating at a lighthouse. Along this boulevard is the famous Majunga baobab, said to be at least 700 of years old with a circumference of 14 metres.

Where to stay
Category A
Zaha Motel (tel: 23 24). At Amborovy beach (not far from the airport, and 8 km from Majunga). Beach bungalows, 30,000 FMG. Excellent swimming and all tourist amenities.

Village Touristique. On a long windy stretch of beach. Always seems to be deserted. About 17,000 FMG with shower and WC.

Hotel de France, Rue Maréchal Joffre. About 20,000 FMG. Shower and WC. in all rooms plus air conditioning.

Category B
Nouvel Hotel. 13, Rue Henri Palu (one block up from sea front), about 13,000 FMG. Its prices put it in the B category but the Nouvel seems the best hotel in town. Clean, attractive, with air conditioning and mosquito nets. 16 rooms.

Kanto Hotel. The best hotel out of the town and excellent value at around 10,000 FMG for cabins (only 4) set on a hill overlooking the sea about 1 km north of the town. Good open air restaurant and bar. A good place to relax in comfort for a few days.

Hotel Restaurant Bombetoka. Along the seafront 1½ km from town. Bungalows 10,000 FMG, poor value but good restaurant.

Category C
Hotel Continental, Rue de la République. Central, but grotty. Shower, fan.

Yaar Hotel. (Near Nouvel) about 7,000 FMG. Shower and bidet in each room but no mosquito nets or screen.

Hotel Boina, Rue Flacourt. Around 6,000 FMG. 12 rooms. Pleasant, screened, good value.

Chez Chabaud (see Katsepy). Mme Chabaud's daughter runs a simple hotel in Majunga (5,000 FMG) and is a marvellous cook. The hotel is near the Hotel de Ville.

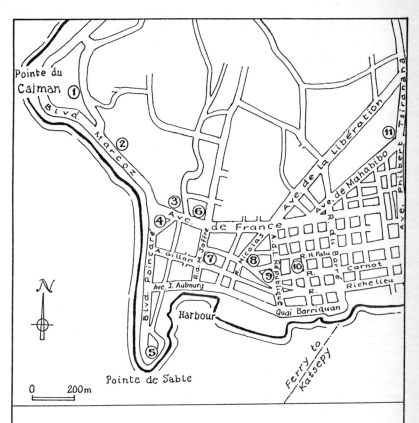

Majunga (Mahajanga)

① Hôtel Kanto   ② Hôtel/Restaurant Bombetoka

③ Air Madagascar   ④ Baobab   ⑤ Lighthouse

⑥ Hôtel Boina   ⑦ Hotel de France   ⑧ Restaurant Sampon d'Or

⑨ Hôtel Continental ⑩ Yaar Hôtel   ⑪ Hôtel de Ville (Town Hall)

Where to eat

Good food in the seafront restaurants of Bombetoka and Kanto, and Chez Chabaud.

Hotel-Restaurant de la Plage (Chez Karon) in the Village Touristique supposedly serves good food. Closed Mondays.

Le Sampan d'Or. Near the Hotel Continental. Chinese.

Restaurant Vietnamese. Near the Hotel de France.

Restaurant Chez Thi-San, Rue Marechal Joffre.

There are several Indian restaurants serving 'carry' (curry) and Samosas (sometimes called Sambos); usually good value.

The Salon de Thé Baba opposite Hotel Continental serves excellent snacks and breakfast (try their pain au chocolat). Also recommended are the Kismet and Kohinoor snackbars near the port: excellent icecream.

Night Club

Le Ravinala. Near the quay. Lively.

Excursions from Majunga

Cirque Rouge

12 km from Majunga and about 2 km from the airport (as the crow flies) is a canyon ending in an amphitheatre of red, beige and lilac coloured rock eroded into strange shapes – peaks, spires, and castles. The canyon has a broad, sandy bottom decorated with chunks of lilac-coloured clay. It is a beautiful and dramatic spot and, with its stream of fresh water running to the nearby beach, makes an idyllic camping place for a few days (but be careful of swimming in the sea – there's a danger of sharks).

The area, a few kilometres north of the Zaha Motel, is popular with Majungans who have holiday beach bungalows there, so if you decide to camp you can probably hitch a ride back to town, particularly at weekends. Bring your own food.

As a day trip a taxi will take you from Majunga and back for around 14,000 FMG. Give yourself at least one hour to look around. Late afternoon is best, when the sun sets the reds and mauves alight.

Katsepy

No visit to Majunga is complete without a meal chez Madame Chabaud. She runs a small beach hotel at Katsepy, a tiny unspoiled fishing village across the bay from Majunga, and also a restaurant of the same name near the Hotel de Ville in Majunga. Trained as a cook in France (Nice) she returned to her home town to practise her art for weekend visitors and the occasional tourist.

Katsepy is an hour's journey by ferry (leaves at 7.30 and 3.30 – but check at the quay as these times are flexible) and costs 200 FMG. The sign on the quay confusingly calls Katsepy 'Avotra'. There is sometimes a noontime boat on Sundays. Be prepared for a 'wet landing' if you arrive at low tide.

On arrival there are rows of stalls selling basic food and coconut milk if you don't want to splash out at the restaurant. Chez Chabaud is signposted. There are ten rather basic bungalows, although mosquito nets are now provided, costing about 7,000 FMG, and three vast meals a day (breakfast 600 FMG, lunch and dinner 3,500 FMG, and a special Sunday lunch for 5,000 FMG). There is one large self-catering bungalow for families or small groups and even a fully equipped tree-house!

In between eating you can lounge or walk on the miles of deserted beach (and perhaps accept an invitation to visit a fishing community), watch mud-hoppers (tree-climbing fish!) skipping around the mangroves, and swim in the murky-red sea.

Except at weekends, it is best to make a reservation in advance (not because Katsepy will be crowded, but Mme Chabaud may not be there) through Chez Chabaud in Majunga (near the Hotel de Ville). 'Food brill, everything excellent – wow!' (Petra Jenkins).

Majunga (Mahajanga) -Area

— Road
—·— Track
— — Poor Track
(MAY BE IMPASSABLE IN THE RAINY SEASON)
····· Footpath

0   5 km

Onward to Mitsinjo

Taxi-brousses sometimes meet the ferry for the onward journey to Mitsinjo (and vehicles taking the ferry are almost certainly bound for that town). The journey takes about 4 hours and costs around 3,500 FMG.

'Mitsinjo is a lovely town with a wide main street, trees with semi-tame sifakas, a general store that has a few rooms available, and Hotely Salana which serves wonderful food and even has a fridge so cold beer! You order your meal in advance, and get a real feast.' (Petra Jenkins).

Not far from Mitsinjo is lake Kinkony (a protected area). Petra reports: 'About once a week in the dry season the fishermen of Lac Kinkony do a supply run to Mitsinjo and you may be able to get a lift. The lake is wonderful. It boasts fish eagles, flamingoes, sacred ibis … need I say more? It is free from bilharzia but the north-east end is a bit silty for swimming. Cadge a lift by pirogue and you've got paradise! Crocodiles are friendly and don't bother swimmers (!).'

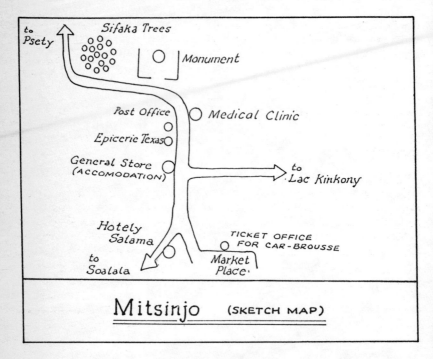

Mitsinjo (SKETCH MAP)

From Mitsinjo you may be able to make your way to Soalala, from where there is an air service (and the possibility of visiting the nature reserve of Tsingy de Namoroka) or you can go on to Besalampy (which is also served by Air Madagascar). Then you can continue to make your way down the coast, taking cars, *pirogues* or whatever transport presents itself. This route is only practical in the dry season and for rugged and self-sufficient travellers. You can fly out of Maintirano, Antsalova, or Belo sur Tsiribihina. Good luck!

Grottoes of Anjohibe

85 km north of Majunga, mostly along a barely motorable track and not checked out personally, these caves are said to be some of the most spectacular in Madagascar. There is a central vault with stalagmites and stalactites, and several grottoes opening off it.

Marovoay

Formerly the residence of the Boina kings, the town's name means 'many crocodiles'. When the French attacked the Malagasy forces assembled in Marovoay in 1895, in their successful drive to conquer Madagascar, it is reported that hundreds of crocodiles emerged from the river to devour the dead and dying. Malagasy hunters have since got their revenge, and you would be lucky to see a croc these days.

Marovoay is accessible by road (72 km) or river from Majunga (pirogue or barge). Reportedly a very enjoyable river trip (but don't take my word for it – I haven't done it and have no idea how long it takes!) through the numerous channels of the Betsiboka estuary, past a variety of scenery. Probably the most sensible course is to take a taxi-brousse to Marovoay and enquire about river transport there. At least, then, you would be taking advantage of the current and the natural friendliness of a small, and seldom-visited town.

SOUTH OF MAJUNGA

The Forestry Station of Ampijoroa

This is part of the Réserve Naturelle Intégrale d'Ankarafantsika. Ampijoroa (pronounced Ampijeroo) is the only protected example of western vegetation and its accompanying fauna easily accessible to visitors. I recommend it highly. The warden, M. Rabemazava, is hard-working and helpful, and for some years Don Reid, a British herpetologist attached to the WWF and Jersey Wildlife Preservation Trust, has been working on a project to breed the highly endangered plowshare tortoise, or Angonoka (*Geochelone yniphora*), at Ampijoroa. The Angonoka is the rarest tortoise in the world, so the first successful egg hatching in 1989 was cause for jubilation. Don described how much research was necessary to ensure that conditions were ideal for mating: foreplay, for instance, involves the male turning the female on her back, and then thoughtfully nudging her the right side up again. Four to five eggs are laid which remain in the ground from 90 to 230 days – a very variable and long period which is dependent on the rainfall to soften the soil sufficiently for the hatchlings to dig their way out. There were also human problems: the

Malagasy bricklayer from the south, contracted to built an enclosure, could not carry out the job because tortoises are *fady* in his part of the island.

Ampijoroa lies about 90 km south of Majunga, to the west of the main road and the nature reserve of Andranofasika, shortly before (if coming from Majunga) the small town of the same name. I got there with Air Route Services from Tana (which dumped me at the gate to the reserve at 2.30 a.m. I crept off into the forest and had a not-at-all-bad night in my sheet sleeping bag and *Zoma* blanket, waking to the sight of a flock of flamingoes silhouetted against the pink dawn sky); a taxi-brousse from Majunga might have been better, although I had no trouble hitching a lift in a private car into Majunga.

Wildlife viewing in Ampijoroa is easy and thrilling. Right beside the warden's house is a tree that Coquerel's sifaka, *Propithecus verreauxi coquereli*, use as a dormitory. They are extremely handsome animals with the usual silky white fur but with chestnut-brown arms and thighs. I watched them for about an hour while they slowly woke up, stretched languidly, then spread their arms to take in the warming rays of the morning sun before starting their breakfast of leaves. Other lemurs to be seen in the forest are brown lemurs, *Lemur fulvus fulvus*, *Lemur mongoz* (if you're very lucky), and *Lepilemur edwardsi* if the warden shows you its tree. I went on a nocturnal search for mouse lemurs (*Microcebus murinus*) but our torches failed to pick out the tell-tale red eyes.

The forest has some good paths and the warden may be able to guide you on an initial orientation tour. Thereafter you are free to wander happily on your own.

At the time of writing there is no accommodation and you must bring your own tent and food. However, bungalows and a restaurant are being built, and Ampijoroa looks destined to join Berenty as one the standard stops for wildlife tours.

Maintirano

This small western port is attractive for people who want to get off the beaten track. Nothing much happens here, but there is a pleasant though basic hotel and a restaurant which turns out excellent food in a primitive kitchen – until the owner gets bored with you! Oenone Hammersley reports: 'The first hotel we went to (Fantara) resembled a cross between army headquarters and a prison. We thought we'd arrived in Colditz – no windows, a cement floor... We moved to a very friendly and clean place, the Laizama Hotel, which overlooks the sea. There were mosquito nets and lots of geckos in the room – both necessary to keep out the prolific insect life. The best restaurant is on the outskirts of town on the airport road – its name is Buvette et Repas Mahateatea and it looks like a garage. Eating there was always a surprise and a pleasure (we booked our meals in advance). Once we were served crab with prawn sauce, and crab salad.

'We spent much of our time sunbathing and swimming in the blood-red sea (it took us a while to find the way to the beach – across a causeway between two lagoons). It's a huge beach with pristine white sand. When not on the beach or eating, we wandered around looking at the big market (lots of fish) and the many Indian shops, all of which seemed to sell the same thing: fabrics and food.'

Maintirano is one of the places served by Air Madagascar (Twin Otter) on its Tana – Majunga run.

MORONDAVA

The Morondava area was the centre of the Sakalava kingdom. Today it is most often visited for the few remaining Sakalava tombs and for the unspoilt beaches with their small fishing communities, magnificent avenues of baobabs, and months of sunshine (it can be very hot). Until the construction of the new road few visitors came here, but this is changing and Morondava is included in many itineraries.

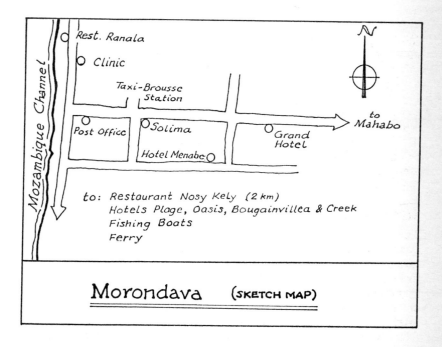

Morondava (SKETCH MAP)

'The town is by a huge beach, only a small part of which is used as a public lavatory. There are some excellent beaches further away and accessible only by pirogue.' (Robert Howie). It's not bad for swimming, the sea is red-coloured as always on the west coast, but it shelves reasonably steeply so you're not wading for miles as so often happens.

Getting there and back

By Road   Morondava is 700 km from Tana served by a very good road. There are regular taxi-brousses which take about 14 hours and cost around 14,000 FMG. The adventurous might like get off at Miandrivazo and continue their journey by river.

By boat   Apart from river possibilities, described in more detail under Miandrivazo, there are supply boats and pirogues plying the coast. You may find one going south to Tuléar. Worth a try.

By air   There is a service from Tana or Tuléar to Morondava on Wednesdays and Saturdays.

Where to stay

Bougainvillea (run by Mme Nelly Dublois). Beach houses, so exposed to a cool breeze, for 18,000 FMG (double) and rooms for rather less.

The Oasis. Another beach hotel, similar to the Bougainvillea but with air-conditioning.

Hotel Menabe. 7,500 FMG to 12,000 FMG. 22 rooms. New, very good value, with private bathroom, hot water, fan, table, chair, etc.

Grand Hotel. 3,500 FMG. Not very grand. Cold showers, but pleasant setting with balcony overlooking main street. Cockroach rating 7/10.

Hotel de la Plage. Beach hotel, 7 rooms, each with basin and communal WC, 4,000 FMG, including good breakfast. Pleasant and clean. Run by Moslems so no alcohol. Indian food (set menu).

Kismat. Basic and clean, but rather noisy. 5,000 FMG.

Where to eat

Renala. On the seafront and serving the best seafood in town.

Nosy Kely. Next to the Bougainvillea, Italian owned, excellent.

Carré d'As (popularly known as Curried Arse, and part of the Village Touristique). Excellent Malagasy food, steak and chips and other goodies. Darts and disco!

The Ebony and the Ivory. English run, specialises in fish or steak.

Excursions

Take the road to **Belo sur Tsiribihina** to see the magnificent avenue of baobabs. The name of the town means 'where one must not dive', supposedly because of the crocodiles. The warning still holds true –

Jane Wilson reports that a woman doing her washing was eaten by a croc in 1986.

Vezo-Sakalava funerary sculpture

The often erotic, carved wooden sculptures of the Vezo people (Sakalava, but with a specialised interest in shore fishing) are not easy to see, and sadly have been desecrated by souvenir hunters. You will need a guide. John R. Jones recommends Nandrasana Farezy, who is found at the Centre Forestier, B.P. 117, Morondava; tel: 520-96. Your hotel manager may have other suggestions.

Analabe reserve

This is another private nature reserve owned by M. Jean de Heaulme. In 1990 it was still not open to tourists, but the plan is to bring it to the level of Berenty, with the area divided into three parcels: scientific study, tourism, and reserve. A hotel is currently being built. No doubt when it opens it will be well advertised.

The reserve lies 60 km north of Morondava, by the de Heaulme sisal plantations near the village of Beroboka Sud. It contains some mangrove areas as well as marshes and lakes typical of coastal plain. Most of the animals, including lemur species, seen at Berenty may be seen here, although they are not yet habituated. The latest WWF report says that the reserve is not protected from fire and charcoal-burners, and some captive lemurs are languishing in poor conditions.

Miandrivazo

Described by Raniero Leto, who spent some time in the south-west, as the hottest place in Madagascar, with an average temperature of 28°C. The town lies on the banks of the Mahajilo, a tributary of the Tsirihina, and is an important centre for tobacco. 'The name comes from when Radama was waiting for his messenger to return with Rasalimo, the Sakalava princess of Malaimbandy with whom he had fallen in love. He fell into a pensive mood and when asked if he was well replied "Miandry vazo aho" – I am waiting for a wife.'

There is a basic hotel and a restaurant, and you can arrange to be taken down river to Belo sur Tsiribihina (a two day trip) by boat. Raniero bought his own boat, and describes the trip here:

The advantage of a river trip are numerous. It is relaxing, as long as you're going downstream, but strenuous enough that at the end of the day you feel you've done something. But the greatest advantage is that it is more or less silent – we managed to drift very close to several troops of lemurs that were drinking.

We bought a small but water-tight pirogue at Miandrivazo for 60,000 FMG (1987), with the help of the local police. We added a balancer similar to the ocean-going pirogues which cost another 1000 FMG. The pirogue was made from heavy wood, so with the three of us and our packs there was only about 6 inches above the water line. The journey took six days, though much of the time was spent looking for food, which was hard to find. There were also strong winds in the late afternoon which produced quite big waves.

We didn't see any crocodiles, but we did see plenty of wildlife including lemurs, chameleons, eagles and a multitude of others. For three days, while passing through the Bemaraha mountains, we saw no trace of humans. The trip was the highlight of our stay and yet also the cheapest part.

SOME MALAGASY PROVERBS

Tantely tapa-bata ka ny foko no entiko mameno azy.
This is only half a pot of honey but my heart fills it up (used when a gift is deemed inadequate).

Aza manontany basy amin' ny Angilisy.
Don't talk to the English about guns. (Don't bring coals to Newcastle.)

Mahavoa roa toy ny dakam-boriky.
Hit two things at once like the kick of a donkey. (Kill two birds with one stone.)

Hazo tokana tsy mba ala.
One tree does not make a forest.

Mividy omby anaty ambiaty.
Buy an ox in the bush (a pig in a poke).

Tsy midera vady tsy herintaona.
Don't praise your wife before a year. (Don't count your chickens before they're hatched.)

Ny omby singorana amin' ny tandrony, ary ny olona kosa amin' ny vavany.
Oxen are trapped by their horns and men by their words.

Lavitry ny maso, lavitry ny fo.
Out of sight, out of mind.

Tondro tokana tsy mahazo hao.
You can't catch a louse with one finger (i.e. co-operate).

Ny alina mitondra fisainana.
The night brings wisdom (I'll sleep on it).

Appendices

HISTORICAL CHRONOLOGY
Adapted from 'Madagascar, Island of the Ancestors' with kind permission of the author, John Mack.

AD 500 | Approximate date for the first significant settlement of the island.

800-900 | Dates of the first identifiable village sites in the north of the island. Penetration of the interior begins in the south.

1200 | Establishment of Arab settlements. First mosques built.

1500 | 'Discovery of Madagascar by the Portuguese Diego Dias. Unsuccessful attempts to establish permanent European bases on the island followed.

1650s | Emergence of Sakalava kingdoms.

Early 1700s | Eastern Madagascar is increasingly used as a base by pirates.

1716 | Fénérive captured by Ratsimilaho. The beginnings of the Betsimisaraka confederacy.

1750 | Death of Ratsimilaho.

1780 | The future Andrianampoinimerina declared king of Ambohimanga.

1795/6 | Andrianampoinimerina established his capital at Antananarivo.

1810-28 | Reign of Radama I, Merina king.

1818 | First mission school opened at Antananarivo.

1820 | First mission school opened at Tamatave.

1828-61 | Reign of Ranavalona I, Merina queen.

1835	Publication of the bible in Malagasy, but profession of the Christian faith declared illegal.
1836	Most Europeans and missionaries leave the island.
1861-1863	Reign of Radama II, Merina king.
1861	Missionaries re-admitted. Freedom of religion proclaimed.
1863-8	Queen Rasoherina succeeds after Radama II assassinated.
1868-83	Reign of Queen Ranavalona II.
1883	Coronation of Queen Ranavalona III.
1895	Establishment of full French protectorate; Madagascar became a full colony the following year.
1897	Ranavalona III exiled first to Réunion and later Algiers. Merina monarchy abolished.
1917	Death of Ranavalona III in exile.
1942	British troops occupy Madagascar.
1947	Nationist rebellion suppressed with many dead.
1958	Autonomy achieved within the French Community.
1960	Madagascar achieves full independence.
1975	Didier Ratsiraka first elected president.

BIBLIOGRAPHY

General – history, the country, the people

Bradt, H., editor. (1988). *Madagascar** (Exotic Lands series). Aston Publications, England. Madagascar in colour photos.

Bloch, M. (1986) *From Blessing to Violence*. Cambridge University Press, UK. History and ideology of the circumcision ritual of the Merina people.

Covell, M. (1987) *Madagascar: Politics, Economics and Society*. Frances Pinter Ltd, London. In the *Marxist Regimes* series.

Crook, S. (1990) *Oceans Apart*. Impact Books, UK. The story of the Sarimanok Expedition by outrigger canoe across the Indian Ocean from Bali to Madagascar.

Drury, R. *Robert Drury's Journal*. Negro University Press, U.S.A. The diaries of a sailor shipwrecked on Madagascar in the 1700s.

Drysdale, H. (1991) *Chasing Shadows: a Journey in Madagascar*. Hamish Hamilton, UK. An account of Helena's journeys (bits of which have been included in this guide). A TV programme on the search for her Malagasy ancestor is scheduled for 1991.

Hennebique, J. (1987) *Madagascar, mon île au bout de monde*. Editions Siloe, Paris. A large 'coffee table' book containing numerous beautiful colour photos. Text in French.

Heseltine, N. (1971). *Madagascar*. London. A detailed and excellent overview of the country.

Kent, R.K. (1962). *From Madagascar to the Malagasy Republic*. Thames and Hudson, London.

Kent, R.K. (ed.) (1979) *Madagascar in History: Essays from the 1970s*. Foundation for Malagasy Studies, Albany, CA, USA. Essays by 14 authors.

Mack, J. (1986) *Madagascar: Island of the Ancestors*. British Museum, London. A scholarly and informative account of the ethnography of Madagascar, published to coincide with the exhibition at the Museum of Mankind, London, the Natural History Museum, New York, and now the President's Palace, Antananarivo. Includes a very detailed bibliography.

Mack, J. (1989) *Malagasy Textiles*. Shire Publications, UK.

A Glance at Madagascar (1973). An excellent little book, sometimes available in Madagascar, giving much useful information on the Malagasy people, their history, traditions, and beliefs. Currently out of print.

*Available from Bradt Publications. We also import maps of Madagascar.

Murphy, D. (1985). *Muddling through in Madagascar.* Murray, London. A marvellously entertaining account of a journey (by foot and truck) through the highlands and south.

Oberlé, P. *Tananarive et l'Imerina* and *Provinces Malgache.* Two excellent and detailed photo guides available in Tana bookshops. French.

Wilson, J. (1990) *Lemurs of the Lost World.* Impact Books, UK. An account of the author's 'Crocodile Caves of Ankarana' expedition.

Natural history.

Readily accessible literature

Attenborough, D. (1961) *Zoo Quest to Madagascar.* Pan, London.

Caufield, C. (1985). *In the Rainforest.* Alfred Knopf, Inc. (U.S.)

Durrell, G. 1983. *Ark on the Move.* Coward-McCann Inc. (US). Descriptions of the Durrell's observations in Madagascar, Mauritius and Rodriques, in the usual inimitable Durrell style.

Haltenorth T. and Diller, H. Trans. by Robert W Hayman. (1980) *Field Guide to the Mammals of Africa including Madagascar.* Wm.Collins & Son Ltd.

Jolly, A. (1980). *A World Like Our Own: Man and Nature in Madagascar.* Yale University Press. The outstanding book on the natural history of Madagascar with a sympathetic approach to the Malagasy people. Written in a highly readable style, this coffee table book is expensive but worth every penny.

Jolly, A. (1987). *Madagascar: A World Apart* (with photographs by F.Lanting), National Geographic Magazine 171, 148- 183.

Jolly, A., Oberle, P., and Albignac, R. Editors. *Madagascar.* Pergamon Press, Oxford. This book in 'The Key Environments' series is mainly a translation of the French *Madagascar: Un Sanctuaire de la Nature.* At present it is the best general reference book on the natural history of Madagascar, although much of the information is now dated. Sections on invertebrates, amphibians, reptiles, birds, lemurs, etc, with two chapters on the vegetation and flora and good coverage of geology.

Langrand, O. (1990) *Field Guide to the Birds of Madagascar.* Yale University Press. The long-awaited definitive guide to the island's birds.

Loetschert, W. and Beese, G., Trans. by Clive King. (1983) . *Collins Guide to Tropical Plants.* Wm. Collins Sons & Co. Ltd.

Oberle, P. (1981). *Madagascar: Un Sanctuaire de la Nature.* Kintana, Antananarivo and Paris. Has some good illustrations, lacking in the English version.

Specialist literature.

Faune de Madagascar, (1956). Tananarive and Paris. To date 64 volumes, birds (vol.35), mammals (vols. 36, 44), reptiles (vols.33, 36, 47), zoogeography (vol. 13) and the remainder invertebrates. In French.

Dee, T.J. (1988). *The Endemic Birds of Madagascar*. ICBP, Cambridge. Scientific data on status, distribution and habitat.

Harcourt, C. (1990). *Lemurs of Madagascar and the Comores*. IUCN, Cambridge. A Red Data book with scientific descriptions of all Madagascar's lemurs.

Jenkins, M.D., editor. (1987). *Madagascar: An Environmental Profile*. IUCN, Gland, Switzerland and Cambridge, U.K. Currently contains the most up-to-date descriptions of the nature reserves, with check-lists of flora and fauna.

Morat, P. (1973). *Les Savanes du Sud-Ouest Madagascar*. ORSTOM, Paris. Includes a map scale 1:500 000 in which there is the 'Massif de Isalo'.

Nicholl, M.E. & Langrand, O. (1989) *Madagascar: Revue de la Conservation et des aires protégées*. WWF, Switzerland. Currently available only in French, but an English edition is in preparation. A detailed survey of the reserves studied by the WWF, lists of species, and excellent maps.

Rauh, W. (1972). *Cactus and Succulent Journal*, (US) 44. 7-16. *The Genus Pachypodium*. Discusses and compares the African and Madagascan species: a large number of photographs.
Reynolds, G.W. (1966). *The Aloes of Tropical Africa and Madagascar*. The Aloes Book Fund, Swaziland.

Richard-Vindard, G. & Battistini, R. (Editors) (1972). *Biogeography and Ecology of Madagascar*. W.Junk, The Hague. Largely in English including chapters on geology, climate, flora, erosion, rodents and lemurs. Each chapter includes an extensive bibliography.

QUESTERS

The world through nature tours

Madagascar, Mauritius and the Seychelles

24 day tours of three Indian Ocean islands, each with their own unique flora and fauna, led by expert naturalists.

Our tour of Madagascar includes Tuléar for baobabs, salt marshes and mangroves, Berenty Reserve and Périnet Reserve for their great variety of flora and fauna, and Nosy Be for snorkeling; in the Seychelles see half a million sooty terns and thousands of snow-white fairy terns on Bird Island, and seek out the unique species on Mahe, Praslin, Cousin and La Digue; Mauritius offers pink pigeons and parakeets, as well as the famous Pamplemousse Botanical Gardens.

With Questers you have ample time to photograph, absorb and reflect. Tour parties are small, accommodation is first class.

Call or write for a copy of our Directory of Worldwide Nature Tours.

QUESTERS
Worldwide Nature Tours
257 Park Avenue South
New York, NY 10010, USA.
Tel: (212) 673-3120

Bradt Publications
Maps & Travel

Sales & Accounts
41 Nortoft Road · Chalfont St Peter · Bucks · SL9 0LA · England Tel: 02407 3478 · Fax: (0) 734 509262 · Telex: 849021 FRAN G
Editorial Office
Grey House (Flat) · Beeches Drive · Farnham Common · Bucks · SL2 3JU · England Tel: 0753 646580

May 2 1990,

Dear Readers,

Following a plea for update information
in the first edition I received some
marvellously entertaining and
informative letters. I do hope you will
keep up the good work for the next
edition. I shall continue to travel to
Madagascar each year, but cannot cover
the whole island while you,
collectively, can.
   So do write, don't put it off, and
please print your name and address so
you can be properly thanked.

Looking forward to hearing from you.

Bon Voyage!

Hilary Bradt

Hilary Bradt

Portrait of the tourist who came after
the hotely closed (and no-one told me!)

INDEX